VISIONS OF A
NEW EARTH

VISIONS OF A NEW EARTH

Religious Perspectives on Population, Consumption, and Ecology

Edited by

HAROLD COWARD
and
DANIEL C. MAGUIRE

State University
of New York
Press

Published by
State University of New York Press, Albany

© 2000 State University of New York

Production by Susan Geraghty
Marketing by Anne Valentine

Printed in the United States of America

For information, address State University of New York
Press, State University Plaza, Albany, N.Y., 12246

Library of Congress Cataloging-in-Publication Data

Visions of a new earth : religious perspectives on population,
    consumption, and ecology / edited by Harold Coward and Daniel C.
    Maguire.
        p.   cm.
    Includes bibliographical references and index.
    ISBN 0-7914-4457-0 (hc). — ISBN 0-7914-4458-9 (pbk.)
        1. Human ecology—Religious aspects. 2. Consumption (Economics)-
    -Moral and ethical aspects. I. Coward, Harold G. II. Maguire,
    Daniel C.
    GF80.V57 2000
    178—dc21   99-24398
                                                                    CIP

10   9   8   7   6   5   4   3   2

CONTENTS

ACKNOWLEDGMENTS

Although this book is in many respects a development of the beginning insights of the earlier volume, *Population, Consumption, and the Environment: Religious and Secular Responses*, edited by Harold Coward (SUNY Press, 1995), the idea for the book was born in an informal meeting of Harold Coward, Daniel Maguire, and José Barzelatto. In addition to the scholars listed as authors, Radhika Balakrishnan gave valuable advice and criticism throughout. The work was undertaken as a joint project of "The Religious Consultation on Population, Reproductive Health and Ethics" and "The Centre for Studies in Religion and Society, University of Victoria."

Thanks are due to the Ford Foundation for providing the funding that made this book-writing project possible. June Bull, the Centre's secretary, is to be thanked for arranging research meetings of the team. Ludgard De Decker, the Centre's administrator, prepared the manuscript for the press and saw to the copyeditor's queries, checking of the page proofs, and Sonia Furstenau prepared the index.

CHAPTER 1

Introduction

Daniel C. Maguire

We have become newly aware of that delicate marvel that made a surprising appearance on the surface of the earth. It is precarious and fragile and weight-wise almost insignificant since it is less than a billionth of the weight of the whole planet. Many things militate against its survival, and that concerns us, because the name we give to this phenomenon— perhaps the only manifestation of it in all the folds of the universe—is *life*.

Life. The systematic effort to know and enhance its values is called *ethics*. The name we give to our response to the preciousness we find in life is *religion*, a preciousness so great that it elicits from us our supreme encomium, our ultimate superlative, *sacred*. Religion is, definitionally, the response to the sacred. Ethics and religion are twinned. What enhances life and its milieu we call moral: its mysterious and awe-filled grandeur we call holy. Some religions conclude to one or many divinities at the root of this grandeur; others say theistic conclusions short-circuit our sense of wonder and detract from the miracle that is life itself. Whatever the explanations of sacrality—theistic or not—the fact remains that the experiences of the good and the holy are concentric— or more simply, the sacred is the nucleus of the good.

This experience of life as good to the point of holy is the foundation of civilization. Law and political and economic theory are liege to our experience of the sanctity of life. The sanctity of life animates literature and ensouls art. Those swirling, symbol-packed movements we call *religions* are the main source of moral attitudes that emerge as the basal assumptions of laws, politics, and economics.

One would assume, then, that in a well-ordered mind-sphere, religion and ethics would be accepted as foundational to the intellectual life. But that underestimates the mischievous vagaries of that talented and

1

bratty life-form we call human. In times recent the linked studies of ethics and religion have been demoted and banished from the mainstreams where decisions over the demise or flourishing of life are made.

Religion, the Missing Dimension of Statecraft is the telling title of a recent study.[1] The volume, which originated in the Center for Strategic and International Studies, makes its case by showing the bungling that occurs when the influence of religion is ignored in international political decisions. This common deficit is a cultural malady, not limited to international politics. All too much of Western thought is phobic on the subject of religion. If the literature of a period were to ignore all reference to love or sexuality we would accuse it of neurotic suppression for its slighting of such a central force in human personality.[2] Yet it is taken as normal when political and economic analyses of contemporary problems treat ethics and religion the way Victorian schoolmarms treated sex.

In much discourse on crisis-level problems such as ecological ruin, overconsumption, and demographic pressure, religion is sidelined and "theology" is a pejorative term that suggests fanciful rather than realistic analysis. At most, religion is allotted mascot status or tolerated as grounding for the odd rhetorical flourish in political oratory.

THE UBIQUITY OF RELIGION

Since religion is a response to the sacred and since no one finds nothing sacred, religion is pan-human. That which we find sacred moves us to awe, and awe is the electricity of the will. It is, in a word, power. When Alexander Pope said that the worst of madmen is a saint gone mad, his poetic allusion was to the power of that form of emotive, appreciative intelligence that we call religion. Ignoring power in the name of realism is surely in the category of the mad. When John Henry Newman said that people will die for a dogma who will not stir for a conclusion, he was at one with Pope in the assessment of religion's power. And when Camus said that whatever the importance of scientific truths, people do not die for them, he was teaching the same lesson in social psychology.

This volume presents scholars from eight of the world's religious classics. Fully aware of the downside that accompanies all historic movements religious or other, these scholars have entered the mines of their traditions searching out the renewable moral energies therein contained and showing the applicability of those traditions to the problem of overconsumption (often called "affluenza") along with the environmental and demographic crises. Note well: all three, consumption, population, and ecology are seen here as conceptually hyphenated and linked. *Indeed, this is the master theme and guiding conviction of this volume: it is impossible to consider overconsumption, population, or ecology separately without including all three.*

The religions represented and creatively probed and applied here were all explosions of reverence. And yet the world is not panting for their wisdom. They are accorded mausoleum status, and one does not go to mausolea to be fed. But before crying "foul" at our exclusion from the most crucial conversation in the history of the world, we had better begin with a penitent pause. Religion and its scholars have contributed to their own excommunication.

THE DEFINITIONAL FAILURE

It's hard to be taken seriously when you're not sure who you are. Definitional confusion invites and abets disparagement. Catherine Bell in a study of religious scholars' recent efforts to define their discipline refers to ours as "a field that is constantly resounding with litanies of alarm." The field, she says indictingly is "in trouble." It suffers from a "crisis of identity," a methodological "impasse," and a theoretical "malaise," making "the professional study of religion muddled and uninfluential."[3] Robert C. Neville in his presidential address to the American Academy of Religion cited the Enlightenment skepticism that permeates the field of religious studies. In his view this systematic suspicion that has been imprinted on our profession has made the study of religion and even the very American Academy of Religion decidedly inhospitable to religious people and to religion itself![4] With enemies like ourselves, our need for friends is dire.

Many historians and social scientists who do not at all ignore religion are very unclear about what it is that they are not ignoring. Wilfred Cantwell Smith calls religion "notoriously difficult to define" noting that there is "a bewildering variety of definitions; and no one of them has commanded wide acceptance."[5] J. W. Bowker agrees: "Nobody seems to know what [religion] is."[6] Fitz John Porter Poole says that anthropologists have "expended enormous, but largely unproductive, efforts in an attempt to define religion," and Maurice Bloch thinks that the "only solution seems to be to abandon the notion of religion as an analytical category."[7] Stewart Guthrie takes the problem as he sees it to its roots: "Writers have speculated on the nature and origins of religion for well over two thousand years but have not produced so much as a widely accepted definition. Instead, there are nearly as many definitions as writers. Religion is difficult to define because definitions imply theories, and no good general theory of religion exists."[8]

So here we are, bickering gibberishly and postmodernly about what we are, and wondering why much of the human community has conversationally stepped around us. We must entertain the possibility that we get no hearing because we have deserved none.

SOLUTIONS

The solution to religion's exile suggested and acted upon in this volume is twofold: (1) recognize that religion is in all of its manifestations *a response to the sacred*, however defined or localized. It can take noxious or helpful forms. In its most helpful mode it spawns moral revolutions rich in symbol and poetic ritual. These revolutions tumble through history, growing and diversifying and acquiring the stability we call tradition and taking on names like Buddhism, Hinduism, Judaism, Christianity, and Islam or walking almost anonymously in rich aboriginal form in places like Africa or North America. Corrupted (as the best can always be) they can support the worst in us, but at their best they are epics of compassion and of the art of wonder. The great religions of the world are *classics*, in-depth plumbings of the human spirit and history-making appreciations of the good of the earth. A classic touches the deepest predicates of human truth experience. A classic is a gifted perception of the true, the good, and the beautiful at its most privileged depths.[9] When a religion manages to achieve these depths, it is, like any classic, worth a hearing. It is also, for our purposes here, a source of power and motivation that can be enlisted in the fight for life on earth.

The religions of the world do indeed carry with them in their histories the encrusted residues of past failings and achievements no longer relevant. But if they do measure up as moral classics they mimic the earth with its hidden interior fires that only occasionally seep out. The heat of wisdom is buried in the belly of a moral classic. Good theology—or sacrology as it would be better called since not all religion, not all experience of the sacred is theistic—releases that heat and shows its applicability to our present and future tenses.

Notice that this definition of religion has a normative thrust. Social science hungering for a normless objectivity is reduced to treating as "religion" whatever anyone describes as such. Even Robert Neville bows to this promiscuity in his address to the American Academy of Religion saying: "By 'religion' I mean whatever any of those disciplines or approaches might mean by religion."[10]

This is a white flag that surrenders to the portrayal of religion as an undefinable conundrum.

A NORMATIVE DEFINITION OF RELIGION

The approach in this volume is to look for experiences of the sacred that enhance the life-values. Not everything that is called religion measures up to this norm. The normativity of this definition could offend only those under the spell of positivist poisons who confuse normlessness with objectivity.

Since values are part of the objective order and are indeed the supreme challenge to discerning intelligence, the objectivity sought in this volume is value-laden. Value claims are to be tested not banished. The authors of this volume do not want to be free of the values that nourish the life-miracle on planet earth, this diminutive masterpiece in our sprawling universe.

And that leads to the second phase of the solution for repatriating religion into the center of human inquiry: *application*. Experience, it has been said, is the plasma of theory. Religion grown into tradition is a system of thought, feeling, and evaluation. Those religions are born in the stream of lived life, but their most dynamic insights can get splashed onto the banks, there to congeal while the waters of life rush on and pass them by. Such is the way of religious decadence. Reform occurs when crises draw them back into the surging life-stream. But to earn a place back in the movement of life, they must pass the most honest of intellectual tests, the *so what?* test.

This test is, after all, the legitimate test of any philosophy or theory. What difference does it make? If religions today stir the heart and produce experiences of enlightenment and joy but say nothing to our eco-crisis, they are tinkling brass and sounding cymbals. To pass the test of relevance today, religion must face the discipline of the *so what?* test foisted on them by grisly facts such as these: on a given day as we now mismanage the earth, we add fifteen million tons of carbon to the atmosphere, eliminate 115 square miles of tropical rainforest, create seventy-two square miles of desert, eliminate forty to one hundred species, erode 71 million tons of topsoil, add twenty-seven hundred tons of CFCs to the stratosphere, and increase world population by 263,000, with our food needs increasing and our feeding capacities in decline.[11] As David Orr writes: "Human breast milk often contains more toxins than are permissible in milk sold by dairies. At death, human bodies often contain enough toxins and heavy metals to be classified as hazardous waste. Male sperm counts worldwide have fallen by 50% since 1938, and no one knows exactly why. Roughly 80% of European forests have been damaged by acid rain. Ultraviolet radiation reaching the ground in Toronto is now increasing at 5% per year."[12] Meanwhile we disenfranchise the female half of the human species and accumulate wealth to obscene levels at the small royal top of our pyramidal economy while squalor marks with death the large and destitute bottom. If the salvation or enlightenment or nirvana or will of God of which traditional religions speak do not relate helpfully to all of this, then they are each and all vain and vapid.

Application to current crises also rescues religions from the self-indulgent abstractions to which they all seem liable. Classical religions begin as moral movements. Even their symbols or dogmas have a moral payload. They are not propositions dutifully accepted but devoid of issue; they are shapers of minds and of behavior—and of social systems. As religions decay, the dogmas can become elaborate boxes, elegantly bedecked and revered, but empty of their primordial moral content. Buddhism, for example, began with refreshing insights, marked by a profound simplicity. It sought to cope with sorrow by taking a middle course between self-indulgence and extreme asceticism so as to lead a well-ordered and harmonious life. However, as one student of Buddhism puts it: "This very simple doctrine was developed in various rather pedantic forms, most important of which was the 'Chain of Dependent Origination' . . . commented on again and again by ancient and modern scholars, and probably not fully understood by anybody."[13]

Buddhist pedants were not alone. Christian speculations on the subsistent relations of the Trinity were far from the straightforward moral thunder of the prophets and the Sermon on the Mount attributed to Rabbi Jesus. When it comes to obscurantist elitism, none of the religions is without sin.

The Religious Consultation on Population, Reproductive Health and Ethics in partnership with the Centre for Studies in Religion and Society at the University of Victoria, with support from the Ford Foundation, the John D. and Catherine T. MacArthur Foundation, and the General Service Foundation, sponsored the study that finds its first fruits in this volume edited by Harold Coward and myself. The Consultation was founded in the belief that religions will play a role, for better or for worse, in the current eco-crisis. If the already advanced terracide is to be curtailed, the unique energy and power of religion must be enlisted. Two thirds of the world actively affiliate with the formalized religions and the other third is surely under the spell of these symbol-laden seismic moral movements. Great religions are born in imaginative power and can shift the tectonic plates of attitude and worldview. Their cultural impact is never confined to the devotees of these movements. The Religious Consultation was founded in the belief that there will be no merely technical solution to the world's current problems: the disempowerment of women, the cult of weaponry and war, the loss of a sense of the common good, the rape of our parental earth, and overpopulation.

Flowcharts and data analysis have their place, but if the flaccid will of our dangerous species is to be stirred to the power-sharing sacrifices and the biophilic discipline needed for our survival, the sense of the sacred must play its quintessential motivational role.

Human motivation without the tincture of the sacred is dried and brittle. Willpower is the yield of reverence and of that full bloom of reverence called love. The classic religions live where reverence germinates.

CRISIS-OPPORTUNITY

The terrestrial crisis is an opportunity for the fullest flowering of human genius and of our capacities for reverence. History has been called a butcher's bench, but there are gentler and nobler forces within us that must be rallied. Our history is not just butchery but also birth and nurture and the generositities of morality and art. Religions rise from the precordial depths of human awareness where these heroic energies, too often dormant, await today an epochal summons. As Larry Rasmussen writes: "Religions typically come to be and take their distinctive shape in the breakup of worlds. . . . [I]t is precisely a deep cultural crisis that initially gives birth to religions and later to their reform."[14] This moment of earth crisis is ripe for such birthing and reform.

This is the first project, the flagship of the Religious Consultation on Population, Reproductive Health and Ethics and it fittingly began with the triple problematic of population-consumption-ecology. Concern for human numbers without concern for overconsuming elites is unjust and unhelpful. A single superconsumer in the rich world does more harm to the earth than hundreds of the poor;[15] 2.9 million in Chicago consume more than 90 million people in Bangladesh.

This volume is only phase one of a multitiered project. Indeed we think of this more as a process than a project. The scholars herein assembled do not subscribe to the belief that the world will be saved by yet one more scholarly volume . . . as important as such works will be. This book will be followed by a policy manual taking the substance of this volume and presenting it in another idiom for an audience of policy-makers and activists. Thereupon will follow a video and presentations by our scholars through the popular communications media. Our goal is to bridge the town-gown divide, in the cause of starting processes and not just publishing thoughts, we will invite artists of every stripe to join in this reimagining of life on earth. It is our plan to initiate international conferences and conversations to critique our work and stimulate movement and we will share our experience of this model with other scholars, urging them to stir their untapped talents for outreach.

We are developing a model pioneered by Harold Coward. We brought the scholars together for four days of intense and pleasant interchange and mutual education to achieve something of a common mind about our project. We proved that the supreme intellectual achievement—conversation—could happen across seemingly deep divides of religion and culture. The authors then repaired to write their chapters and we met again ten months later for four days of mutual critique. We knew each other by then and the critiques were vigorous and fruitful. We were joined in this second session by Drs. José Barzelatto, Marjorie Muecke, and Robert Franklin of the Ford Foundation, who brought a wealth of international experience to the table. Glenn Yocum, editor of the *Journal of the American Academy of Religion* also joined us, as did Radhika Balakrishnan, a political economist, natively of India, and now at Marymount College in Manhattan. This rich mix was followed by months of final revisions and the product of it all now awaits our readers.

Theory needs firm footing in the facts of life. Thus the volume opens with chapters by two economists. David Loy is a Buddhist economist living in Japan. His cosmic sense of interconnectedness and attention to reality gives bright focus to the full plight of our *oikos*. Loy strips away the secular and "realist" pretenses of our market capitalism and shows that it now functions as a religion, in fact the "first truly world religion, binding all corners of the globe into an increasingly monolithic worldview." The religion of the market inculcates a set of values whose religious role we overlook only because we insist on seeing them as "secular." The market does what religions do; it tells us what is sacred.

David Korten continues this unmasking, showing that the Bretton Woods agreements of 1944 were the symbol-setters of the postwar world. In the final days of World War II, the United Nations Monetary and Financial Conference at Bretton Woods became the Vatican of the market religion, issuing edicts and founding the institutions that would shape the dogmas of the new capitalism. The doctrine of prosperity without limits was proclaimed. The earth was "infinitely blessed," with "no fixed limits," and "not a finite substance." Planetary limits were erased in this halcyon faith. Growth is God with trickling down grace benefitting all. Bretton Woods with its fideistic and naive confidences issued into the World Bank and the International Monetary Fund. The groundwork was also laid for what would later become the General Agreement on Tariffs and Trade (GATT). Untrammeled trade was the sacrament of this new age economics. These assumptions now ensconced as policy changed the political economy, leading to the creation of corporate giants that dwarf states. The fruit of this? Today, of the world's one hundred largest economies, fifty are corporations—not including banking and financial institutions—and these giants that now bestride the earth are not encumbered with democratic structure, constitutions, or Bills of Rights. The planet and the poor of the world are not experiencing this rampage as salvation.

Harold Coward goes right to the core of ethical inquiry. In the dominant culture of the West, self is defined individualistically. Self is a lonely isolate that may reach out contractually to others or might, by inference, remain by itself alone. Of course this is a fiction since the atoms in our bodies are the cousins of the stars and our reality is social from conception to birth to death. Genes, the building blocks of our bodies are sacraments of our sociality. The sense of aloneness and non-connectedness is the ultimate illusion.

Coward traces out the devilment that comes from assuming that the ethical agent is an ontologically separated "choosing individual." The power to choose is our glory; ignorance of the social matrix of our choosing is fatal. Coward explores cultures where the self is a "we-self" not an "I-self." The results of this shift are seismic and speak to our current crisis.

Alberto Múnera brings to this volume the voice of the "third world." Residing and working in Latin America, this Jesuit priest theologian shows how the dominant religion of that region, Roman Catholicism, has in its teachings a theory of social and distributive justice that undercuts the rawness of individualistic capitalism. He musters neglected teachings of scripture and the popes that champion the rights of the poor. His *cri de coeur* cites the facts of injustice, and shows how with fatal irony the poverty caused by gross maldistribution of wealth generates population increases, unmanageable migrations, and a wrecking of the earth. Living with and speaking with the poor of the world, Múnera excoriates the devastating consumerism of the greedy "First World." He also shows the neglected liberal ethical theories that developed in Catholic history and are applicable to reproductive ethics.

Catherine Keller indicts Protestantism for its "collusion with the most potent forces of social, economic, and ecological injustice" and she does so because a religious and moral tradition can only cure what it first diagnoses in itself. Keller recognizes that the antinature "virus" is not only Protestant but infects the core of all of traditional Christianity. She illumines brightly however the contorted path the Protestant story followed in the West and its powerful role in the creation of "the peculiar North American dynamic of cheerful capitalist optimism" joined to a blithe readiness to destroy the ecological matrix of the very prosperity capitalism promises. With the indictment in place, Keller still finds hope in old places and hints at creative possibilities that would be good news both to us and to the lilies of the field.

Early Israel was not just a religious movement; it was a workshop for a new humanity. All the key categories of social existence were rethought in radical ways. Laurie Zoloth looks at the legacy of the Jews, "the collective progeny of the slaves of Exodus." She finds in their stories a "hint of the infinite possibility of a world healed." Wakeup calls boom loudly from Israel's scrolls and stories for a world "lulled into a somnambulant despair by the pursuit of commodities." Israel does not romanticize untended nature; nature would be "a restless wilderness without our hands." In a new and creative leap, Zoloth takes the image of Exile and brings it into international ethics. She applies it to a world alienated. In her hands the Exile becomes a paradigm for the recovery of reverence and solidarity, for "sleepless responsibility" for the other, especially the poor, for a social definition of ownership, and for a characteristically Jewish invigoration of our capacities for critique and dispute. She also defends small acts of ecological integrity. She does not say that empires will crumble under the weight of these practices but that they will bring water to the streams of our integrity.

All the authors of this volume are painfully aware of the sins of their religious traditions. Vasudha Narayanan does not proffer a romantic view of the Hindu traditions. Natalism is a strong thrust in Hinduism. "Almost all dharmic texts of Hinduism praise the joys of having children," she notes and rituals and charms abound to encourage childbearing. Sterilization, almost always of women, accounts for 72 percent of all the contraception in India. The situation in her native India is not promising on the issues that concern this volume. "India is on the fast track to repeat the mistakes of the West." Cultural invasions survive longer than military incursions and India was clearly invaded culturally.

Yet there is rich blood pulsing in the heart of Hinduism. There are lessons in the traditions about the seductions of materialism. As with all classical religious traditions there are wise and subversive insights on ownership. No serious philosophy could lack this and these religions are serious philosophies. Religious rituals in Hinduism have been directed to ecologically benevolent practices including tree planting. Also, and importantly, recognizing that education does not just come from staring at words, the Hindu cultures exalt the power of dance and ritual to teach and motivate. It instructs us who have a too narrow view of epistemology on the use of the arts as we confront the prospects of a ruined earth.

Just as Narayanan shows that Hindu lands are not Hindu enough, Nawal Ammar points to the hopes for a more genuinely Muslim Islam. Early in the Christian ecumenical movement, Robert MacAfee Brown spoke of the need for "caricature assassination." Muslim scholars like Ammar confront this need in the West where noxious caricatures of

Islam abound. Ammar does this without fudging the negatives in Islamic countries. She concedes that "in most Muslim countries the patriarchal, misogynist local cultures favor interpretations of the Qur'an that debase women." And yet there are other kindly and potentially influential traditions in the Islamic traditions that are central to the spirit of Islam and that support a vigorous feminism.

All of the classical religions have the seeds of significant economic and political theory. Islam has a highly developed sense of the common good that is antidotal to greedy Western individualism. Its taxation principle is grounded in redisributive justice; the wealth and power of the rich are to be redirected to the poor. Taxes are justified to meet the essential needs of all. Also, whatever the abuses in practice, the Qur'anic ideal of political authority is the liberation of all people. Islam also inculcates a respectful stewardship of the earth and its treasures. It exalts the ideal of *hay'a*, which Ammar translates interestingly as "a dignified shyness" before the goodness of the earth and the rich diversity of peoples and cultures.

Rita Gross's development of a Buddhist environmental ethic illustrates that the major religions are also exercises in social psychology. Buddhism, particularly, has specialized in the critique of egoism and the separatist "I-self" discussed by Harold Coward. As such it contains potent critiques of personal, corporate, and national greed and how that greed disrupts the essential interdependency of the ecosystem. Buddhism see us as part of that ecosystem, not as towering gods who bestride that system in a dominative mode. Again, the surgery here on much of Western individualism and on issues such as "private property" is as delicate as it is radical. Western theories of ownership are in sorry debt to Roman law's concept of absolute property rights, rights that allow us to use, profit from, and abuse what we possess: *ius utendi, fruendi, et abutendi*. This vicious and asocial and even hostile conception of property kills the solidarity that is necessary for biotic and human flourishing.

Gross also directs a Buddhist critique to reproductive behavior, arguing that much of it is fueled by individual or communal greed and ego and is therefore just as suspect as greed for assets. Gross does not avoid the hard questions and works to the conclusion that "involuntary fertility regulation and involuntary limits to consumption are not always inappropriate."

Like all the authors of this volume, Chün-fang Yü challenges the Western illusion that the eco-crisis can be solved by technical and strictly rational considerations. She insists that our "values and beliefs" must change before our lifestyles and ways of thinking will take a more benign turn. Chinese religion, unlike the Abrahamic religions, has no creator God or no afterlife for postmortem refuge. This earth and its enveloping heavens are our mother and father; we do not have some invisible removed deity as parent. In substance we are one with the universe. The truly "great" person sees the self, others, and the world as one body. Yü traces out the economic and ecological implications of this unitive sense of reality.

This and other chapters in this volume show that theism is neither univocal or universal. There is a fluid multiplicity in the theism of Hinduism, plus a pronounced nontheism in Buddhism, and roles for ancestors in aboriginal religions where godlike qualities are discernible in personifications of nature. The Abrahamic religions tend more toward an ontological rigidity when it comes to God-talk and interreligious dialogue must be sensitive to this.

Jacob Olupona insists that you cannot understand Africa outside the context of its unique exploitation by Europe and America and its postcolonial militarism and mismanagement. Many African nations cannot be called "developing" because they are in worse condition than they were pre-independence.

Like India, Africa suffers still from the cultural invasion inflicted by the imperialists. Benign social attitudes toward sharing and ownership were dislodged. The British, for example, foisted their notion of private property on the Kikuyu, displacing their notion of communal ownership of land. The social disruption from this endures. In the native African religions, land ultimately belonged to Ngai, the Supreme God. In a way that parallels Leviticus, humans were tenants only and the earth is a sacred trust. But in a way that does not parallel Leviticus, nature is endowed with the same ontological status as humans. Animals and plants share a common spiritual energy. There is striking ecological reverence in the rituals, in the African sense of the common good of all of nature, and in their developed sense of collective guilt for misuse of the earth. Like all the chapters in this volume, this is a study of the roots of motivation.

All the chapters in this volume show that the barriers we erect between our disciplines and religions are increasingly artificial. The implications of that touch all the social sciences. These studies signal strongly that the rigor of facing a common problematic bonds all participants, intellectuals and policymakers alike. Our collaborative efforts also illustrate the natural union of religion and ethics. The authors invite the readers into the new kind of conversation and strategizing needed on this generous host of an earth, an earth that can only survive by thriving.

NOTES

1. Douglas Johnston and Cynthia Sampson, eds., *Religion, the Missing Dimension of Statecraft* (New York: Oxford University Press, 1994).

2. Carol Bly, *Bad Government and Silly Literature* (Minneapolis: Milkweed Editions, 1986), p. 3.

3. Catherine Bell, "Modernism and Postmodernism in the Study of Religion," *Religious Studies Review* 22.3 (July 1996): 179.

4. Robert Cummings Neville, "Religious Studies and Theological Studies: AAR 1992 Presidential Address," *Journal of the American Academy of Religion* 51 (1993).

5. Wilfred Cantwell Smith, *The Meaning and End of Religion* (New York: The New American Library, 1962), p. 21.

6. J. W. Bowker, "Information Process, Systems Behavior, and the Study of Religion," *Zygon* 2:361.

7. Fitz John Porter Poole, "Metaphors and Maps: Toward Comparison in the Anthropology of Religion," *Journal of the American Academy of Religion* 53.3:423. Maurice Bloch, "Religion and Ritual," in *The Social Science Encyclopedia*, ed. Adam Kuper and Jessica Kuper (London: Routledge and Kegan Paul, 1985), p. 698.

8. Stewart E. Guthrie, *Faces in the Clouds: A New Theory of Religion* (New York: Oxford University Press, 1993), p. 8.

9. On the five marks of a genuine classic, see Daniel C. Maguire, *The Moral Core of Judaism and Christianity* (Minneapolis: Fortress Press, 1993), pp. 59–66.

10. Robert Cummings Neville, "Religious Studies and Theological Studies," p. 186.

11. David W. Orr, *Ecological Literacy: Education and the Transition to a Postmodern World* (Albany: State University of New York Press, 1992), p. 3.

12. David W. Orr, *Earth in Mind: On Education, Environment, and the Human Prospect* (Washington, D.C.: Island Press,1994), p. 1.

13. A. L. Basham, *The Wonder That Was India: A Survey of the Culture of the Indian Sub-Continent before the Coming of the Muslims* (London: Sidgwick & Jackson, 1954), p. 269.

14. Larry L. Rasmussen, *Earth Community Earth Ethics* (Maryknoll, N.Y.: Orbis Books, 1996), p. 14.

15. See Alan Durning, *How Much Is Enough? The Consumer Society and the Future of the Earth* (New York: W.W. Norton, 1992).

CHAPTER 2

The Religion of the Market

David R. Loy

Religion is notoriously difficult to define. If, however, we adopt a functionalist view and understand religion as what grounds us by teaching us what this world *is,* and what our *role* in that world is, then it becomes obvious that traditional religions are fulfilling this role less and less, because that function is being supplanted—or overwhelmed—by other belief systems and value systems. Today the most powerful alternative explanation of the world is science, and the most attractive value-system has become consumerism. Their academic offspring is economics, probably the most influential of the "social sciences." In response, this chapter will argue that our present economic system should also be understood as our religion, because it has come to fulfill a religious function for us. The discipline of economics is less a science than the theology of that religion, and its god, the Market, has become a vicious circle of ever-increasing production and consumption by pretending to offer a secular salvation. The collapse of communism makes it more apparent that the Market is becoming the first truly world religion, binding all corners of the globe into a worldview and set of values whose religious role we overlook only because we insist on seeing them as "secular."

So it is no coincidence that our time of ecological catastrophe also happens to be a time of extraordinary challenge to more traditional religions. Although it may offend our vanity, it is somewhat ludicrous to think of conventional religious institutions as we know them today serving a significant role in solving the environmental crisis. Their more immediate problem is whether they, like the rain forests we anxiously monitor, will survive in any recognizable form the onslaught of this new religion. The major religions are not yet moribund but, on those few occasions when they are not in bed with the economic and political powers that be, they tend to be so preoccupied with past problems and outmoded perspectives (e.g., pronatalism) that they are increasingly irrelevant (e.g., fundamentalism) or trivialized (e.g., television evangelism). The result is that up to now they have been unable to offer what is most needed—a meaningful challenge to the aggressive proselytizing of market capitalism, which has already become the most successful religion of all time, winning more converts more quickly than any previous belief system or value system in human history.

This situation is becoming so critical that the environmental crisis may actually turn out to be a positive thing for religion, for ecological catastrophe is awakening us not only to the fact that we need a deeper source of values and meaning than market capitalism can provide, but to the realization that contemporary religion is not meeting this need either.

ECONOMICS AS THEOLOGY

> It is intolerable that the most important issues about human livelihood will be decided solely on the basis of profit for transnational corporations.
> —Herman E. Daly and John B. Cobb Jr.,
> *For the Common Good*

In 1960 countries of the North were about twenty times richer than those of the South. In 1990—after vast amounts of aid, trade, loans, and catch-up industrialization by the South—countries of the North had become *fifty* times richer. The richest 20 percent of the world's population now have an income about 150 times that of the poorest 20 percent, a gap that continues to grow.[1] According to the UN Development Report for 1996, the world's 358 billionaires are wealthier than the combined annual income of countries with 45 percent of the world's people. As a result, a quarter million children die of malnutrition or infection every week, while hundreds of millions more survive in a limbo of hunger and deteriorating health. . . . Why do we acquiesce in this social injustice? What rationalization allows us to sleep peacefully at night?

> [T]he explanation lies largely in our embrace of a peculiarly European or Western [but now global] religion, an individualistic religion of economics and markets, which explains all of these outcomes as the inevitable results of an objective system in which . . . intervention is counterproductive. Employment is simply a cost of doing business, and Nature is merely a pool of resources for use in production. In this calculus, the world of business is so fundamental and so separate from the environment . . . that intervention in the ongoing economic system is a

threat to the natural order of things, and hence to future human welfare. In this way of thinking, that outcome is just (or at least inevitable) which emerges from the natural workings of this economic system, and the "wisdom of the market" on which it is based. The hegemony achieved by this particular intellectual construct—a "European religion" or economic religion—is remarkable; it has become a dogma of almost universal application, the dominant religion of our time, shoring up and justifying what would appear to be a patently inequitable status quo. It has achieved an immense influence which dominates contemporary human activity.[2]

According to Dobell, this theology is based on two counterintuitive but widely accepted propositions: that *it is right and just* (which is why "the market made me do it" is acceptable as a defense of many morally questionable activities); and that *value can be adequately signaled by prices*. Since natural resources are unpriced, harvesting techniques such as drift nets and clearcuts are acceptable and often necessary in order to be competitive, despite the fact that "more or less everybody now knows that market systems are profoundly flawed, in the sense that, left on their own with present pricing and practices, they will lead inevitably to environmental damage and destruction of irreplaceable ecological systems."[3]

The basic assumption of both propositions is that such a system is "natural." If market capitalism does operate according to economic laws as natural as those of physics or chemistry—if economics were a genuine science—its consequences seem unavoidable, despite the fact that they are leading to extreme social inequity and environmental catastrophe. Yet there is nothing inevitable about our economic relationships. That misunderstanding is precisely what needs to be addressed—and this is also where religion comes in, since, with the increasing prostitution of the media and now universities to these same market forces, there seems to be no other moral perspective left from which to challenge them. Fortunately, the alternative worldviews that religions offer can still help us realize that the global victory of market capitalism is something other than the attainment of economic freedom: rather, it is the ascendancy of one particular way of understanding and valuing the world that need not be taken for granted. Far from being inevitable, our economic system is one historically conditioned way of organizing/reorganizing the world; it is a worldview, with an ontology and ethics, in competition with other understandings of what the world is and how we should live in it.

What is most impressive about market values, from a religious perspective, is not their "naturalness" but how extraordinarily persuasive their conversion techniques are. As a philosophy teacher I know that whatever I can do with my students a few hours during a week is practically useless against the proselytizing influences that assail them outside class—the attractive (often hypnotic) advertising messages on television and radio and in magazines and buses that constantly urge them to "buy *me* if you want to be happy." If we are not blinded by the distinction usually made between secular and sacred, we can see that this promises another kind of salvation, that is, another way to solve our unhappiness. Insofar as this strikes at the heart of the truly religious perspective—which offers an alternative explanation for our inability to be happy and a very different path to become happy—religions are not fulfilling their responsibility if they ignore this religious dimension of capitalism, if they do not emphasize that this seduction is deceptive because this solution to our unhappiness leads only to greater dissatisfaction.

Instead of demonstrating their inevitability, the history of economic systems reveals the contingency of the market relationships we now take for granted. Although we tend to view the profit motive as universal and rational (the benevolent "invisible hand" of Adam Smith), anthropologists have discovered that it is not traditional to traditional societies. Insofar as it is found among them it tends to play a very circumscribed role, viewed warily because of its tendency to disrupt social relations. Most premodern societies make no clear distinction between the economic sphere and the social sphere, subsuming economic roles into more general social relationships. Precapitalist man "does not act so as to safeguard his individual interest in the possession of material goods; he acts so as to safeguard his social standing, his social claims, his social assets. He values material goods only in so far as they serve this end." But in a capitalist society "instead of economy being embedded in social relations, social relations are embedded in the economic system."[4]

Tawney discovered the same perspective on market forces in the pre-Renaissance West: "There is no place in medieval theory for economic activity which is not related to a moral end, and to found a science of society upon the assumption that the appetite for economic gain is a constant and measurable force, to be accepted like other natural forces, as an inevitable and self-evident datum, would have appeared to the medieval thinker as hardly less irrational and less immoral than to make the premise of social philosophy the unrestrained operation of such necessary human attributes as pugnacity and the sexual instinct."[5]

The crucial transformation evidently began in the late Middle Ages—which, by no coincidence, is when the prevailing religious interpretation of the world began to lose its grip on people's lives. As profit gradually became the engine of the economic process, the tendency was for gradual reorganization of the entire social system and not just of the economic element, since *there is no natural distinction between them.*[6]

"Capital had ceased to be a servant and had become a master. Assuming a separate and independent vitality it claimed the right of a predominant partner to dictate economic organization in accordance with its own exacting requirements."[7] It is another example of the technological paradox: we create complex systems to make our lives more comfortable, only to find ourselves trapped within the inexorable logic of their own development. The monster in Shelley's *Frankenstein* expresses it more brutally: "You are my creator, but I am your master."

The scholar who did the most to uncover the religious roots of market capitalism was Max Weber. His controversial theory not only locates the origins of capitalism in the "this-worldly asceticism" of Puritan ethics but suggests that capitalism remains essentially religious in its psychological structure. According to *The Protestant Ethic and the Spirit of Capitalism,* Calvinist belief in predestination encouraged what became an irresistible need to determine whether one was among the chosen; economic success in this world came to be accepted as demonstrating God's favor; this created the psychological and sociological conditions for importing ascetic values from the monastery into worldly vocations, as one labored to prove oneself saved by reinvesting any surplus rather than consuming it. Gradually this original goal became attenuated, yet inner-worldly asceticism did not disappear as God became more distant and heaven less relevant. In our modern world the original motivation has evaporated but our preoccupation with capital and profit has not disappeared with it; on the contrary, it has become our main obsession. Since we no longer have any other goal, there being no other final salvation to believe in, we allow the means to be, in effect, our end.

Weber's sociology of religion distinguishes more ritualistic and legalistic religions, which adapt themselves to the world, from salvation religions, more hostile to it. Salvation religions are often revolutionary due to the prophecies that motivate them, and missionary because they seek to inject a new message or promise into everyday life. Their efforts to ensure the perpetuation of grace in the world ultimately require a reordering of the economic system. Weber noticed that adherents of this type of religion usually "do not enjoy inner repose because they are in the grip of inner tensions."

This last point, which not only describes Puritan this-worldly ascetics but reminds us of our own situation, suggests that market capitalism began as, and may still be understood as, a form of salvation religion: dissatisfied with the world as it is and seeking to inject a new promise into it, motivated (and justifying itself) by faith in the grace of profit and concerned to perpetuate that grace, with a missionary zeal to expand and reorder (rationalize) the economic system. Weber's arguments imply that although we think of the modern world as secularized, its values (e.g., economic rationalization) are not only derived from religious ones (salvation by injecting a revolutionary new promise into daily life), they are largely the same values, although transformed by the loss of reference to an otherworldly dimension.

Our type of salvation still requires a future-orientation. "We no longer give our surplus to God; the process of producing an ever-expanding surplus is in itself our God."[9] In contrast to the cyclic time of premodern societies, with their seasonal rituals of atonement, our economic time is linear and future-directed, since it reaches for an atonement that can no longer be achieved because it has disappeared as a conscious motivation. As an unconscious incentive, however, it still functions, for we continue to reach for an end that is perpetually postponed. So our collective reaction has become the need for growth: the never-satisfied desire for an ever-higher "standard of living" (because once we define ourselves as consumers we can never have too much) and the gospel of sustained economic expansion (because corporations and the GNP are never big enough).

THE GREAT TRANSFORMATION

> Engels tells the story of remarking to a Manchester manufacturer that he had never seen so ill-built and filthy a city: "The man listened quietly to the end, and said at the corner where we parted: 'And yet there is a great deal of money made here; good morning, sir.'"
>
> —Kirkpatrick Sale, *Rebels against the Future*

The critical stage in the development of market capitalism occurred during the industrial revolution of the late eighteenth century, when new technology created an unprecedented improvement in the tools of production. This led to the "liberation" of a critical mass of land, labor, and capital, which most people experienced as an unprecedented catastrophe because it destroyed the community fabric—a catastrophe recurring today throughout much of the "developing" world. Karl Polanyi's *The Great Transformation* (1944) is an expression of outrage at these social consequences as well as an insightful explanation of the basis of this disfiguration: the way that the world became converted into exchangeable market commodities in order for market forces to interact freely and productively. Earlier the commercialization of English agriculture had led to enclosure of the common pasturage land that traditionally belonged to the community. The plague of industrial commodification proved to be much worse. The earth (our mother as well as our home) became commodified into a collection of resources to be exploited. Human life became commodified into labor, or work time, valued according to supply and demand. Social patrimony, the cherished inheritance laboriously accumulated and preserved for one's descendants, became commodified into fungible capital, a source of unearned income for the lucky few and a source of crushing debt for the rest.

The interaction among these commodifications led to an almost miraculous accumulation of capital and an equally amazing collapse of traditional community life, as villagers were driven off their land by these new economic forces. "To separate labor from other activities of life and to subject it to the laws of the market was to annihilate all organic forms of existence and to replace them by a different type of organization, an atomistic and individualistic one," emphasizes Polanyi. Such a system "could not exist for any length of time without annihilating the human and natural substance of society." The laissez-faire principle, that government should not interfere with the operations of the economic system, was applied quite selectively: although government was admonished not to get in the way of industry, its laws and policies were needed to help reduce labor to a commodity. What was called noninterference was actually interference to "destroy noncontractual relations between individuals and prevent their spontaneous re-formation."[9]

Is it a coincidence that the same doublespeak continues today? While so-called conservatives preach about liberating the free enterprise system from the restraining hand of government, federal subsidies are sought to support uneconomic industries (e.g., nuclear power) and underwrite economic failures (the Savings-and-Loan scandal), while international policies are designed to make the world safe for our multinational corporations (GATT, NAFTA, and the Gulf War). Until the last few centuries there has been little genuine distinction between church and state, between sacred authority and secular power, and that cozy relationship continues today: far from maintaining an effective regulatory or even neutral position, the U.S. government has become the most powerful proponent of the religion of market capitalism as the way to live, and indeed it may have little choice insofar as it is now a pimp dependent upon skimming the cream off market profits.

A direct line runs from the commodification of land, life, and patrimony during the eighteenth century to the ozone holes and global warming of today, and those commodifications have also led to another kind of environmental destruction that, in a different way, is just as problematic: the depletion of "moral capital," a horrible term that could only have been devised by economists, to describe another horrific social consequence of market forces. As Adam Smith emphasized in his *Theory of Moral Sentiments*, the market is a dangerous system because it corrodes the very shared community values it needs to restrain its excesses. "However much driven by self-interest, the market still depends absolutely on a community that shares such values as honesty, freedom, initiative, thrift, and other virtues whose authority will not long withstand the reduction to the level of personal tastes that is explicit in the positivistic, individualistic philosophy of value on which modern economic theory is based."[10] A basic contradiction of the market is that it requires character traits such as trust in order to work efficiently, but its own workings tend to erode such personal responsibility for others. This conflict tends toward a breakdown that is already quite advanced in many corporations. Massive "downsizing" and a shift to part-time workers demonstrate diminishing corporate concern for employees, while at the top astronomical salary increases (with lucrative stock options), and other unsavory practices such as management buy-outs reveal that the executives entrusted with managing corporations are becoming more adept at exploiting or cannibalizing them for their own personal benefit. Between 1980 and 1993 Fortune 500 firms increased their assets 2.3 times but shed 4.4 million jobs, while C.E.O. compensation increased more than sixfold, so that the average C.E.O. of a large corporation now receives a compensation package of more than $3.7 million a year.[11]

In such ways the market shows that it does not accumulate "moral capital"; it "depletes" it and therefore depends upon the community to regenerate it, in much the same way it depends upon the biosphere to regenerate natural capital. Unsurprisingly, long-range consequences have been much the same: even as we have reached the point where the ability of the biosphere to recover has been damaged, our collective moral capital has become so exhausted that our communities (or rather, our collections of now-atomized individuals each looking out for "number one") are less able to regenerate it, with disturbing social consequences apparent all around us. This point bears repetition because the economic support system that was created to correct the failures of capitalism is now blamed for the failures of capitalism. But the social rot affecting so many "developed" societies is not something that can be corrected by a more efficient application of market values (such as getting unmarried mothers off welfare so their work will contribute to society); rather, it is a direct consequence of those market values. The commodification that is destroying the biosphere, the value of human life, and the inheritance we should leave for future generations also continues to destroy the local communities that maintain the moral fiber of their members. The degradation of the earth and the degradation of our own societies must both be seen as results of the same market process of commodification—which continues to rationalize its operation as natural and inevitable.

The cumulative depletion of "moral capital" reminds us that a community is greater than the sum of its parts, that the well-being of the whole is necessary for the well-being of each member. This, however, is something that contemporary economic theory cannot factor into its equations. Why not? The answer brings us back to the origins of economic thought in the eighteenth century, origins embedded in the individualistic philosophy of utilitarianism prevalent at that time. Philosophy has developed considerably since then, yet economic theory remains in thrall to utilitarian values, all the more for being ignorant of its debt.[12] According to utilitarianism, society is composed of discrete individuals seeking their own personal ends. Human values are reduced to a calculus that maximizes pleasures (with no qualitative distinctions between them) and minimizes discomfort. Rationality is defined as the intelligent pursuit of one's private gain. In Adam Smith's understanding of this, "individuals, are viewed as capable of relating themselves to others in diverse ways, basically either in benevolence or in self-love, but they are not constituted by these relationships or by any others. They exist in fundamental separation from one another, and from this position of separateness they relate. Their relations are external to their own identities."[13] Inasmuch as the discipline of economics seems to have attained priority among the social sciences, this view of our humanity has come to prevail at the same time that its presuppositions have been thoroughly discredited by contemporary philosophy, psychology, and sociology— not to mention religion, which has always offered a very different understanding of what it means to be a human being. Nonetheless, as market values lead to a decline in the quality of our social relationships, "[s]ociety becomes more like the aggregate of individuals that economic theory pictures it as being. The 'positive' model inevitably begins to function as a norm to which reality is made to conform by the very policies derived from the model."[14] We have learned to play the roles that fit the jobs we now have to do and the commercial images that constantly assail us.

Given the influence today of neo-Malthusian thinking about population, it is important to notice that Malthus stands within this tradition. His *Essay on the Principle of Population* (1798) argued for an iron law of wages: a subsistence wage is the just wage, because higher wages lead only to rapid population growth until that growth is checked by poverty. It follows that poverty is not a product of human institutions but the natural condition of life for most people. The influence of this way of thinking has been in inverse proportion to the (lack of) empirical evidence for it, for world demographic trends have provided little. The rapid population increase that occurred in nineteenth-century England, which occurred after many people had been driven off their land and into factory work, supports the contrary conclusion, that people are not poor because they have large families, but require large families because they are poor (there was a great demand for child labor). Morally, Malthusianism tends to gloss over the issue of who is actually consuming the earth's resources. Theoretically, its major propositions—that population grows geometrically while food increases arithmetically—arbitrarily isolate two causal variables from the complexity of historical factors, while assuming as constant perhaps the most important variables of all: the "naturalness" of an unfettered market and the competitive, self-seeking "rational" individual that neoclassical economics still presupposes.[15]

Our humanity reduced to a source of labor and a collection of insatiable desires, as our communities disintegrate into aggregates of individuals competing to attain private ends . . . the earth and all its creatures commodified into a pool of resources to be exploited to satisfy those desires . . . does this radical dualism leave any place for the sacred? for wonder and awe before the mysteries of creation? Whether or not we believe in God, we may suspect that something is missing. Here we are reminded of the crucial role that religions can serve: to raise fundamental questions about this diminished understanding of what the world is and what our life can be.

THE ENDLESS HUNGER . . . ARE WE HAPPY YET?

> It is not the proletariat today whose transformation of consciousness would liberate the world, but the consumer.
> —Daniel Miller, *Acknowledging Consumption*

From a religious perspective, the problem with market capitalism and its values is twofold: greed and delusion. On the one hand, the unrestrained market emphasizes and indeed requires greed in at least two ways. Desire for profit is necessary to fuel the engine of the economic system, and an insatiable desire to consume ever more must be generated to create markets for what can be produced. Within economic theory and the market it promotes, the moral dimension of greed is inevitably lost; today it seems left to religion to preserve what is problematic about a human trait that is unsavory at best and unambiguously evil at its worst. Religious understandings of the world have tended to perceive greed as natural to some extent, yet rather than liberate it they have seen a need to control it. The spiritual problem with greed—both the greed for profit and the greed to consume—is due not only to the consequent maldistribution of worldly goods (although a more equitable distribution is of course essential), or to its effect on the biosphere, but even more fundamentally because greed is based on a delusion: the delusion that happiness is to be found this way. Trying to find fulfillment through profit, or by making consumption the meaning of one's life, amounts to idolatry, that is, a demonic perversion of true religion; and any religious institution that makes its peace with the priority of such market values does not deserve the name of genuine religion.

In other words, greed is part of a defective value-system (the way to live in this world) based on an erroneous belief-system (what the world is). The atomistic individualism of utilitarianism, which "naturalizes" such greed, must be challenged and refuted intellectually and in the way we actually live our lives. The great sensitivity to social justice in the Semitic religions (for whom sin is a moral failure of *will*) needs to be supplemented by the emphasis that the Asian enlightenment traditions place upon seeing through and dispelling delusion (ignorance as a failure to *understand*). Moreover, I suspect that the former without the latter is doomed to be ineffective in our cynical age. We are unlikely ever to solve the problem of distributive social justice without also overcoming the value-delusion of happiness through individualistic accumulation and consumption, if only because of the ability of those who control the world's resources to manipulate things to their own perceived advantage. That is not to demonize such people, for we must recognize our own complicity in this system, not only through our own levels of consumption but also through the effects that our pension funds have upon the workings of the market.

According to the French historian Fernand Braudel, the industrial revolution was "in the end a revolution in demand"—or, more precisely, "a transformation of desires."[16] Since we have come to look upon our own insatiable desires as "natural," it is necessary to remember how much our present mode-of-desiring is also one particular, historically conditioned system of values—a set of habits as manufactured as the goods supplied to satisfy it. According to the trade journal *Advertising Age,* which should know, in 1994 the United States spent $147 billion for advertising—far more than on all higher education. This translated into a barrage of 21,000 television commercials, a million magazine advertising pages, 14 billion mail-order catalogs, 38 billion junk-mail ads, and another billion signs, posters, and billboards. That does not include related industries affecting consumer taste and spending, such as promotion, public relations, marketing, design, and most of all fashion, which amounted to another $100 billion a year.[17] Put together, this constitutes probably the greatest effort in mental manipulation that humanity has ever experienced—all of it to no other end than creating consumerist needs for the sake of corporate profit. No wonder a child in the developed countries has an environmental impact as much as thirty times that of a child in the Third World.

If the market is simply the most efficient way to meet our economic needs, why are such enormous industries necessary? Economic theory, like the market itself, makes no distinction between genuine needs and the most questionable manufactured desires. Both are treated as normative. It makes no difference why one wants something. The consequences of this approach, however, continue to make a great difference. The pattern of consumption that now seems natural to us provides a sobering context to the rapid deterioration of ecological systems over the last half-century: according to the Worldwatch Institute, more goods and services have been consumed by the people living between 1950 and 1990 (measured in constant dollars) than by all the previous generations in human history.[18]

If this is not disturbing enough, add to it the social consequences of our shift to consumption values, which, in the United States at least, has revolutionized the way we relate to each other. "With the breakdown of community at all levels, human beings have become more like what the traditional model of *Homo economicus* described. Shopping has become the great national pastime. . . . On the basis of massive borrowing and massive sales of national assets, Americans have been squandering their heritage and impoverishing their children."[19] So much for their patrimony. Our extraordinary wealth has not been enough for us, so we have supplemented it by accumulating extraordinary amounts of debt. How ingenious we have been to devise an economic system that allows us to steal from the assets of our descendants! Our commodifications have enabled us to achieve something usually believed impossible, time-travel: we now have ways to colonize and exploit even the future.

The final irony in this near-complete commodification of the world comes as little surprise to anyone familiar with what has become addictive behavior for so many millions of people in the United States. Comparisons that have been made over time and between societies detect little difference in self-reported happiness. The fact that we in the developed world are now consuming so much more does not seem to be having much effect on our level of contentment.[20]

This comes as no surprise to those with a more religious orientation to the world. The best critique of this greed for consumption continues to be provided by traditional religious teachings, which not only serve to ground us functionally but show us how our lives can be transformed. In Buddhism, to cite the example of my own religion, the insatiable desires of the ego-self are the source of the frustration and lack of peace that we experience in our daily lives. Overconsumption, which distracts and intoxicates us, is one of the main symptoms of this problem.

Later chapters in this book explore the ways Buddhism and other religions diagnose and attempt to resolve this problem. If we contrast their approaches with market indoctrination about the importance of acquisition and consumption—an indoctrination that is necessary for the market to thrive—the battle lines become clear. All genuine religions are natural allies against what amounts to an idolatry that undermines their most important teachings.

In conclusion, the market is not just an economic system but a religion— yet not a very good one, for it can thrive only by promising a secular salvation that it never quite supplies. Its academic discipline, the "social science" of economics, is better understood as a theology pretending to be a science.

This suggests that any solution to the problems they have created must also have a religious dimension. That is not a matter of turning from secular to sacred values, but the need to discover how our secular obsessions have become symptomatic of a spiritual need they cannot meet. As we have consciously or unconsciously turned away from a religious understanding of the world, we have come to pursue this-worldly goals with a religious zeal all the greater because they can never be fulfilled. The solution to the environmental catastrophe that has already begun, and to the social deterioration we are already suffering from, will occur when we redirect this repressed spiritual urge back into its true path. For the time being, that path includes struggling against the false religion of our age.

NOTES

1. David C. Korten, *When Corporations Rule the World* (West Hartford, Conn.: Kumarian Press, 1995), pp. 107–8.

2. A. Rodney Dobell, "Environmental Degradation and the Religion of the Market," in *Population, Consumption, and the Environment*, ed. Harold Coward (Albany: State University of New York Press, 1995), p. 232.

3. Ibid., p. 237.

4. Karl Polanyi, *The Great Transformation* (Boston: Beacon Press, 1944, 1957), pp. 46, 57.

5. R. H. Tawney, *Religion and the Rise of Capitalism* (New York: Harcourt, Brace, 1926), p. 31.

6. This implies that an alternative to our market religion would not require eliminating the market (and the failure of twentieth-century socialism suggests that it should not be eliminated), but restoring market forces to their proper delimited place within community social relations.

7. Tawney, *Religion and the Rise of Capitalism*, p. 86.

8. Norman O. Brown, *Life against Death* (New York: Vintage, 1961), p. 261. Since every God needs a Devil, and every religion a theory of evil, members

of the market religion find evil in that which threatens their surplus: especially taxes, inflation, and (for corporations) governmental regulation, e.g., trade barriers.

9. Polanyi, *Great Transformation*, pp. 163, 3.

10. Herman E. Daly and John B. Cobb Jr., *For the Common Good*, 2nd ed. (Boston: Beacon Press, 1994), p. 50. I am much indebted to their highly recommended book, which presents a detailed critique of modern economic theory and demonstrates how our environmental and social problems can be solved if we have the will to do so.

11. Korten, *When Corporations Rule the World*, p. 218.

12. "Economics sprang at least half-grown from the head of Adam Smith, who may very properly be regarded as the founder of economics as a unified abstract realm of discourse, and it still, almost without knowing it, breathes a good deal of the air of the eighteenth-century rationalism and Deism." (Kenneth E. Boulding, *Beyond Economics* [Ann Arbor: University of Michigan Press, 1968], p. 187.)

13. Daly and Cobb, *For the Common Good*, p. 160.

14. Ibid., p. 162.

15. For an incisive critique of Malthusianism, see Mohan Rao, "An Imagined Reality: Malthusianism, Neo-Malthusianism and Population Myth," *Economic and Political Weekly*, 29 January 1994, pp. 40–52.

16. Fernand Braudel, *The Wheels of Commerce*, trans. Sian Reynolds (New York: Harper & Row, 1982), 183.

17. Alan Durning, *How Much Is Enough* (New York: Norton, 1992), p. 122.

18. Ibid., p. 38.

19. Daly and Cobb, *For the Common Good*, p. 373.

20. Durning, *How Much Is Enough*, pp. 38–40.

CHAPTER 3

Sustainability and the Global Economy

David C. Korten

What is the relationship between our hopes for a sustainable future and the dynamics of the global economy?

To answer that question, it is necessary to travel back in time more than fifty years to the meeting of world leaders held in Bretton Woods, New Hampshire, a meeting that played a historic role in the creation of three major institutions that have led the drive to globalize the world's economies.

The fame of Bretton Woods dates back to July 1944 when the United Nations Monetary and Financial Conference was held there. The world was in the throes of World War II. Mussolini had been overthrown. The Allies had landed at Normandy, but Hitler would last another ten months. War also continued to rage in the Far East, and Japan would not surrender for another thirteen months. The United Nations Charter was still a year away. In that context, the economic leaders who quietly gathered were looking beyond the end of the war with hopes for a world united in peace through prosperity. Their specific goal was to create the institutions that would promote that vision.

At the opening session, Henry Morgenthau, U.S. Secretary of the Treasury and president of the conference, read a welcoming message from President Roosevelt and gave his opening speech, which set the tone and spirit of the gathering. Morgenthau envisioned the "creation of a dynamic world economy in which the peoples of every nation will be able to realize their potentialities in peace and enjoy increasingly the fruits of material progress on an earth infinitely blessed with natural resources." He called on participants to embrace the "elementary economic axiom . . . that prosperity has no fixed limits. It is not a finite substance to be diminished by division."[1]

Thus Morgenthau set forth one of several underlying assumptions of the economic paradigm that guided the work of the architects of the Bretton Woods system. Many of these assumptions were reasonably valid. But two of the most important were deeply flawed. The first is that economic growth and enhanced world trade would benefit everyone. The second is that economic growth would not be constrained by the limits of the planet.

By the end of the historic meeting, the World Bank and the International Monetary Fund (IMF) had been founded and the groundwork laid for what later became the General Agreements on Tariffs and Trade (GATT). In the intervening years, these institutions have held faithfully to their mandate to promote economic growth and globalization. Through structural adjustment loans, the World Bank and the IMF have pressured the countries of the South to open their borders and focus their economies on export production. Trade agreements negotiated through the GATT have reinforced these actions, opened economies in both North and South to the increasingly free flow of goods and money, and eliminated controls on corporate practices.

As we look back at the intervening fifty years we can see that the Bretton Woods institutions have indeed met their goal. Economic growth has expanded fivefold. International trade has expanded by nearly twelve times and foreign direct investment has been expanding at a rate two to three times that of trade expansion. Yet tragically, while these institutions have met their goal, they have failed in their purpose. The world has more poor people today than ever before. We have an accelerating gap between the rich and the poor. Widespread violence is tearing apart families and communities nearly everywhere. And the planet's ecosystems are deteriorating at an alarming rate.

Yet the prevailing wisdom continues to maintain that economic growth offers the answer to poverty, environmental security, and a strong social fabric—and that economic globalization—which involves erasing economic borders to allow the free flow of goods and money— is the key to growth. Indeed, the more severe the mounting economic, environmental, and social crises become, the stronger the policy commitment to these same prescriptions, even as evidence mounts that they are not working. Indeed, there is a growing consensus outside of official circles that they *cannot* work, for reasons I will elaborate. Yet official institutions seem unable to take a badly needed fresh look.

In 1944, those who gathered at Bretton Woods were living in a world gripped by war, struggling to look beyond it to a new world order. Today, we live in a world gripped by a particular economic paradigm that we are struggling to look beyond. In so doing, we must envision a very different world order that embodies a more advanced understanding of the reality of our planet and the potential of our species. Such a vision, which puts a new frame on our global crisis, is emerging out of the struggles of growing numbers of individuals and organizations from around the world, mostly outside the mainstream. Many are dependent on private philanthropy to carry forward their important work.

My intention is to present a synthesis of some of this thinking. The issues I will address are complex and not well understood. I will necessarily have to simplify some very complex realities. Regardless of whether I convince you of my arguments, I hope you will at least recognize the profound significance of the issues addressed and seek out other opportunities to examine them in greater depth. I will begin with four concepts that in my mind provide an orienting perspective fundamental to understanding that the worldview that informed the original Bretton Woods meeting and subsequent policy is dangerously wrong.

A FULL WORLD

As the founder of ecological economics, Herman Daly, regularly reminds us, the human economy is embedded in and dependent on the natural ecosystem of our planet (see figure 3.1).[2] Up until the present moment in human history, however, the scale of our economic activity relative to the scale of the ecosystem had been sufficiently small that in both economic theory and practice we could get away with ignoring this fundamental fact.

We have now crossed, however, a monumental historical threshold. Because of the fivefold economic expansion since 1950, the environmental demands of our economic system now fill the available environmental space of the planet. We now live in a full world.

The first environmental limits that we have confronted, and possibly exceeded, are not the limits to nonrenewable resource exploitation, as many once anticipated, but rather the limits to our use of renewable resources and to our use of the environment's sink functions—its ability to absorb our wastes. These are limits related to the loss of soils, fisheries, forests, and water, to the absorption of CO_2 emissions, and to destruction of the ozone layer. We could argue about the details of whether a particular limit was hit at noon yesterday or will be passed at midnight tomorrow. The details are far less important than coming to terms with the basic truth that we have no real option other than to recreate our economic institutions in line with the reality of a full world.

The existing Bretton Woods structure is geared by both structure and ideology to an ever continuing expansion of economic output—eco-

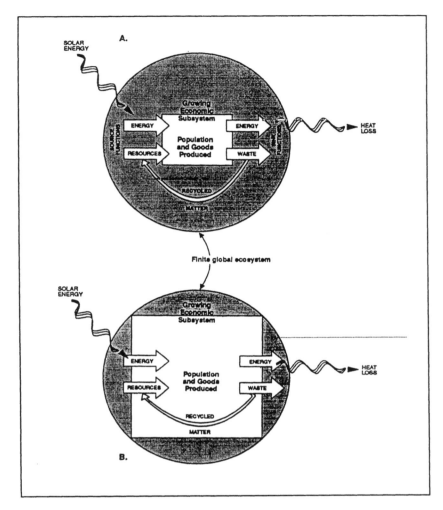

FIGURE 3.1
Transition to a Full World

Source: Goodland, Daly, & El Serafy, *Population, Technology and Lifestyle*

nomic growth—and to the integration of national economies into a
seamless global economy. The consequence is to intensify competition
for already overstressed environmental space. In a full world, this inten-
sified competition accelerates destruction of the regenerative capacities
of the ecosystem on which we and future generations depend; it crowds
out all forms of life not needed for immediate human consumption pur-

poses; and it increases competition between rich and poor for control of ecological resources. In a free market—which responds only to money, not needs—the rich win this competition every time. We see it happening all over the world. Hundreds and millions of the financially weak are simply displaced as their lands, waters, and fisheries are expropriated and converted to uses serving the wants of the more affluent.

So long as resources remain, the demands of the rich can be met—which may explain why so many of the rich see no problem. The poor experience a very different reality, but in a market economy their experience doesn't count.

As Herman Daly regularly notes, the market is unable to deal with questions relating to the appropriate scale of economic activity. There are no price signals indicating that the poor are going hungry because they have been forced off their lands. Nor is there any price signal to tell polluters that too much CO_2 is being released into the air or that toxics should not be dumped into soils or waters. Steeped in market ideology and highly responsive to corporate interests, the Bretton Woods institutions have demonstrated little capacity to give more than lip service either to environmental concerns or to the needs of the poor. Rather, their efforts have de facto centered on assuring that people with money have full access to whatever resources remain—with little regard for the broader consequences.

A new Bretton Woods meeting to update the institutional system would serve a significant and visionary need—if it were based on a realization that economic growth is no longer a valid public policy priority. Indeed, whether the global economy grows or shrinks is largely irrelevant. Having crossed over the threshold to a full world, the appropriate concern is whether the available planetary resources are being used in ways that: (1) meet the basic needs of all people; (2) maintain biodiversity; and (3) assure the sustained availability of comparable resource flows to future generations. Our present economic system is failing on all three counts.

THREE SOCIO-ECOLOGICAL CLASSES

In *How Much Is Enough?* Alan Durning divided the world into three consumption classes that we might characterize as: overconsumers, sustainers, and marginals (see figure 3.2).[3]

The overconsumers are the 20 percent of the world's people who consume roughly 80 percent of the world's resources—those of us whose lives are organized around automobiles, airplanes, meat-based diets, and the use of wastefully packaged disposable products. The marginals, a

OVERCONSUMERS 1.1 Billion > US $7,500 per capita (Cars-Meat-Disposables)	SUSTAINERS 3.3 Billion US $700-7,500 per capita (Living Lightly)	MARGINALS 1.1 Billion < US $700 per capita (Absolute Deprivation)
Travel by car & air	Travel by bicycle & public service surface transport	Travel by foot, maybe donkey
Eat high fat, high calory meat-based diets	Eat healthy diets of grains, vegetables and some meat	Eat nutritionally inadequate diets
Drink bottled water and soft drinks	Drink clean water plus some tea and coffee	Drink contaminated water
Use throw-away products & discard substantial wastes	Use unpackaged goods and durables & recycle wastes	Use local biomass & produce negligible wastes
Live in spacious, climate-controlled, single family residences	Live in modest, naturally ventilated residences, with extended multiple families	Live in rudimentary shelters or in the open; usually lack secure tenure
Maintain image-conscious wardrobe	Wear functional clothing	Wear second-hand clothing or scraps

FIGURE 3.2
Earth's Three Socio-Ecological Classes

Based on Alan Durning, *How Much is Enought?*, Worldwatch Institute

corresponding 20 percent of the world's people, live in absolute deprivation. Given the reality of a full world, we have little choice but to
acknowledge that the deprivation of this group is a direct consequence
of our own overconsumption.

Another important, and somewhat more encouraging insight
embedded in this figure is the fact that roughly 60 percent of the world's
people are already members of the sustainer class. Their basic needs are
being met in more or less sustainable ways. This insight makes the problem seem somewhat less formidable.

Unfortunately, by embracing the premise of infinite physical abundance articulated by Morgenthau, the Bretton Woods system has pursued a development vision that defines prosperity in terms of bringing
both sustainers and marginals into the overconsumer class. In a finite
world, this is a physical impossibility. The vision of Bretton Woods is an
illusion; its failure of purpose was inevitable.

Even more tragic, however, policies and projects directed to achieving the impossible dream have made, and continue to make, life in the
sustainer class ever more difficult. For example, the more human habi-
tats become structured around the automobile, which has become one
of our most environmentally and socially destructive technologies, the

more difficult it becomes to live without a car—even though it is entirely possible to structure a built environment so that a car serves no real need. Our goal must be to make life in the sustainer class as secure, comfortable, and fulfilling as possible and to assist the world's overconsumers and marginals in becoming sustainers. This requires a fundamental reorientation in development thinking.

Population growth is also a relevant concern. The larger the total population, the more constrained the sustainer lifestyle must ultimately be. I will not dwell on the population problem here as it is addressed in other chapters in this volume.

THE CHAMPAGNE GLASS OF ECONOMIC INJUSTICE

The United Nations Development Programme's *Human Development Report* for 1992 introduced the champagne glass as a graphic metaphor for a world of extreme economic injustice (see figure 3.3).[4] The bowl of the champagne glass represents the abundance enjoyed by the 20 percent of people who live in the world's richest countries, receive 82.7 percent of the world's income, and consume a comparable share of resources. Down at the bottom of the stem, where the sediment settles, we find the poorest 20 percent of the world's people who barely survive on 1.4 percent of the total income. The combined incomes of the top 20 percent are sixty times larger than those of the bottom 20 percent. Furthermore, this gap has doubled since 1950—when the top 20 percent enjoyed only thirty times the income of the bottom 20 percent. And the gap continues to grow.

Figure 3.3 actually understates the true inequality in the world because it is based on national averages rather than actual individual incomes. If we take into account the very rich people who live in poor countries and the very poor people who live in rich countries, it turns out that the incomes of the richest 20 percent of the world's people are approximately 150 times those of the poorest 20 percent. That gap is growing as well. An even more dramatic illustration of inequality is the fact that, today, the world's 350-plus billionaires have a combined net worth equal to the total annual income of the poorest 45 percent of the world's people.

Robert Reich, the former U.S. Secretary of Labor, explained in his book *The Work of Nations*, that the economic globalization the Bretton Woods institutions has advanced so successfully has served to delink the interests of the wealthy classes from a sense of national interest and thereby from a sense of concern for and obligation to their less fortunate neighbors. A thin segment of the superrich at the very lip of the cham-

pagne glass has formed a stateless alliance that defines the global interest in a way that happens to be synonymous with the personal and corporate financial interests of its members.⁵

This delinking has been occurring in nearly every country in the
world to such an extent that it is no longer meaningful to speak in terms
of a world divided into Northern and Southern nations. The more
meaningful North-South divide is not geography, it is class.

The free-trade market and free-trade polices advanced by the Bret-

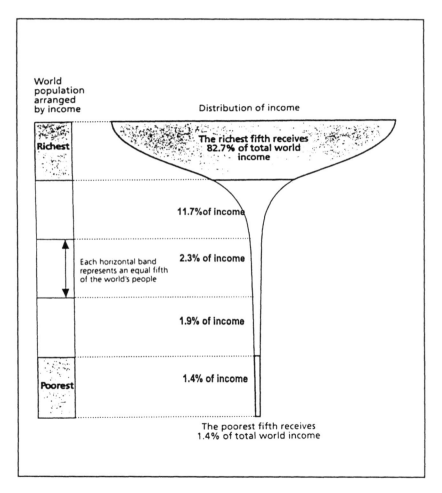

FIGURE 3.3
Economic Injustice

ton Woods institutions give precedence to the interests of money over other human and environmental concerns and are thus aligned almost entirely with the narrow interests of the ruling economic elite. It is difficult to conceive of a more powerful proof of this assertion than the rapid growth of the gulf that separates the small strata of the superrich from the rest of society. Whether intended or not, the policies so successfully advanced by the Bretton Woods institutions have inexorably strengthened the ability of the superrich to lay claim to ever more of the world's wealth at the expense of other people, species, and the viability of the planet's ecosystem.

DEMOCRATIC PLURALISM

The issue is not the market per se. Trying to run an economy without markets is disastrous, as the experience of the Soviet Union demonstrated. However, there is a fundamentally important distinction between markets and *free* markets. Figure 3.4 speaks to this difference.

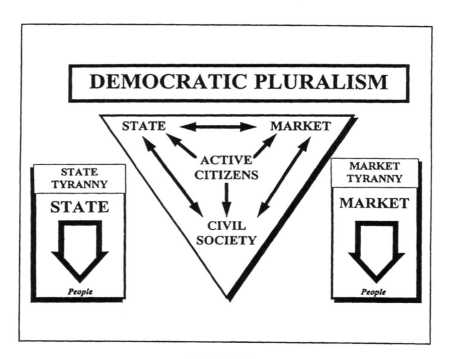

FIGURE 3.4
Democratic Pluarlism

A struggle between two extremist ideologies has been a central feature of the twentieth century. Communism called for all power to the state. Market capitalism calls for all power to the market—a euphemism for giant corporations. Both ideologies lead to their own distinctive form of tyranny. The secret of Western success in World War II and the early postwar period was not a free market economy. It was the practice of democratic pluralism built on institutional arrangements that seek to maintain a balance between the institutions of the state and the market and protect the right of an active citizenry to hold both institutions accountable to the public interest.

Contrary to the claims of ideologues who preach a form of corporate libertarianism, markets need governments to function efficiently. It is well established in economic theory and practice that markets allocate resources efficiently only when firms internalize the costs of their production and when markets are competitive. Governments must set and enforce the rules that make cost internalization happen, and since successful firms invariably grow larger and more monopolistic, governments must regularly step in to break them up and restore competition.

For governments to play their necessary role in balancing market and community interests, governmental power must be concentrated at the same system level as market power. If markets are national, then there must be a strong national government. By expanding the boundaries of the market beyond the boundaries of the nation state through economic globalization, we almost inevitably place the concentration of market power beyond the reach of government. This has been an important consequence of both the structural adjustment programs of the World Bank and IMF and the trade agreements negotiated under the GATT. The effective result is to transfer governance decisions from governments, which at least in theory represent the interests of all citizens, to the dominant institutions of the market—corporations—which by their nature serve the interests of their shareholders. One result is a loss of ability of societies everywhere on the planet to address environmental and other needs.

Relieved of constraints to their own growth, enormous economic power is being concentrated in the hands of a very few global corporations. Antitrust actions to restore the conditions of market competition by breaking up these concentrations has been one of the many casualties of globalization. Indeed, current government policies encourage national firms to merge into ever more powerful concentrations to strengthen their position in global markets.

The fact that large corporations have been shedding employees at a rapid rate has created an impression in some quarters that the large firms are losing their power. It is a misleading impression. The Fortune 500 firms did shed 4.4 million jobs between 1980 and 1993. During this same period, however, their sales increased by 1.4 times, assets by 2.3 times, and CEO compensation by 6.1 times. Although these large firms employ just one twentieth of 1 percent of the world's population, they control 25 percent of the world's output and 70 percent of world trade. This concentration has progressed to the point that of the world's one hundred largest economies, fifty are now corporations—not including banking and financial institutions.

Any industry in which five firms control 50 percent or more of the market is considered by economists to be highly monopolistic. *The Economist* magazine recently reported that five firms control more than 50 percent of the *global* market in the following industries: consumer durables, automotive, airlines, aerospace, electronic components, electrical and electronic, and steel. Five firms control over 40 percent of the global market in oil, personal computers, and—especially alarming for its consequences on public debate on these very issues—media.

Such firms have enormous political power and they are actively using it to reshape the rules of the market in their own favor. The GATT has become one of their most powerful tools for this purpose. Under the new GATT agreement, a World Trade Organization, the WTO, has been created with far-reaching powers to provide the world's largest corporations with the legal protection they feel they need to continue expanding their far-flung operations without responsibility for serving any interest other than their own bottom line.

The WTO will hear disputes brought against the national and local laws of any country that another member country considers to be a trade barrier. Complaints will be heard by secret panels comprised of three unelected trade experts whose rulings can be overturned only by a unanimous vote of the member countries. In general, any health, safety, or environmental standard that exceeds a maximum set by an international standards body dominated by industry representatives is likely to be assumed to be a trade barrier unless the offending government can prove it has a valid scientific basis. The burden of proof is on the defendant. If the WTO panel rules that a law constitutes a trade barrier, the government for whom the decision is taken may demand payment from the transgressing government equal to the presumed loss. The GATT agreement also guarantees global patent protection—a move that gives large corporations virtual monopoly rights over a wide range of technologies and even life-forms.

A FINANCIAL SYSTEM OUT OF CONTROL

As powerful as the large corporations are, they function increasingly as instrumentalities of a global financial system that has become the world's most powerful governance institution. The power in this system lies with a small group of private financial institutions that have only one objective—to make money in massive quantities. A seamless electronic web allows anyone with proper access codes and a personal computer to conduct instantaneous trades involving billions of dollars on any of the world's financial markets. The world of finance has become much like a gigantic computer game. In this game, the smart money does not waste itself on long-term commitments to productive enterprises engaged in producing real wealth to meet the needs of real people. Rather it seeks short-term returns from speculation in erratic markets and from simultaneous trades in multiple markets to profit from minute price variations. In this game, the short term is measured in microseconds; the long term in days. The environmental, social, and even economic consequences of financial decisions involving more than a trillion dollars a day are invisible to those who make them.

Joel Kurtzman, former business editor of *The New York Times* and editor of the *Harvard Business Review*, estimates that for every dollar circulating in the productive economy today, twenty to fifty dollars circulate in the world of pure finance.[6] Since these transactions take place through unmonitored international computer networks, no one knows how much is really involved. The $1 trillion that changes hands each day in the world's international currency markets is itself 20 to 30 times the amount required to cover daily trade in actual goods and services. If the world's most powerful governments act in concert to attempt to stabilize exchange rates in these same markets, the best they can manage is a measly $14 million a day—little more than pocket change compared to the amounts mobilized by speculators and arbitragers.

The vast bulk of these free-floating funds are controlled by large investment houses, banks, mutual funds, and retirement funds. Each pool of money is managed by professional investment managers whose reputations depend on their financial performances relative to that of their colleagues. The mutual fund managers see their results reported for public scrutiny each day in every major newspaper around the world. Some people may put their money in these funds for the long term, but the professionals who manage these funds have to show daily and quarterly results.

The corporations that invest in real assets are forced by the resulting pressures to restructure their operations in ways that maximize their immediate short-term return to shareholders. One way to do this is by downsizing, streamlining, and automating their operations, using the most advanced technologies to eliminate hundreds of thousands of jobs. The result is jobless economic growth. Contemporary economies simply cannot grow fast enough to create jobs faster than technology and a dysfunctional economic system are shedding them. In nearly every country in the world we now have a labor surplus, and those lucky enough to have jobs are increasingly members of the contingent workforce without either security or benefits. The resulting fear and insecurity makes the jobs versus environment issue a crippling barrier to essential environmental action.

Another way to increase corporate profits is to externalize ever more of the cost of the firm's operations into the community. This is accomplished by pitting localities against one another in a standards-lowering competition to offer subsidies, tax holidays, and freedom from environmental and employment standards. Similarly, workers are pitted against one another in a struggle for survival that pushes wages down to their lowest common denominator. This is what global competitiveness is about—competition among localities—not among the corporations, which are engaged in minimizing the competition among themselves through mergers and strategic alliances.

Any corporation that does not play this game to its limit is likely to find itself a takeover target by a corporate raider who will buy out the company and profit by taking the actions that the previous management—perhaps from a fit of social conscience and loyalty to workers and community—failed to take. The basic point is that the globalizing economic system is reconstructing itself in a way that makes it almost impossible for even highly socially conscious and committed managers to operate a corporation responsibly in the public interest.

CONCLUSION

We are caught in a terrible dilemma. We have reached a point in history that requires us to rethink the very nature and meaning of human progress in fundamental ways. Yet the vision and decisions that emerged from Bretton Woods more than fifty years ago set in motion events that have transformed the governance processes of societies everywhere on the planet in ways that make the necessary actions virtually impossible. It has happened so quickly and is so foreign to our culturally imbedded assumptions that few among us even realize what has happened. The real issues are seldom discussed in a media dependent on corporate advertising.

There is a compelling case to be made that sustainability in a growth-dependent globalized economy is what Herman Daly would call an impossibility theorem. What is the alternative? Among those of us who are devoting significant attention to this question, the answer is the opposite of globalization. It lies in promoting greater economic *localiza-*

tion—breaking economic activities down into smaller, more manageable pieces in ways that link the people who make decisions to the consequences of those decisions, both positive and negative. It means rooting capital in place and distributing its control among as many people as possible.

We must recognize that our global development models and the myths on which they are based reflect the values and institutions of an earlier industrial era. Corporations, concentrating enormous economic resources in centrally controlled institutions and unleashing the power of capital-intensive technologies to exploit the world's natural and human resources to benefit the few, have been the cornerstone of that era. But as globalization accelerates the exploitation of the earth and its people, the industrial era is likely to exhaust itself as it exhausts the human and natural resource base on which all of our lives depend.

Powerful interests stand resolutely in the way of achieving such a reversal of current trends. The biggest barrier, however, is the limited extent of public discussion on the subject. The starting point must be to get the issues out on the table and bring them into the mainstream policy debates in a way that is not now happening.

NOTES

1. U.S. Department of State, *Proceedings and Documents of the United Nations Monetary and Financial Conference, Bretton Woods, New Hampshire, July 1–22, 1944*, vol. 1, pp. 790–83, as cited by Bruce Rich, *Mortgaging the Earth* (Boston: Beacon Press, 1994), pp. 54–55.

2. Herman Daly et al., *Population, Technology and Lifestyle: The Transition to Sustainability* (Covelo, Calif.: Island Press, 1992).

3. Alan Durning, *How Much Is Enough? The Consumer Society and the Future of the Earth*, Worldwatch Institute Environmental Alert Series (New York: Norton, 1992).

4. United Nations Development Programme, *Human Development Report* (New York: Oxford University Press, 1992).

5. Robert B. Reich, *The Work of Nations: Preparing Ourselves for 21st-Century Capitalism* (New York: Vintage Books, 1992).

6. Joel Kurtzman, *The Death of Money* (New York: Simon & Schuster, 1993), p. 65.

CHAPTER 4

Self as Individual and Collective: Ethical Implications

Harold Coward

Most modern Western ethical analysis in matters of reproduction, consumption, and ecology assumes that the ethical agent is "the choosing individual." This is especially true of much analytical philosophy. I want to critically examine this assumption and suggest that it has two potential flaws: (1) it does not fit with many traditional religious societies where the ethical agent is seen to be the collective rather than the individual; and (2) the focus on the choosing individual as the ethical agent leads to a concentration on rights rather than obligations (witness the language of recent United Nations declarations). Both of these points can be interpreted as "flaws" if they lead to a separation of the individual from the larger context of humanity or nature in which he or she is an interdependent part. Being a "chooser of options" is in itself not the problem. Deliberative choice is in many ways the hallmark of mature personhood. Indeed, the modern Western focus on the choosing individual and his or her rights has achieved many positive gains in terms of equal justice for women and the oppressed. The contention of this chapter, however, is that these gains—valuable though they are—have had a price, namely, the loss of our sense of collective interrelationships with other humans and with the natural environment that makes our continued life possible. The problem is in the isolation and estrangement, not in the choosing power itself. This chapter argues that a recovery of our collective sense of self-identity, to at least balance our current bias toward seeing ourselves as atomistic, isolated choosing individuals, is essential for an ethical analysis of the population/consumption/ecology problematic.

"I-SELF" AND "WE-SELF" IN ETHICAL ANALYSIS

Those of us shaped by a modern Western upbringing and cultural context tend to experience our personal identity as created by being a chooser of options. This is the modern liberal concept of individuals as choosers. Our identity in a liberal society is a construct of the choices we make or fail to make. We see ourselves first and foremost as consumers or as constructors of options. Our natural, social, and economic environments are then for us not givens but potentially manipulable elements in our never ceasing struggle for, in the words of Thomas Hobbes, "power after power."[1] This leads us to seek the maximum benefits for our individual selves here and now over against the good of other persons now, or future generations, or nature itself. We tend to structure the world so that the individual choices we make in reproductive, economic, or environmental situations will bring us maximum benefit. The ethic encouraged is one of self-interest defined in individualistic utilitarian terms[2] rather than self-interest through identification with the larger whole, for example, humanity or the cosmos. It produces a focus upon human rights (often defined as isolated individual rights in law and public policy) as a way of ensuring that each person gets his or her fair share. It fosters an economy that, when meshed with modern technology, constantly expands to supply enlarging needs (with increasing levels of consumption) and to keep pace with the world's rapidly growing population. The result is an unsustainable degradation of nature in the name of serving human needs defined as human rights. Human beings, and their needs, are put at war with the sustainability of nature—which according to some readings of the Bible and Qur'an is created for the purpose of supporting humans. This one-sided ontology may have helped foster the modern liberal emphasis on the individual. When put together with utilitarian secular ethics and the market economy, the results for the global ecosystem may be devastating (see the greenhouse effect projections of environmental scientists).[3]

Although the individual as atomistic, isolated chooser is the identity that dominates the self-understanding of most modern Europeans and North Americans, for much of the rest of the world identity is understood quite differently. In traditional Jewish, Islamic, Hindu, Buddhist, Chinese, and Aboriginal societies self-identity is constructed not by individual choices but by participating in a "family" that may extend out to include caste, tribe, and all humans as well as plants, animals, and the cosmos. For example, in the Chinese worldview it is never the isolated, individual "self" but the self as interrelated in community, nature, and with heaven that is the ethical agent. Identity is in one's harmonious interrelationships, not in one's choices/rights, powers, and privileges.

Such a broadened self-understanding leads to a focus on obligations to the whole rather than an emphasis on individual human rights—although the safeguards of the latter are an important defense against abuses of the individual (especially children and women) that the former has sometimes produced, and therefore they need to be retained but balanced. Let me move from the level of broad social, political, and economic analysis to that of psychological processes to further explore the different understandings of the self as an ethical agent that I have sketched above. I begin with a personal illustration.

Several years ago when I was just beginning my career as a university professor, I ended up going to a conference with a colleague who was Hindu, born in India. I am a Canadian Protestant Christian. Now I knew all about Hinduism—in fact I taught it in the university. But until this trip I had not really understood the tradition from within. The difference began when we selected our seats on the plane. Of course, we would sit together, but the seats should be chosen so as to avoid certain inauspicious numbers. When we got to the hotel room that we were sharing, other things began to happen. I noticed my friend using my toothpaste. For me, this seemed to be an invasion of my privacy and property, without even the courtesy of asking permission. For him, there was no clear separation of ownership because we were together—our identities and possessions were merged into a collective unity. It was our toothpaste, and as it looked interesting, he was trying it. I soon came to understand that being together also meant that whenever we left the room to attend sessions, eat, or do some sightseeing, we did it together. This was quite different from my usual conference-going experience of room sharing where the only time you might see your roommate was at night or on waking in the morning. Being with my Hindu colleague and sharing his worldview meant we did everything together. The two of us were merged into one. For me to go off to do something on my own would have caused a serious rupture in our collective personhood. No longer was I an autonomous individual. We made our decisions as a shared identity.

This collective as opposed to individual identity has important implications for issues of population, consumption, and ecology. As doctors, nurses, or ethicists dealing with reproductive issues, for example, it means we are not interacting with an autonomous person (our usual experience), but with a person who understands self-identity in terms of a larger whole such as an extended family.

Alan Roland, a New York psychiatrist, reports just such an experience.[4] He found that his Indian Hindu patients (highly educated professionals) did not respond to his usual modern Western therapies, which assumed a strongly individualized sense of self—an I-ness characterized by a self-contained set of ego boundaries with sharp distinctions between self and others. By contrast he found his South Asian patients to be a familial or "we-self" that enabled them to function within extended families. Rather than the self-contained ego boundaries of the typical North American "I-self," which allows us to function in a highly autonomous society, the "we-self" of his Indian patients had highly permeable ego boundaries opening the way for the constant empathy and receptivity to others necessary for life in an extended family. Instead of actualization of the individual self, the personal and spiritual goal of the South Asian is the reciprocal responsibility required to live in harmony within the hierarchical structure of family, society, and ideally all of nature. Whereas the North American I-self sharply separates between self and others, self and nature, often in a competitive fashion, the we-self of Asian cultures extends outward to include family, caste-group, linguistic-ethnic culture, and even the natural environment. From the Buddhist perspective, which is dominant in the cultures of East and Southeast Asia, it is our false attachment to the I-self and its selfish desires that is the cause of unethical action and suffering. Understanding ourselves as but a tiny interdependent part of the complex we-self of the cosmos leads to compassionate action and nirvana. Yet within that complex we-self, observes Rolland, a highly private ego is maintained.

What does all this mean for reproductive issues in health care? First, diagnosis and treatment in many cultures will have to pay more attention to the extended family and the environmental context in which the person lives—the we-self. For example, my wife, a nurse, working in a family practice unit serving prairie Stoney Aboriginal patients had frequent we-self experiences. When a young woman or older teenage girl would arrive with gynecological problems, she would be accompanied by her mother, aunts, and grandmother. All would insist on going back to the examining room together (a room designed to hold just two or three). When the doctor was taking the history, often it would be the grandmother who would do the talking, saying when the girl had had her last period, and so forth. Everyone knew everything, naturally, as they were a we-self. And everyone expected to be involved in the treatment and any ethical decisions to be made. This raises the second point, namely, that issues of consent have to take seriously that the ethical decision-maker in such a culture is not just the individual, but the we-self of which they are but a respected part. Recognition of this fact should cause us to reexamine our methods and forms for obtaining consent which, for the most part, are devised on the assumption that the person is an autonomous individual—an I-self, sharply separated from others in one's family or society. The existence of cultures with we-self expanding identities challenges autonomous conceptions of health and human rights often assumed in UN declarations, especially relating to women and children. We should not be surprised to discover that the feminist movements in traditional cultures do not always express the goal for women in terms of individual women's rights. Rather it is the just and respected place of women within the we-self of the family and even the environment that is the focus of ethical analysis. When ethical issues surrounding reproduction arise, a woman within the we-self ideally ponders the good of the extended family and the sustainable capacities of the environment, along with her own desires, in coming to a decision. Nor should we be surprised to find that in such cultures the idea that children or adolescents have ethical standing independent of the family raises reactions of incomprehensibility and hostility.

While our modern Western notions of individual autonomy and human rights can serve to highlight ethical abuses and exploitation that can and do arise in the extended family (an important contribution often liberating to women and children), the other side of the coin is that the we-self ideals of mutual responsibility and respect between ourselves, others, and the environment are a much needed corrective to a self-centered selfishness that our modern Western competitive I-self so successfully generates. Indeed at a time of rapid population increase or tightened resources in health care, ethical questions of who gets treatment and in what order of priority are made very difficult, if not impossible to resolve, when the rights of individual autonomy reign supreme. A collective we-self, by contrast, provides a more practical and helpful ethical approach, one that strives to balance the needs of the individual with those of the larger interdependent whole. In our current and future scarce-resources scenarios, we may find wisdom in the way traditional we-self cultures have developed ethical guidelines for solving such problems. Inuit grandparents used to go off to freeze to death in the snow when there was not enough food for the young. While our technological capacities should enable us to avoid the prescription of freezing to death, the ethical value of the we-self in giving priority to the young in times of scarce resources is one we should carefully consider.

The experience of death in different cultures offers another illustration as to how great sensitivity is demanded in understandings of self-identity. Our autonomous I-self focus has led us to give great attention to such things as advance directives or living wills. This is in sharp contrast to we-self societies where it is inconceivable to think of the death of an individual independent from the community of which he or she is a part. Of course, individuals must have the right to some definite say about their own dying place, even in communitarian societies.

Peter Stephenson, a medical anthropologist, offers an example from a Hutterite community in southern Alberta.[5] In contrast to the fast (and therefore supposedly "painless") "ideal death" of an individual in modern Western culture, the Hutterite ideal of a good death is one that is slow and drawn out surrounded by family and community. Everyone is anxious to see the "fortunate one" who is preparing to enter a better heavenly life. Death-bed time is needed for dying Hutterites for it is a time when, together with the members of their community, "they are to 'relive' their lives, to forgive others and to be forgiven."[6] Dying is not an isolated matter for the individual self but an obligation to be lived through with the we-self of the whole community—allowing for the socialization of all into the prospect of a better heavenly life.

How does all of this become an ethical issue for doctors, nurses, and communities? Stephenson tells the story of his Hutterite friend, Paul, who at forty-eight died of lymphosarcoma. Paul was taken from his home colony to the hospital in the city. Because of limited visiting hours and distant travel, few members of the community were able to visit Paul and together with him prepare for a good death. Finally after nearly two weeks, Paul was returned to his colony by ambulance arriving in the evening but dying at 4:00 a.m. In the eyes of the community, Paul's death was "too quick." Paul's isolated time in the hospital represented a lost opportunity for the collective self of Paul and his community to prepare a good death. Stephenson concludes: "When Paul died he was still too much alive—he was still among the [living] and not yet with 'the dead.'"[7] He did not have time to put his we-self to rest.

"WE-SELF" AND INDIVIDUAL ETHICAL ACTION

Having described the distinction between the I-self and the we-self in ethical analysis, let us now carefully examine the relationship between the we-self and engagement of the individual in ethical action—as for example in responding to the challenges of overpopulation, excess consumption, and degradation of the environment. Does understanding oneself as a we-self rather than an I-self make any difference to the way one responds to these ethical challenges? David Loy certainly thinks so. In his chapter in this book he suggests that the atomistic individualism of utilitarianism, which "naturalizes" such greed, must be challenged and refuted intellectually and in the way we actually live our lives. Consumerism fosters exaggeration of selfish I-ness. He goes on to say that the sensitivity to social justice of the Western religions, where sin is a moral failure of *will*, needs to be supplemented by the emphasis that the Asian religions place on seeing through and dispelling illusion (ignorance as a failure to *understand*).

Loy's analysis is supplemented by the contemporary Japanese writer

Yuasa, who argues that the Asian way of seeing the mind-body problem helps in overcoming our atomistic I-ness. Yuasa, in his book *The Body: Toward an Eastern Mind-Body Theory*,[8] argues that Western theories either deny the mind-body unity (following Descartes) or see it as occurring by some substantial unchanging link such as the pineal gland, the soul, or the brain, which is present in all people but not developed to the perfection in which action mirrors thought in a fused unity of body-mind awareness. Kasulis, commenting on Yuasa's analysis, puts it this way: "It is as if the grid of Western thought has a place for the concept of an achieved body-mind unity, but that place is hidden behind the crosshatching of the Western concepts. The Western tradition can recognize the possibility, but its concepts intersect so that a blindspot occurs precisely where the body-mind unity can be found—in the enlightened state achieved through years of spiritual and physical cultivation."[9] It is a problem of *will* obstructed by sin. As Paul puts it in Romans 7:14, "I do not do what I want, but I do the very thing I hate." But for God's grace there is no hope. However, for the West, neither does *understanding* guarantee the desired action—especially not since Descartes separated mind from body. As the poet T. S. Eliot puts it:

> Between the idea
> And the reality
> Between the motion
> And the act
> Falls the shadow . . .

the shadow that makes us modern Westerners "The Hollow Men."[10] Even Kant concluded we cannot know reality—the things in themselves, although thinkable, are not knowable.[11] For Westerners, the "shadow" of sinful will and flawed understanding make it difficult to fully unify thought and action, mind and body. Nor does Western thought (theology or philosophy) seem to offer a way out. Perhaps, suggests Yuasa, that is because Western thought has been too focused upon the mind-body relationship in the common (universal) rather than the exceptional person (the religious and artistic masters). In such perfected persons, the shadow has been overcome and a perfect unity of mind and body obtains allowing full awareness of reality and spontaneous action in accordance with that awareness (variously called *śunya* (Buddhism) or *wu-wei* (Daoism). The gap between the theoretical and the practical, the will and the action, the mind and the body is closed. But how, we ask as Westerners, is this miracle to be accomplished? Yuasa replies that it is through Eastern techniques of yoga or meditation that the intellectual and the physiological, the mind and the body are integrated. In more familiar psychological terms, what is achieved through these techniques is nothing short of the full integration of the conscious with the unconscious and the disappearance of the individual ego (the I-self) as the focal point of the personality.

While Yuasa's analysis contains much truth, it oversimplifies Western thought and leaves out key strands that do not fall into the polarized mind-body dualism that he categorizes as representative of the West. Such dualism did not characterize Paul's thought in Romans. And Catherine Keller[12] points out that a stress on community identity was present in the Hebrew background of Jesus and in primitive Christian metaphors such as the Body in which "we are members of one another." However, she admits that such seed ideas failed to take root and flower as Western thought evolved through the teachings of the Church Fathers, Augustine, Aquinas, Descartes, Kant, and Hegel. Hume does challenge this body-soul bifurcation and adverts to an elusive feeling of connection as the ground for the inherence of perceptions. Thandeka's recent *The Embodied Self* persuasively argues that "the self embedded in nature slipped through the gap [the absence of a link between the noumenal and empirical self] in Kant's theory and lost its body."[13] This gap for Schleiermacher became a precognitive state of "feeling"—the feeling of the self as embedded in nature. William James, too, in his *Psychology* (1893) saw no mind-body duality in the self as a stream of consciousness.[14] The philosophers Whitehead and Lonergan also could be mentioned in this same connection.

Of wider current influence among contemporary Western thinkers who reject mind-body or body-soul duality are feminists like Gilligan and Chodorow. Even more important for our current argument, however, is their assertion that women through the ages have not typically felt themselves to be cleanly separated as selves from the surrounding world of persons, plants, and animals. Thus women are far less likely to have eradicated the sense of connection to others, nature, and self that is dominant in many men and typifies modern Western society.[15] However, as Van Herik[16] and Joy[17] point out, the stronger we-self of women in the West may well be the result of the way females have been socialized by patriarchical culture rather than by biological difference. Keller cites Chodorow's psychological analysis that "Girls come to experience themselves as less differentiated than boys, as more continuous with and related to the external object-world."[18] Like the we-self of traditional societies, girls' experience of self, Keller suggests, contains permeable ego-boundaries out of which the basic feminine sense of being connected to others and to nature and yet at the same time differentiated can evolve.[19] One's connectedness, says Keller, becomes more and more differentiated by taking in more and more of what is different. Such self-development, however, has not flourished in women due to the dominance of individualistic and autonomous values in modern Western education, socialization, and business. Consequently, the continuing relevance of Yuasa's admittedly overly simplistic analysis.

This excursus into "the mind-body problem," as it is usually called, was prompted by my question, "Does understanding oneself as a we-self rather than an I-self make a difference to the way one responds to the population, consumption, ecology problematic?" I want to suggest that a we-self as opposed to an I-self identity opens the way to a fuller realization of individual ethical action, and that Yuasa's mind-body analysis explains why. Yuasa suggests that in each of us there are two layers of consciousness.[20] There is the surface level of self-conscious awareness, which is the realm of thought. This "I think" level can be abstractly imagined, as Descartes did, to be disembodied and has been the object of most Western philosophy of the mind. It is the realm of the I-self. However, this level of self-conscious awareness does not stand on its own but is merely the surface level of something deeper, which Yuasa calls the "dark" consciousness. It includes what Freud called the unconscious but also the neurophysiological supports of the body—the brain, the autonomic nervous system, and so forth, parts that are necessarily engaged when we act. The goal is to unify the two levels. This is the achievement of exceptional individuals but also of all of us in particular moments of the sort I will illustrate in a moment. The more fully we unify these two levels, the more of a we-self we manifest, and the more spontaneous will be the unification of thought and action, mind and body. The illustration of how we all experience moments of such unification, even in our mostly I-self lives is offered by Yuasa as follows. Imagine that you are driving a car that goes into an unanticipated but controlled swerve to avoid hitting a dog. If you are asked how you avoided running over the dog, you will reply that you "simply reacted." How did you know when and how to move the car out of the way by the complicated maneuver of steering, braking, and timing? Certainly not by thinking it out at the moment for there was no time. Your response was a unity of thought and action, a conditioned response triggered by many years of driving practice. At the first instant of seeing the dog, you spontaneously valued the dog and attempted to avoid harming it. Momentarily the dog was part of your extended we-self. Had you had time to think, you may have been reluctant to swerve because that might place you and your car in danger of crashing, thus damaging yourself or your valuable possession, the car—a more selfish I-self response. Each of us seems to react in an unselfish spontaneous way in sudden situations like our automatic swerve to avoid the dog. Such a reaction is also evident when we suddenly come upon an accident on the highway. Seeing the car in the ditch, our immediate impulse is to stop and help—the foot comes off the accelerator and onto the brake. But then in a flash of thought, our I-self mind goes to work: am I really the right person to help, since I am not a doctor or nurse I might not do the right thing and might be sued, therefore, better leave it for someone else more qualified and, besides, if I stop I will be late for my important appointment—and so the foot goes back on the accelerator. In the extraordinary or perfected person, by contrast, the shadow of selfish thought never darkens the immediate compassionate impulse, the car is braked to a full stop and help given. The injured person is part of one's larger we-self identity and caring action comes spontaneously, just as it did in Jesus' parable of the good Samaritan. While the Western religions of Judaism, Christianity, and Islam clearly require the extension of our we-self identities to include all other humans—women, children, the foreigner, and even our enemy—Asian and Aboriginal teaching pushes further until all animals, all organic and inorganic nature are included. Such an all-inclusive we-self is I think potentially present in each of us. We do seem to impulsively pull back from hurting animals, killing plants, or polluting earth, air, and water. But this momentary we-self impulse rapidly disappears under the stronger self-interest of the I-self. Even when our thinking adopts ideals that value social and economic justice along with respect for animals, plants, earth, air, and water, our actions do not always follow suit. A mind-body split remains.

For the Western religions, the way to overcome this barrier to compassionate action is through the surrender of one's I-self to God in obedience. When focused on social justice issues this approach has produced some fine theology (e.g., Reinhold Niebuhr's *The Nature and Destiny of Man*),[21] and some exemplary action including: the Quakers' emancipation of women, opposition to slavery, campaigns for prison reform, and the extension of education to all classes of society; the Mennonites' willingness to fight hunger and poverty, and to work for peace; and Martin Luther King Jr.'s movement to liberate Blacks in the United States. Until recently, however, Western religious examples of the unification of mind and body into compassionate action that transcends the I-self seem restricted to the human realm. Only in Western mystical thought (e.g., the Kabbalists of Judaism and the Sufis of Islam or Saints like Francis of Assisi) do we find a strong impulse to extend the we-self beyond humans to identification with animals, plants, and the whole of the cosmos. The Kabbalists teach that just as God voluntarily limited his omnipresence to make room for the creation of humans, animals, plants, and so forth, so also, following God's example, humans must voluntarily limit their I-selves—their rate of reproduction, their use of natural resources, and their production of fouling wastes.[22] By the actions of limiting our reproduction and our wants (our I-self) we make room for coexistence with our environment in this and future generations (the ethics of an extended we-self). In the Sufi view nature is the manifestation of God's breath. The Sufi mystic Ibn' Arabī teaches that nature in its innocence manifests God's Compassionate Breath (*nafas al-Rahmān*) through its regularity and beauty.[23] Obedience requires the surrender of the I-self to God and identification in a unity of thought and action with the Compassionate Breath within us and around us in all creatures and entities of the cosmos—a large and extended we-self indeed! Today it is no longer just the esoteric witness of the mystics that is pushing the extension of the we-self to include all of nature. As the main thrust of these chapters makes clear, it is the challenges of overpopulation, unsustainable consumption, and the threatened destruction of the natural ecosystem itself that is forcing Jews, Christians, and Muslims toward an extended we-self of the sort earlier mystics pioneered.

While the Asian approaches of Hinduism, Buddhism, Chinese Religion, and the Aboriginal traditions have all advocated an extended we-self (inclusive of animals, plants, earth, air, and water) from the start,[24] the degree to which this has resulted in more enlightened action in these societies seems open to question. Callicot and Ames have suggested that the differences among religions do not seem to make much difference when we examine how humans have interacted with nature to date. In both the East and the West the environment has been ruthlessly exploited. In the view of Callicot and Ames it is our innate aggressiveness as *homo sapiens*, inherited from prehuman savanna primates, that is at the root of the problem.[25] This might lead us to the pessimistic conclusion that what religions teach about ecology does not matter after all, for we as humans are simply driven by our biological inheritance strongly manifested in our modern Western I-selves. However, neither the religions discussed in these chapters nor secular ethics would accept such a deterministic position. There is simply too much evidence that humans can and do change their behavior—sometimes in radical fashion. And it is with regard to just such conversions of thought and action that religions have demonstrated success down through the ages. This brings us back to Yuasa's analysis of mind-body theory.

The particular claim Yuasa makes for the Asian traditions is that the perfected realization of the extended we-self in action is seen as a possibility that everyone of us can achieve—indeed, in Hinduism and Buddhism we will each be reborn as many times as needed until we realize perfection by practicing what we preach. In addition, points out Yuasa, not only do these religions teach the ideas that each person is perfectible in the fully extended we-self but they also offer teachers and disciplines

(Yoga or meditation techniques) by which we may transform our I-self behavior into we-self behavior and so fully unify mind and body in harmony with the cosmos. In Yuasa's more psychological terminology this result would be a unification of the two levels, our ordinary conscious awareness and our unconscious including our neurophysiological body, into a single mind-body unity—a we-self that is fully aware of the ecosystem of which it is but an interdependent part, and integrated with it in spontaneous ethical action. The advantage Yuasa thinks the Asian approaches offer over the modern West's male-dominated individualism is that for the West the perfectibility of mind-body unification in an extended we-self is seldom suggested even as a possibility to be striven for.[26] And should one want to realize such an "impossible possibility," there are few spiritual masters or disciplines available in the modern West to help one on the way.

In the first section of this chapter, we contrasted the I-self typical of modern European and North American society with the we-self that characterizes women and traditional Muslim, Hindu, Buddhist, Chinese, and Aboriginal cultures. It is evident that in these traditional cultures, the we-self of the vast majority of persons would fall far short of the fully expanded and realized we-self described in the paragraphs above. In Chinese thought, for example, Mencius distinguishes between the actual and the ideal we-self. The question then needs to be raised as to what difference there is between the average actual we-self in a traditional Hindu, Buddhist, Chinese, Muslim, or Aboriginal society and the typical modern European or North American I-self—especially with regard to ethical action relating to the population, consumption, ecology problematic. As the section made clear, the we-self in traditional cultures made ethical decisions not from an individualistic I-self perspective but with reference to the larger collective we-self of which the individual was but a part. With regard to reproduction decisions this means that it is not just the wishes of the woman or the husband and wife that must be considered. The we-self invokes the extended family and, at times, as in contemporary China, the carrying capacity of the city or country in the action decision.[27] From a Buddhist perspective, concern that population growth may exceed the capacity of the earth may lead to a we-self decision to moderate both reproduction and consumption.[28] If the we-self in these traditions takes ethical concern for others no further than the extended family, caste, tribe, or nation, then limiting consumption and making it more just for all people on earth may not happen. Indeed the extended family can be just as powerful a force for greed and environmental exploitation as the individual I-self. Even within the extended family there can be negative results from we-self identity—women can be oppressed and led to adopt unhealthy "martyr" roles and children can be looked upon as "pawns" to be moved around for the enhancement of family power and fortune. In Japan, for example, we-self identification incorporated in industrialism has been most destructive both within and outside of the country in terms of social equity and environmental sustainability. The company functions as a quasi-family providing cradle to grave social security but in turn requiring unquestioning dedication, loyalty, and self-sacrifice from its employees. Individual employees may regret spending so little time at home with the family or feel guilt over participation in industrial practices that damage the environment, but the we-self consciousness that the company has carefully nourished overrides the I-self conscience of the person as a responsible husband, father, and citizen. Other abuses occurred in Japan during World War II when the we-self identification was mobilized for fighting—each citizen was called a *sekishi* (a child of the Emperor) and expected to unquestioningly do as the Emperor, his government, or military officers commanded. Similar destructive we-self identifications are seen in some "guru-led" organizations like the Om Sinrikyo cult, which allegedly sprinkled poisonous gas in the Tokyo subway system. These are the authoritarian or totalitarian we-self dangers that need an I-self sense of individual rights and critical conscience so as to maintain a healthy balance. The potential advantage of the person in the extended family is that (as Roland's research demonstrates) from the beginning identity is experienced in a we-self rather than I-self form. The lack of individualized ego in the we-self personality may well make it easier to extend the already existing we-self personality structure to include justice for all humans and respect for animals, plants, earth, air, and water. An added advantage is that many of these we-self traditions have a fully expanded we-self identity as the built-in religious goal to be realized—along with the practical techniques for doing it. But what they sometimes lack is the parallel goal of individual critical self-consciousness that is necessary for the development of a nonauthoritarian we-self. Such a we-self might be characterized as having "unity within diversity"—a person with sufficient individuality as to be able to develop a critical evaluation of those in power and yet retain a sense of being connected to others and to nature leading to compassionate, spontaneous action. This contrasts with the we-self of a totalitarian kind, which is characterized as "unity without diversity." To the outside world this we-self can show aggressiveness and chauvinistic denial—as the Japanese examples demonstrate.

To conclude this second section, let us briefly review. In this part of the chapter we have analyzed the we-self in relation to its ability to produce ethical action on the issues of population, consumption, and ecology. Does being a we-self rather than an I-self bring any advantage in this regard? By employing Yuasa's mind-body analysis we demonstrated that the nonauthoritarian we-self identity, especially in its Asian or Aboriginal manifestations, opens the way to a more complete realization of ethical action on population, consumption, and ecology, than the modern Western I-self identity offers. Not only is a fully unified mind-body we-self provided, but in its religious ideal it is extended to include all humans, animals, plants, earth, air, and water as the harmonious whole of which the individual is an interdependent part. Further this ideal is fully realizable in that the ordinary everyday "we-self" (which may begin by including only the extended family) is expandable via the disciplines of meditation to include all of the cosmos. The practical effect of an expanded and realized we-self is that in our ethical choosing we are spontaneously restrained, just, and compassionate in all matters of reproduction, consumption, and ecology. However, this is an ideal that the average we-self in a traditional Hindu or Buddhist society may take many, many lifetimes to perfect. The we-self does, however, offer the comparative advantage over the modern Western I-self of already being a collective identity that by cultivation through spiritual discipline is expandable beyond the family, city, or country to identity with the cosmos.

WE-SELF AND ETHICS IN PUBLIC POLICY DECISIONS

Does conceiving of identity in we-self rather than I-self terms make a difference at the level of ethics in public policy decision making? This is an important question for modern democracies that have officially embraced a pluralism premise that promises to respect the differing worldviews of minority cultural/religious/ethnic communities. For example, it is a key question for Canada since Canada has embraced a public policy that claims to be multicultural. Although the mainstream host culture of Canada clearly sees itself in I-self terms and correspondingly adopts an individualistic human rights approach on public policy issues, many of Canada's ethnic communities (e.g., Aboriginals, Hindus, Sikhs, Chinese and Japanese Buddhists, and South Asian Muslims) experience their identity in we-self terms.

Earlier I noted some of the practical problems that result when we-self identities interact with I-self contexts in the public arena—remember the case of the young Aboriginal woman consulting the doctor together with mother, grandmother, and aunts on a reproductive problem? From the too-small size of the examining room to the expectation in the training of doctor and nurse that they would deal with the *individual* Aboriginal woman alone for purposes of diagnosis and ethical decision making, the I-self and we-self cultures are in a state of tension and conflict. Such examples are common, not only in health care but also in law and education. In law, especially the I-self emphasis upon rights as a way to resolve problems and ensure justice runs into problems in that by law rights are usually attached to human individuals and their property. Thus identities that understand themselves in a collective we-self sense simply do not fit and are therefore passed by in ethical decision making. There is enough difficulty in dealing with collective identities among humans—think of the discombobulation that results when the I-self world of law, economics, and politics is asked to deal with a we-self that includes and gives ethical standing to animals, plants, and even inorganic nature—the earth, air, and water.

Scholars working within the liberal I-self worldview are attempting to cope with this problem by developing a communitarian ethic—one that extends identity and rights to communities.[29] Basing itself on Kant's ideal of respect for persons, "welfare liberals" as they are called in philosophy, have argued that there is a positive duty on the state to protect the cultural conditions such as language, religion, and culture, which allow for the development of autonomous persons. One's identity is seen as acquired not just as an individual, but as a member of a community. Thus the need for collective rights to provide linguistic and cultural security for members of minority immigrant religious and other groups.

But there is a fatal weakness in this welfare-liberal defense of collective rights. First, the only groups to which the welfare liberal will extend collective rights are those whose cultures support the formation of autonomous individuals—namely, only those that meet the liberal individualist criterion of autonomous individual identity. This rules out many groups in pluralistic society. Second, welfare liberals actively discourage groups that reject the liberal identity presupposition. Groups that do not facilitate the growth of autonomous individuals for religious or other reasons (e.g., Amish, Hindus, Muslims, Chinese, and Aboriginal peoples) will be confronted by the activist welfare-liberal state in areas like education (e.g., residential schools) or health care (e.g., treat the individual not the family/environment). Individual autonomy trumps all values and so renders non-liberal-based immigrant groups as "not counting." What is needed is a liberal approach in which communities are treated as fundamental units of value while at the same time retaining a sense of personal individual dignity.

Can the classical liberal concerns with individual rights, freedoms, and interests (which we rightly value highly) be revisioned into a more holistic conception of ethics in public policy in which communities would matter in their own right? And could "communities" ever be extended, as the Aboriginal, Kabbalists, Sufis, Daoists, Hindus, Buddhists, and some feminists do, to include animals, plants, earth, air, and water—the ecosystem itself? This is the urgent ethical challenge facing the I-self world, with its powerful possessions of prosperity, science, and technology, that somehow must be ethnically shared and used for the good of all.

Would a public-policy ethic based on the principle of we-self obligation do better? I think it might. It certainly receives strong support from the religious traditions. In the Hebrew Bible, one has the obligation to extend hospitality to the sojourning stranger and respect the land. The Bible offers three perspectives that inform the laws concerning the sojourner: (1) Israel is to remember that once she was a sojourner in Egypt where God saw her oppression and delivered her into a bounteous land; (2) the God who saved Israel is the protector of the poor, the weak, and the disinherited—therefore Israel has the obligation to help any in need ("You shall not oppress a stranger for you were a stranger in the land of Egypt" Exod. 23:9); (3) all people in Israel, the Israelites and the strangers among them, must conform to God's law and keep the land holy.[30] But the Bible even goes further and describes everyone, including Israel, as strangers and sojourners before God and in God's land.[31] The obligation then according to the Bible is that there is to be no "identity difference" between ourselves and the foreign other, since we are all immigrants or sojourners before God. All individuals and groups share the same obligations and rights in God's law; we are God's children obliged to follow God's law and to love one another as God loves us. But that is not all. We are also obliged to respect the land, the good environment God created and to keep it holy. Therefore citizens and foreigners both have an obligation to be co-stewards with God and not despoil the land by overuse, which our individual choice ethic has led us to do. We are to remember, as Ps. 39:1 puts it, that we are all God's passing guests or sojourners. Christianity states the Hebrew Bible teaching in the form that all people in the world are God's children and therefore we are obliged to show one another the same love God shows us. In this context the I-self concept of the separate other vanishes. Such a universal obligation requires one to live in we-self identity with the sojourner/immigrant in Torah, if a Jew, or to live together in God's love through the grace of Christ, if Christian.

The Hindu ethic has an equally demanding obligation, although stated in differing degrees depending on one's stage of life. In its fullest form (that of the *sannyasin*) one is required to treat all others as if they were members of one's own family. No longer can one regard one's own family members more lovingly than others. All persons on earth are seen as one's mother, father, sister, brother, husband, or wife—as part of one's we-self. Clearly there is no room left for perceptions of social distance; Buddhists extend the analysis to include the animals. A Tibetan Buddhist meditation focuses on the idea that the animal in question may have been one's mother in a previous life and thus is deserving of all the love one feels toward one's mother. And since all of the universe is a manifestation of the Buddha-Nature, everything (humans, animals, plants, earth, water, and air) is to be accorded the respect one would accord the Buddha. Not only must any felt "social distance" to other humans be overcome, but also to plants, animals, and the whole of the cosmos.

The fundamental problem with the modern liberal assumption that equates identity with the choosing individual as the autonomous ethical agent is that it creates for us the perceptions of "social distance" that characterize humans or nature outside of our I-self as the foreign other. A sense of identity that focuses on us as part of a larger we-self or interdependent whole (differently conceptualized by each religious tradition) rather than an atomic choosing/rights-demanding individual gives us a basis for a better public policy.

Does Sensitivity to Other Cultures and Concepts
of Self-Identity Lead to Moral Relativism?

So far, I have suggested that the we-self identity of many cultures has important ethical implications. Even if I have convinced you that this is the case, you may have a worry that seems more fundamental— namely, that being sensitive to various cultures and concepts of self-identity will lead us into a state of moral relativism where anything goes. The worry goes something like this. If I am to be tolerant of and sensitive to all cultures or religions and their differing self-concepts, beliefs, and practices, I will end up having to uncritically accept whatever values they hold, whether or not such values are right. In fact, with this approach everything seems relative to the beliefs of one's culture/religion and therefore it would seem "anything goes!" Some Somali mothers request genital mutilation of varying degrees of severity for their daughters and some South Asian families desire sex selection of the fetus to obtain sons. Sensitivity to cultural/religious differences seems to leave health care and other professionals and institutions no choice but to go along with culturally based actions that fly in the face of the values of Hippocrates or Florence Nightingale. But is this necessarily true? Let us see if there is a way of making ethical distinctions between culture/religion norms that does not render them all equally good.

Jay Newman has proposed that we can have cultural tolerance without ethical relativism in the following way.[32] What is called civilized by one culture may be dismissed as savagery by another. Yet we can agree on a way of making ethical judgments between the norms and practices of cultures/religions.

1. We are not so ethnocentric that we cannot recognize real or ideal values in other cultures as better than our own. We can all identify shortcomings in our own culture and can admire institutions and values of radically different ethnic and religious groups. For example, our dawning awareness in the modern West that valuing nature as a commodity to be limitlessly exploited for our own use is properly challenged by the Hindu/Buddhist/Daoist view that humans are an interdependent part of nature and thus must respect it, or the Aboriginal view that the plants and animals are peoples just as we are and therefore deserving of equal respect.

2. There appear to be certain *transcultural values* that are taught in most religions or cultures—values that become more dominant as a society develops and recede as a society disintegrates. For example, when we study such diverse great works as the Hindu *Bhagavad Gita*, the Buddhist *Tripitaka* or Confucius's *Analects* we find ethical teaching that sounds very similar to the Torah, the Bible, the Qur'an, and some modern philosophers. All teach that we are to respect and not abuse nature. The prescription against killing others is virtually universal. Confucius's saying, "A great man is conscious only of justice; a petty man only of self-interest" is paralleled by the requirements for justice taught by the great prophets of the Torah and the Bible. Honesty and truthfulness are valued in the Hindu *Yoga Sutras* as well as the Bible and Qur'an.

While all the values of all traditions are not the same, there are some basic values that keep us from sliding into the moral morass of "anything goes." But we might then ask, if there is a universal ethical foundation of common values, why are they so little practiced in the world? Common values are essentially *ends*, and people in different religions or cultures disagree as to what the appropriate *means* to these *ends* are. Plato's *Republic*, the Bible, and the *Communist Manifesto* all deal with issues related to justice and peace, but offer different means to reach these ideal ends. The crucial question for any society then is how much its ideal ends are realized in practice.

What is the implication of all of this for ethics in a pluralistic public-policy context? It means that there are ethical standards we can look to in each tradition—standards that we can all embrace. In the example of the desire of some Muslim Somali mothers to have clitorectomy performed upon their daughters so as to make them marriageable, a careful study of the Qur'an reveals that this practice is not approved by the Qur'an but is primarily a matter of culture.[33] Nor is sex selection for sons allowed in Hindu ethics. The effective and sensitive way to deal with this issue is not to reject the practice on the basis of Western liberal I-self values, but to help mothers or families see that such practices are not sanctioned by the authority of their own tradition, the Qur'an or Veda. Common values can only be appealed to successfully by pointing to their presence in the religion/culture of the person to whom one is speaking, for example, the Somali mother or the Hindu family. Attempts to apply a value by superimposing it from your culture upon them is imperialistic, insensitive, and in the long run will not work. The other way, namely, appealing to the manifestation of the common value present within their tradition requires that we educate ourselves in the cultures/religions of others. Such education is today a prerequisite for doctors, nurses, social workers, policymakers, or ethicists working with people from various cultures. With education we will be able to sensitively appeal to the transcultural value we wish to actualize in a given situation without regressing to moral relativism *or* engaging in cultural imperialism. Only then will we have a sustainable basis for environmental, consumption, or population ethics.

Another helpful approach to this problem is offered by Susan Sherwin in her book *No Longer Patient: Feminist Ethics and Health Care*. She identifies a feminist basis from which to show that practices such as genital mutilation are wrong regardless of the culture in which they occur. Just as male dominance of women is an international practice, so feminist ethics can critique oppressive practices of male dominance in other cultures. Sherwin notes that: "Genital mutilation is linked to interests associated with male dominance—assurances of sexual fidelity, tight vaginas for sexual pleasure, protection against women's demands for sexual satisfaction, and cruelty to women. Unless there is evidence that women would agree to this practice if they were free of patriarchal coercion, we cannot treat it as an acceptable local custom, even if the majority of citizens in areas where it is customarily practiced now approves of it."[34] But how does one intervene in another culture/religion to oppose such morally unacceptable practices. Here Sherwin counsels caution against any move that could be viewed as imperialism. She says feminists from outside should not impose their solutions without the support of at least some of the women who are part of that culture. The idea is that one can assist from outside by working to support those within a culture who, as a minority, are opposing a cruel and oppressive practice. But, warns Sherwin, sensitivity to the other culture and respect for the democratic practices of moral decision making must always be maintained.

It should be a basic postulate of intercultural dialogue that no culture is perfect, that we can always critique each other and learn from each other. Mutual critique, when done nonimperiously, is not only legitimate but necessary.

CONCLUSION

In this chapter I have distinguished contemporary Western conceptions of the self as individual (I-self) from traditional conceptions of the self as collective (we-self) and briefly explored the ethical implications of the two conceptions for our threefold problematic of population pressure, excess consumption, and degradation of the environment of which we are an interdependent part. Roland's psychological studies showed that persons growing up in we-self cultures had highly permeable ego boundaries opening the way for the constant empathy and receptivity to others necessary for life in extended families. Instead of actualizing the self-contained boundaries of the typical modern Western I-self, necessary for life in a highly autonomous society, the nontotalitarian we-self spiritual goal in traditional cultures is the reciprocal sensitivity and responsibility required to live in harmony with all other humans and all of nature. Yuasa suggested that this approach entailed a mind-body unity that ideally resulted in spontaneous ethical action of the sort that would greatly help our problems of population, consumption, and ecology. Section three of the analysis, however, pointed to a major conflict that introduction of the we-self generates—namely a clash of values between the host I-self society and the minority religious/ethnic we-self cultures. This conflict becomes especially problematic in public policy decision making where sensitivity to other cultures threatens to land us in the moral relativism of "anything goes." By contrast, I argued that by being sensitive to the other and the values inherent in one's own traditions, one could appeal to a common ethic that would become part of a we-self identity we could all share—and thus form a firm foundation for public policy decisions.

NOTES

1. Thomas Hobbes, *Leviathan.*
2. See David Loy's chapter, "The Religion of the Market."
3. Kenneth Hare, "The Natural Background," in *Population, Consumption, and the Environment* (Albany: State University of New York Press, 1995).
4. Alan Roland, *In Search of Self in India and Japan: Toward a Cross-Cultural Psychology* (Princeton, N.J.: Princeton University Press, 1988).
5. Peter Stephenson, "'He Died Too Quick!' The Process of Dying in a Hutterite Colony," *Omega* 14.2 (1983–84).

6. Ibid., p. 129.

7. Ibid., p. 132.

8. Yuasa Yasua, *The Body: Toward an Eastern Mind-Body Theory*, ed. T. P. Kasulis and trans. Nagatomo Shigenori and T. P. Kasulis (Albany: State University of New York Press, 1987).

9. Ibid., pp. 2–3.

10. T. S. Eliot, "The Hollow Men" in *A Little Treasury of Modern Poetry*, ed. Oscar Williams (New York: Charles Scribner's Sons, 1952), p. 286.

11. Immanuel Kant, *Critique of Pure Reason*, trans. Norman Kemp Smith (Toronto: Macmillan, 1929), pp. 27, 74, 87, 149.

12. Catherine Keller, *From a Broken Web* (Boston: Beacon Press, 1986), 169ff.

13. Thandeka, *The Embodied Self* (Albany: State University of New York Press, 1995).

14. William James, *Psychology* (New York: Henry Holt, 1893).

15. Keller, *From a Broken Web*, p. 15.

16. Judith Van Herik, *Freud on Feminity and Faith* (Berkeley: University of California Press, 1982).

17. Morny Joy, "Mindfulness of the Selves," in *Healing Deconstruction*, ed. David Loy (Atlanta, Ga.: Scholars Press, 1996).

18. Keller, *From a Broken Web*, p. 130.

19. Ibid., p. 133.

20. Yasua, *The Body: Toward an Eastern Mind-Body Theory*, pp. 4–5.

21. Reinhold Niebuhr, *The Nature and Destiny of Man*, 2 vols. (New York: Charles Scribner's Sons, 1964).

22. I. Schorsch, "Trees for Life," *The Mellon Journal* 25 (Spring 1992): 3–6.

23. S. H. Nasr, "The Cosmos and the Natural Order," in *Islamic Spirituality: Foundations*, ed. S. H. Nasr (New York: Crossroads, 1987), p. 346.

24. Harold Coward, "Religious Responsibility," in *Ethics and Climate Change: The Greenhouse Effect*, ed. Harold Coward and Thomas Hurka (Waterloo, Ont.: Wilfrid Laurier University Press, 1993), pp. 48–59.

25. J. B. Callicott and R. T. Ames, "Epilogue: On the Relation of Idea and Action," in *Nature in Asian Traditions of Thought: Essays in Environmental Philosophy*, ed. J. B. Callicott and R. T. Ames (Albany: State University of New York Press, 1989), p. 281.

26. Yasua, *The Body: Toward an Eastern Mind-Body Theory*, p. 3.

27. See Jordan Paper and Li Chuang Paper, "Chinese Religions, Population and the Environment" in *Population, Consumption, and the Environment: Secular and Religious Responses*, ed. Harold Coward (Albany: State University of New York Press, 1995), pp. 173–91.

28. See Rita Gross, "Buddhist Resources for Issues of Population, Consumption and the Environment," in Harold Coward, *Population, Consumption, and the Environment*, p. 159.

29. See Michael McDonald, "Should Communities Have Rights? Reflections on Liberal Individualism," *Canadian Journal of Law and Jurisprudence* 4 (1991): 217–37.

30. Exod. 22:21–24, and Deut. 21:23

31. Lev. 25:23.

32. Jay Newman, *Foundations of Religious Tolerance* (Toronto: University of Toronto Press, 1982), p. 65ff.

33. Sami A. Aldeeb Abu-Sahlieh, "To Mutilate in the Name of Jehovah or Allah" (Lausanne, Switzerland: Institute of Comparative Law). The author concludes the teaching of the Qur'an is "God does not mutilate." This issue is also given extended discussion in Sandra R. Lane and Robert A. Rubinstein, "Judging the Other: Responding to Traditional Female Genital Surgeries," in *Hastings Centre Report*, May–June 1996.

34. Susan Sherwin, *No Longer Patient: Feminist Ethics and Health Care* (Philadelphia: Temple University Press, 1992), p. 74.

CHAPTER 5

New Theology on Population, Ecology, and Overconsumption from the Catholic Perspective

Alberto Múnera, S. J.

INTRODUCTION

Ecological disaster, overconsumption, and uncontrolled population growth are each a particularly great problem for humankind, and interconnected as they certainly are, they may even seem overwhelming. There are many perspectives from which it is possible to analyze these problems. But in the Roman Catholic perspective of liberation theology, there is only one: these problems must be considered and interpreted in terms of justice theory from the perspective of the poor and oppressed. This perspective includes poor people and the poor embattled earth.

Like every major religion that has achieved tenure on this earth, Roman Catholicism has historically manifested a rich variety of themes and accents, not all of them complementary and not all of them helpful. This chapter, like all the chapters in this volume, looks to recover what is best in the tradition and apply that to the problems of population, ecology, and the greed of overconsumption. Evolution is a rule of religion as well as of life. There are neglected ingredients in the Catholic tradition that can be developed to produce remedies to these current world crises. As Joseph Cardinal Ratzinger has said: "The Church is not the petrification of what once was, but its living presence in every age. The Church's dimension is therefore the present and the future no less than the past."[1] The perennial challenge is to draw from the past a living theology that meets the needs of the present and the future. I will stress three ways in which Catholicism can do that: (1) in its justice theory currently being renewed in "liberation theology"; (2) in its nature-friendly traditional insistence that nature and grace are not antithetical; and (3) in its capacity to underwrite or at least tolerate moral pluralism in contentious areas such as reproductive ethics.

JUSTICE THEORY

The liberation theology perspective has deep roots in the biblical traditions of Judaism and Christianity and in the traditional social and distributive justice theory that grew up in Catholic moral teaching. The great Protestant theologian, Emil Brunner, wrote in 1949 that "while the Catholic Church, drawing on centuries of tradition, possesses an impressive systematic theory of justice, Protestant Christianity has had none for some three hundred years past."[2] Catholic justice theory always manifested—in theory at least—the biblical preoccupation with the poor: it must now be extended also to address the poverty of our battered earth-home and the rest of the terrestrial biological community. From this perspective we are able to see that the uncontrollable population growth in poor nations, overconsumption with destruction of nonrenewable resources in developed nations, and the consequent ecological disaster, are all due—in the final analysis—to the great injustice produced by the economic systems and structures with their supporting ideologies that are sustained by the rich masters of the world economy. Ecocide and genocide are siblings. Even though the three problems we are considering have their particular causes and origins, I assume that they have a common cause in the great injustice of the world: the incredible gap between the rich and the poor, the inequity in the distribution of wealth, resources, incomes, and goods.

A Catholic approach to this problem must be taken from the same perspective that Jesus clearly demonstrated in his daily dealing with the poor, the oppressed, the marginalized, the weak, the rejected, and those considered the debris of his world. This approach calls for a perspective of deep knowledge of the concrete situations and a religious reaction of justice-love that requires an effective praxis capable of transforming such a terrible reality. Liberation theology's justice theory requires all of this.

An elementary overview of the situation from the perspective of the poor and oppressed enables us to identify the gigantic injustice by which the oppressed of the world are subjected to an inhuman slavery that leads to an unavoidable ecological and demographic disaster that will be the undoing of everyone. According to the UNDP Human Development Report for 1992, the richest fifth of the world receives 82.7 percent of the total world income and the rest of the world receives 17.3 percent. The scandal is that the comfortable of the world live placidly (more or less) with the ticking time bomb of greedy consumption and ecological decay.

From my perspective of living and working in the poor part of the world, I can see that the main problem is the rapaciousness of the rich with their insatiable consuming patterns. This is not to say that there is no relationship between poverty and uncontrolled population growth. Indeed, the population of the poorest countries grows at very high rates and the population of the richest countries remains stable or decreases. The resources of the earth are finite, which means that population possibilities are also finite. When St. Thomas Aquinas commented on Aristotle's *Politics* he agreed with Aristotle that the number of children generated should not exceed the resources of the community and that this should be insured by law as needed. Thomas eschewed the suggestion that homosexuality be used for birth limitation, but he did not shrink from the need for limiting births. If more than a determined number of citizens were generated, he said, the result would be poverty, which would breed thievery, sedition, and chaos. As Johannes Messner says, it is "not without surprise that one finds St. Thomas suggesting the restriction of procreation after a certain number of children."

The population problems reflect the distributional inequities. In each country as well as in the world at large, the richest population even in poor countries remains the same or declines. The poorest population in these countries always multiplies. When the death rate among children is high, people will have more children so that they will at least end up with a few.

There is also a relationship between poverty and migration of poor populations, which magnifies the immense injustice and inequity in the distribution of resources. The growth of poor populations generates migrations, and migrations increase poverty in quantity and quality. The fast growth of poor populations and migrants frequently leads them to establish their settlements in fragile environmental places or in marginal suburban areas where inhuman standards of life deteriorate the environment. They suffer from the lack of education, economic incapacity, and from the very harm they must do the environment simply to survive. The poor also bear the brunt of environmental damage since the rich gobble up the rare resources. The majority of the world's peoples are poor and they are the prime victims—along with future generations—of the ecocide that is ongoing.

We can conclude that increasing uncontrolled population growth, overconsumption, and ecological instability enlarge economic and social injustice and the gap between rich and poor. The injustice in all of this is outrageous. This should be obvious to all people of good will. It is painfully obvious to me since I live in "the Third World" and I see the results daily of this lethal savagery that is blithely called "the global economy."

The economically powerful have all the possibilities of acquiring lands and goods and of transforming any kind of resources for their own benefit. They not only have the financial power but—and this is so important at this moment of history—they are also the producers and owners of technology. What can the poor do in this absolutely unequal and unjust competition for consumption? It is true that some in many countries have acquired great prosperity because of the free market. But it is also true and tragic that the cost of the prosperity of the few rich is the poverty and death of millions of the poor. The concept of need is key to any Catholic economic theory and to any biblical theory of justice. It has no status in global capitalism. At most it begets cynical gestures.

Liberation theology is concerned with the distribution of power. Global capitalism is revolutionizing power in the modern world. The tyranny imposed by the free market profiting from the democratic pluralism has invented a new system in which the creation of incredibly large transnational corporations not regulated by the laws of each country are capable of legislating for all the countries where they operate, through mechanisms not controlled by the democracies but only by corporate interests. It is rule of the greedy, for the greedy, and by the greedy.

Large financial institutions, the World Bank, and the International Monetary Fund have an incredible power. The result of this power is often not benign for the poor. Workers are brutalized by unjust "austerity" requirements to meet our debts to the First-World rich. An unholy competition has been created among the jobless for the jobs that are fewer as automation takes its toll and no political imagination is used to create more and different kinds of job opportunities. Financial institutions do not demonstrate any interest in ecological issues, because ecology does not produce money in a short term . . . although it is the basis of all economies. When the only objective is to produce money in great quantities quickly, it does not matter if that production supposes the destruction of the earth's resources. That they are sawing the limb on which they sit seems not to occur to them.

Capitalism, as both Loy and Korten show, can be understood from a religious perspective as having certain theological foundations. It promises salvation through consumption. It is a diabolic faith system. The ethical content of this understanding holds that the norm of morality is the benefit of the individual asocially conceived. According to this principle, any activity is justified in the economic system established for this purpose. This economic system and its structures are demolishing the present and the future possibilities of the whole human race to survive and thrive. The fact is that this economic system based on such principles has damaged the availability of resources at an incredible speed thanks to the madness of the consumerism supported by the greed for profit and the gross disinterest in the fate of the earth.

In Catholic social-justice theory, government is not an evil to be minimized. It is the prime agent of distributive justice. Its natural role is the furtherance of the common good and the protection of the powerless and the poor. However, one of the primary sources of the world's poverty is the inefficiency of political systems to really govern, together with widespread political corruption. Suspicion of government is such that the idea is growing that public services and the enterprises of the state should be handled like private companies for profit. Of course the costs of public services permanently grow at a rate that only the richest can pay, and people, especially poor people, become more unprotected and poor. Increasing unemployment grows with privatization since the right to a job is not recognized as a human right by profit-driven corporations or by governments that start to think like businesses. The system aspires to reduce public expenses, in order to have greater efficiency through more production with less costs. To reduce the costs means that many workers lose their jobs. Joblessness increases the numbers of the poor, especially in the great urban centers. Injustice grows and social problems for the whole society substantially augment. The free-market system defends free competition in trade and business but such "free" competition does not begin with equal possibilities for all the participants. For instance, the giant airlines of the richest countries swallow up smaller airlines, and so it is in all industries. Without a strong government committed to justice, the situation is desperate.

The rich countries insist that their products be bought at the prices they propose, and the poor have to accept this if they hope to sell their own products to the rich. Of course, the prices of these products are determined by the rich countries. The results are evident: the rapid increase of wealth in the most powerful countries and the terrible rape of the poor.

At the basis of all this, as we have said, there is an interpretation of the world and of the human being: a philosophy, a religious perspective, a theology and it is at odds with Catholic justice theory because it dignifies greed, destroys God's earth, has no sense of companionship with the rest of nature, and has no effective concern for the poor.

NATURE AND GRACE

Space here permits little development of this theme but it has important implications for the concerns of this volume. Over the centuries, Catholicism developed a conviction that there is no incompatibility between faith and reason or between nature and grace. The notion of grace referred to the impact of the divine upon the human. At times this notion was used in a way that was antithetical to nature since grace was seen as precisely supernatural, something that pointed to our destiny beyond this life in an afterlife with God. Understood in this way, it contributed to the *fuga mundi* (flight from the world) kind of spirituality. That was not helpful. However the stronger tendency—and the one that can be best appropriated now for the purposes of our discussion—was to see grace as activating the potential of the natural. This was a way of seeing the sacredness of nature as a gift from God. Out of this there grew a sacramental view of nature. All of nature reflected the glory of its divine creative source, God. Just as reason is not at odds with faith so nature can be seen as illumined in its value by its being a sacrament of the invisible God.

The Catholic tradition held that the Holy Mystery is perceived through the whole created world—*invisibilia per visibilia*, the invisible through the visible. This was a sensuous, nature-friendly approach that saw the whole world as a mirror of God. A rich repertoire of natural elements thus wove themselves into Catholic liturgy: water, oil, wine, bread, salt, wax, fire, ashes, incense, vestments, touching, music. This sacramental penchant took color, glass, and stone and exploded into cathedrals and other forms of art. Creative, ecologically sensitive adaptations of Catholic liturgy could emphasize in new ways the closeness of the natural order to the reality of God.

Since we are not passive pawns of a divine force called grace, since grace is an invitation to co-action with God in caring for the earth, grace is not an invitation to flee the earth, but to care for it. Each of us is in Thomas Aquinas's phrase "a participant in divine providence," charged to care for the earth as cocreators and coproviders with the caring God in whose image we are made.

THE CATHOLIC CASE FOR MORAL PLURALISM

Contrary to widespread impressions, the Catholic moral teaching at its best fought against undue dogmatism in debatable moral matters. This can have important applications to current debated issues in reproductive ethics. Catholicism developed a system called Probabilism that taught that in moral matters, "where there is doubt there is freedom" (*ubi dubium, ibi libertas*). On issues where good people with good reasons disagree and where no infallibility is possible, persons may follow a truly probable opinion, one supported by good reasons and good authorities—even though other good authorities with good reasons may disagree. As Father Henry Davis, S.J., put it years ago: "When the truth of an opinion or the sufficiency of available evidence is debatable, one can never say that either the affirmation or the negation of it is certainly true. The greater probability of one opinion does not and cannot destroy the probability of its contrary."[3] The less probable opinion may be followed in good conscience since it "may be the true one." Probabilism sprang from the realization that Church authorities in the past sometimes taught that something was always wrong, for example, taking any interest at all on a loan, only to discover later that this was based on misinformation and a misinterpretation of the Bible.

Probabilism was a manifestation of humility in the face of moral complexity where good people cannot agree. It gives freedom to the individual conscience. It is based on insight, not on permission from authorities. The insight it is based on is either that of reliable experts (this was called extrinsic probability) or on one's own insight (intrinsic probability). And as Father Davis said: "It is the merit of Probabilism that there are no exceptions whatever to its application; once given a really probable reason for the lawfulness of action in a particular case, though contrary reasons may be stronger, there is no occasion on which I may not act in accordance with the good probable reason that I have found."[4] This is a liberative Catholic tradition and its resurrection today could ease tensions in some of the most sensitive issues where authoritarian approaches marked by an unecumenical and unwarranted dogmatism cause unnecessary tensions.

RECENT PAPAL TEACHING

Recent popes have shown a great interest in the moral implications of the ecological situation of the world and in consumerism. As with probabilism, much of this is unknown to many people. In their desire to have and enjoy rather than to be and to grow, people consume the resources of the earth and their own life in an excessive and disordered way. At the root of the senseless destruction of the natural environment lies an anthropological error that, unfortunately, is widespread in our day. Humankind, having discovered the capacity to transform and in a certain sense create the world through action, forgets that this is always based on God's prior and original gift of the things that are.[5]

The concept of overconsumption is presented by John Paul II in a context of "superdevelopment" of a few groups, which makes people slaves of possessions. Concerning overconsumption we can recognize that an ascetic interpretation of the history of Jesus has moved Catholicism to preach austerity as the most acceptable lifestyle; and the austere example of saints old and new has been proposed as the way to acquire eternal life. This could be stressed today to preach the modern needed virtue of frugality.

This superdevelopment, which consists in an excessive availability of every kind of material goods for the benefit of certain social groups, easily makes people slaves of "possession" and of immediate gratification, with no other horizon than the multiplication or continual replacement of the things already owned with others still better. This is the so-called civilization of "consumption" or "consumerism," which involves so much "throwing-away" and "waste." An object already owned but now superseded by something better is discarded, with no thought of its possible lasting value in itself, nor of some other human being who is poorer.[6]

Based in the biblical tradition, Catholicism has been pronatalist. We all know the general doctrine of the Catholic hierarchy against contraception, which of course must be balanced by the Catholic doctrine of probabilism. The Second Vatican Council clearly proposes a responsible family planning: in planning their families, Catholic couples will thoughtfully take into account both their own welfare and that of their children, those already born and those who may be foreseen. For this accounting they will reckon with both the material and the spiritual conditions of the times as well as of their state in life. Finally, they will consult the interests of the family group, of temporal society, and of the Church herself.[7]

Pope John XXIII considered the relationship between population growth and the lack of resources both a world problem and a particularly difficult problem for poorest countries. How can economic development and the supply of food keep pace with the continual rise in population? This is a question that constantly obtrudes itself today—a world problem, as well as one for the poverty-stricken nations.[8]

The problem of population growth presents a quite disconcerting situation in the Catholic Church. Catholic practice has changed. In Catholic countries like those of Latin America, there is a rapid decrease of population in the last years due to the use of contraception. Some statistics state that almost 80 percent of Catholics in the world use contraception for family planning. The Vatican II Council was very clear in denouncing the great injustice contained in the gap between rich and poor persons and nations due to the use and accumulation of goods that God has designated for the use of all.

While an enormous mass of people still lack the absolute necessities of life, some, even in less advanced countries, live sumptuously or squander wealth. Luxury and misery rub shoulders. While the few enjoy very great freedom of choice, the many are deprived of almost all possibility of acting on their own initiative and responsibility, and often subsist in living and working conditions unworthy of human beings.[9]

In the encyclical "Sollicitudo Rei Socialis," one of the most important documents of the official social doctrine of the Church, Pope John Paul II analyzes the negative signs of the actual social situations: innumerable multitudes of people suffer an intolerable poverty that has worsened. This is unacceptable in the perspective of Jesus.

I wish to call attention to a number of general indicators, without excluding other specific ones. Without going into an analysis of figures and statistics, it is sufficient to face squarely the reality of an innumerable multitude of people—children, adults, and the elderly—in other words, real and unique human persons, who are suffering under the intolerable burden of poverty. There are many millions who are deprived of hope due to the fact that, in many parts of the world, their situation has noticeably worsened. Before these tragedies of total indigence and need, in which so many of our brothers and sisters are living, it is the Lord Jesus himself who comes to question us (cf. Matt. 25:31–46).[10]

In spite of all these inspirational teachings, in terms of practice the Catholic Church presents some anomalous situations:

First, these social teachings and documents are not known by the great majority of Catholics. As a painful matter of fact, many Catholics in the world, and even more painfully in many undeveloped countries the richest Catholic capitalist owners of resources, are the most conservative defenders of ideological capitalism and of the free market. Some of them think that Pope John Paul II in his encyclical "Centesimus Annus" has approved capitalism as a wonderful system. This is not true. It is a self-serving and distorted interpretation of the encyclical and clearly goes against the whole of his social teaching.

Second, the prolonged Vatican critique of communism produced and continues to produce the fortification of extremely conservative positions of many economically powerful Catholics in the world, as though the blessed opposite of communism is a rapacious capitalism.

Third, the past and present opulence and economic power of the clergy of the Catholic Church, in open contradiction to the ideas and practice of Jesus and of the New Testament, has weakened the credibility of the Church's social doctrines.

Catholic moral theology in the past has used a particular method that perhaps explains why the majority of Catholics do not practice the social teaching of the Church. This method was based more on a philosophical Aristotelian epistemology than on an authentic religious experience. The foundation and support of this theology was the philosophical interpretation of the human being in terms of a universal abstract nature: human nature was seen to possess some intrinsic characteristics from which it is easy to establish which behaviors are moral and which are not. This is what has generally been called the "natural law," which is supposed to be universal, absolute, and the origin of obligation for every human being. In this theology moral doctrines are proposed as commandments revealed and imposed by God for the whole of humankind. This was particularly done in reproductive ethics.

This theology does not sufficiently recognize the influence of history and cultures in the construction of particular ethics. Moral theology today is of course against any flaccid relativism but it does cope with the inevitable relationality and historicity of ethical inquiry in the concrete. I believe that one of the most serious problems in the Catholic world today is the incoherence of Catholics in their moral behavior. They may know the helpful and inspiring doctrines cited above but the moral practice of most believers is based on different structures that are the product of the specific cultures and circumstances of the different moments of history. In consequence, many Catholics follow in their moral practice the religion of the market and not the religion of Jesus as explained in the teachings cited above.

Instead of trying to establish theoretical propositions, contemporary Catholic moral theology seeks to take seriously the acceptance and following of Jesus. New Catholic theology follows a method that initially could be seen as more inductive: it demands careful analysis of specific, particular, and concrete situations. It does this in the light of the biblical and traditional Catholic teachings on social and distributive justice. This new theology born in Latin America includes other specificities in its method, which allowed it to assume the name of "liberation theology": It proposes that the object of Theology is "praxis." This is not simply "practice" understood as the application of principles to one's own reality. Praxis is the commitment of a person to the struggle for liberation from the injustice that oppresses the majority of mankind. Most liberation theologians agree with Gustavo Guiérrez who sees theology as critical reflection on praxis in the light of the Word.

The needs of the poor give perspective to this method. And it is the Christian and biblical perspective, for throughout the entire history of God's self manifestation, the divine predilection for the poor is evident. God decides to become a poor man, Jesus Christ, to preach the Gospel to the poor and to liberate them from all injustice and oppression (Luke 4:16–21; citing Isa. 61:1–2). This is why practicing theology according to this method supposes first of all following the poor Jesus, assuming his commitment to the liberation of the poor and oppressed. It means practicing theology from the perspective of the poor and oppressed and for their benefit.

The stress on praxis in order to transform the situation of injustice by the struggle for liberation is the heart and soul of Catholic liberation theology. Theology must offer solutions to the real problems of the people, specifically a real liberation from the concrete injustices and from any kind of oppression and poverty.

In the texts of the New Testament, especially in John and Paul, the following of Christ implies a transformation of the human being so structural that it can be compared to a new birth (1 Pt. 2:2), a new creation, the formation of a new person (Eph. 2:15; 4:24), who does not have the same characteristics as the old person, who is left behind completely (Rom. 6:6). It is like returning to the womb (John 3:1ff.), or a definitive passing from darkness to light (2 Cor. 4:6; Eph. 5:8; 1 Pt. 2:9), from blindness to vision (John 9:1ff.), from silence to word (Matt. 9:33), from leprosy to cleanness (Matt. 8:3), from paralysis to movement (Matt. 9:6), from exile to home (Luke 15:20), from being lost to being found (Luke 15:6), from separation to proximity (Eph. 2:12–13), from death to life (Rom. 6:13; John 5:24; 1 John 3:14).

This substantial transformation of the human being and of society through the following of Jesus is profoundly symbolized in the paschal process of baptism: it is an immersion into the depths of death to emerge risen to a new life (Rom. 6:3; Col. 2:12). Immersion in water had the meaning of passing through darkness (Rev. 3:5) in order to acquire a new light (Eph. 5:7–8). It is the passage from the past to the future (2 Cor. 5:17), from the fragility of this world to the strength and vigor of an imperishable world. It is the transition from corruption to eternal life (1 Cor. 15:42–43). It is the seed that dies under the soil to raise as a tree full of life with fruit a hundredfold (John 12: 24).

The Christian understanding of the world and of the human being, and the experience of being transformed in a replica of Jesus are at the basis of Christian moral conduct regarding the relationship with both the world and the human person. Practically the whole New Testament is oriented toward love of others and of the whole cosmos and history as the only commandment, the only norm of morality for human behavior.

How to transform a world of injustice is no easy task. In Catholic religious terms it begins with the determination of a radical change in the most profound interior of the heart by a conversion to God and a commitment to justice. This religious and ontological transformation leads to a change in attitudes, in systems of life, and in decisions regarding the struggle for the liberation from the injustice suffered by the poorest. The God-given dignity of all persons not only grounds human rights but encourages the followers of Jesus even to lay down their lives for others, but at least to live lives marked by sacrificial sharing and solidarity. This Gospel is challenged today by the egoistic cult of consumerism and its corporate high priest.

All earthly resources and goods have been created for the benefit of the whole human race. Nature is God's creation and is worthy of supreme respect and care. The use of resources should be ordered and limited by the moral parameters dictated by love of others, a love that demands equity, generosity, solidarity, and a fair distribution of wealth. If the causes are the ideological systems of some people, such as a wild and savage capitalism oriented to an absolute free market that operates without any consideration regarding the universal common good, the struggle must be fought on this ideological field.

If the causes are the decisions of the governments of the most powerful nations, the struggle should be in the field of international politics based on the union of the poorest nations seeking respect and creating strategies and mechanisms to resist and to oppose injustice.

If the cause is the creation of gigantic international corporations and the globalization of the economy, the struggle must be located in the creation and multiplication of economic groups oriented toward the establishment of more independent local economies capable of obstructing the concentration of power.

The new Catholic theology believes in empowering the poor and the weak. Maybe that means that the real Church is not constituted by those rich who produce injustice and oppress their brothers and sisters through inhuman and sinful structures of injustice. Maybe a new Church called and gathered from among the poor and the marginalized and fortified with God's help and moved by the Holy Spirit toward a struggle for the justice in every field will receive the strength and the energy that proceed from our Lord Jesus Christ who has won over the power of evil. This is the same strength and energy used by God to liberate his poor and feeble people from the slavery in Egypt.

In a patriarchal and discriminative religion like Catholicism, we have to learn from feminist theology in which we find a serious promotion of justice, a wise control of population growth, an effective and balanced domestic economic management especially in poor populations, and a sensitive ecology.

We have to analyze how to face capitalism. From the Catholic perspective and from our new theology we must fight against its sinful structures in order to establish justice. But the fact remains: we are within a capitalist system and we move within capitalist structures. Could the reli-

gions of the world unite to try to socialize capitalism and bring conscience to it? It is not possible to totally and quickly change the present
situation, but unflagging resistance is our vocation. The challenge is to
mitigate and conscientize capitalism. International corporations are feeling now the reaction of poor countries because of the increasing gap
between rich and poor. The global economy does not care about justice
but maybe it can become interested in the survival of humankind.

Finally I feel that all the world's religions must unite to confront the
real causes of injustice and ecological collapse in the world. We can mar-
shal our vigorous spiritualities to confront uncontrolled population
growth, overconsumption, and ecological disaster. Two-thirds of the
world's peoples affiliate with some religion. There is power in religion.
We have been too naive and too slow to activate that power in the cause
of saving the earth and its threatened people.

NOTES

1. Joseph Ratzinger, "The Dignity of the Human Person," in Herbert Vor-
grimler, ed., *Commentary on the Documents of Vatican II* (New York: Herder
and Herder, 1969), 5:116.
2. Emil Brunner, *Justice and the Social Order* (London: Butterworth,
1945), p. 7.
3. Henry Davis, S.J., *Moral and Pastoral Theology*, Vol. 1 (London &
New York: Sheed and Ward, 1949), p. 93.
4. Ibid., p. 96.
5. Pope John Paul II, "Sollicitudo Rei Socialis," p. 34.
6. Ibid., p. 28.
7. Vatican Council II, "Gaudium et Spes," p. 50.
8. Pope John XXIII, "Mater et Magistra," p. 185.
9. Vatican Council II, "Gaudium et Spes," p. 63.
10. Pope John Paul II, "Sollicitudo Rei Socialis," pp. 25, 28.

REFERENCES

Cobb, John B., Jr. *Sustainability: Economics, Ecology, and Justice.* Maryknoll,
    N.Y.: Orbis Press, 1992.
Dobell, Rodney A. "Environmental Degradation and the Religion of the Mar-
    ket." In *Population, Consumption and the Environment*, ed. Harold Cow-
    ard. Albany: State University of New York Press, 1996, pp. 229–50.
Gutiérrez, Gustavo. *A Theology of Liberation.* Maryknoll, N.Y.: Orbis Press,
    1973.
Korten, David C. "Sustainability and the Global Economy: Beyond Bretton
    Woods." Paper presented at the People-Centered Development Forum,
    13–15 October 1994.

————. *When Corporations Rule the World*. West Hartford, Conn.: Kumarian Press, 1995

John XXIII. "Mater et Magistra." 15 May 1961.

John Paul II. "Sollicitudo Rei Socialis." 30 December 1987.

Maguire, Daniel C. "Catholicism and Modernity." *Horizons* 13.2 (1986).

Messner, Johannes. *Social Ethics*. Herder Book Co., 1964.

Rasmussen, Larry L. *Earth Community, Earth Ethics*. Maryknoll, N.Y.: Orbis Press, 1996.

Rich, Bruce. *Mortgaging the Earth: The World Bank, Environmental Impoverishment, and the Crisis of Development*. Boston: Beacon Press, 1995.

Rifkin, Jeremy. *The End of Work: The Decline of the Global Labor Force and the Dawn of the Post-Market Era*. New York: G. P. Putnam's Sons, 1996.

Swimme, Brian and Thomas Berry. *The Universe Story*. New York: Harper, 1992.

Thomas Aquinas. "Sententia Libri Politicorum."

Vatican Council II. "Gaudium et Spes," 1965.

CHAPTER 6

The Lost Fragrance: Protestantism and the Nature of What Matters

Catherine Keller

> How portentous all Nature is! I read the omen in the flight of birds, in their cries, in the playful flap of the fish against the surface of the water, in their vanishing into its depth, in the distant baying of the hounds.
>
> —Søren Kierkegaard, *Either/Or*

I

One might from this lush passage imagine Kierkegaard a nature contemplative, reading significance from the text of the universe. Such a spirituality could be poised to motivate action in our own age of environmental trauma. However, it turns out that the speech represents not the voice of the author but of his literary device, Johannes the Seducer. Indeed, this portentous ejaculation belongs to the entry written on the day in which Johannes "enjoys his reward"—the consummation of his long and calculating seduction of Cordelia. Written the day after, the last entry indicates his chilling indifference to her: "I do not wish to be reminded of my relation to her; she has lost the fragrance."[1] Johannes figures for Kierkegaard as an allegory of the aesthetic sensibility, a naturalism to which he can juxtapose first that of the ethical and then, supremely, that of "the knight of faith."[2] For this paper, Johannes serves as a trope of the standard Protestant theology of nature, which Kierkegaard, for all his rhetorical originality, merely rejuvenates—and which, I will suggest, offers a thorny obstacle to any adequate Protestant

79

response to such matters as overconsumption, overpopulation and eco-logical degradation, and will continue to do so until adequately coun-tered from within.

II

Within the practice of a specific interreligious conversation on global crisis, I have been asked to speak for Protestantism. I do so in glad protest against and therefore also with that endlessly self-diversifying, heterogenizing set of Christian traditions variously rooted in the protests of the Reformation. This essay specifically considers how North American Protestant Christianity might support evolution toward the kind of just, inclusive, and sustainable world order David Korten advo-cates as post–Bretton Woods "people-centered development." This peo-ple-centeredness does not entail anthropocentrism. On the contrary, for purposes of the present project, even the bland "and" of "social *and* ecological" responsibility does not suffice. Rather, we seek theologically to re-embed the human within the planetary society of mostly nonhu-man life, as a sustainable, civil, and humane economy *within* nature—as part of the interdependent *oikonomia,* the economic-ecological household, of our planet's life. I presuppose the Protestant theological evolution represented by the work of John B. Cobb Jr. with Herman Daly, as does in our project David Loy, which assesses the global reli-gion of growth through "free trade" as the most formidable though cer-tainly not only idolatry of our epoch.[3] Religion is a response to the sacred, as Daniel C. Maguire writes in the introduction to this volume. False sacreds, as defined by market capitalism (functioning as a world religion) are the idols that are shaping our values and our economic and political structures. I propose in this chapter that some significant mass of Protestants can function as an asset rather than an obstacle in the needed global process of idol critique and in so doing contribute to a progressive coalition of religions, without in any way excusing our reli-gion from its collusion with the most potent forces of social, economic, and ecological injustice. On the contrary, a faith can only cure what it first diagnoses in itself.

I will contend that a certain characteristically Protestant gesture of denaturalization inhibits the needed reform of Protestantism itself and of its worlds of influence.[4] I deliberately choose the conflicted semantic site inhabited by the term "nature," out of favor with postmodern sec-ular theory as well as perennial Protestant piety, rather than less prob-lematic notions such as "universe," or "physical world," or for theol-ogy, "creation." If nature signifies the entire matrix of interdependent interactions constituting the energetic contents of the universe, creation designates that same all-encompassing complex in its relation to a creator. While the doctrine of creation mistakenly tends to operate with the distant purity of a divinely detonated Big Bang, for present purposes let me work toward its reconstruction indirectly, through the consideration of the far more ambiguous, intimate, and ecologically current signifying field of "nature." The discourse of nature—that human and nonhuman nature corrupted according to orthodox doctrine by original sin—theologically marks the material intersection of specifically human suffering with our degradation of the nonhuman earth. The fact that progressive thinkers are so prone to speak of nature as precondition and resource of human culture, or that postmodern thinkers treat "nature" as the ploy of a colonizing cultural productivity, in either case echoing the Protestant binary of nature and grace, seems to me all the more reason not to avoid the term. Of course, the present project cannot far indulge abstract explorations of the idea of nature, and the choice of term is not the point. But the ambivalence surrounding nature, as the zone where nonhuman and human life co-materialize, conjures the entire heritage of Western resistance to our finitude: our materiality, our sex, our death, our limitation, and therefore also the range of shining antinature, epitomized in the popular Protestant "heaven," which has assuaged our anxiety and supported our irresponsibility. So the sense that nature itself, like an exploited woman, has "lost the fragrance"—does suggest a theological point of entry into the practical realities we face.

I will examine key paradigms of Protestant theology, especially those of Jean Calvin, Karl Barth, and Søren Kierkegaard, for insight into the Protestant ambivalence about "nature" and therefore all matters of materiality. For these theological habits do matter—they materialize in the economic practices that delimit our social and ecological possibilities. For example, the Puritan virtue of "thrift" would seem inherently to militate against the late capitalist vision of infinite growth. But appeal to an old and betrayed virtue remains an exercise in nostalgia if it does not engage its internal self-contradictions. So we will turn to Max Weber for help in accounting for the inexorable growth of wealth that thrift repeatedly produced and for the function of that wealth once the spirituality that disciplined it evaporated. We may link Weber's thesis as to the spirit of capitalism's Protestant sources to the originary Protestant ambivalence toward our worldly natures and the natural world. Even progressive Protestantism, I fear, has yet to face up to the animus against "nature" carried like a virus in the core of all traditional Christianity, an antimatter that continuously undermines interest in an equitable and joyous configuration of the material lives of all earthly creatures.

Here is a way to pose the theological challenge within the Protestant tradition: only inasmuch as material life—the "nature" of creation—is felt to *matter for its own sake* and not merely for the sake of a transcendent Creator and the *after*life "He" promises can the Protestant tradition challenge its own economically successful constituencies to take responsibility for their material practices. Yet there are already stirrings of a renaturalizing movement within Protestantism, a kind of materializing of the spirit as "protest" on behalf of the earth and its interlocked life-forms. This chapter will suggest that the prophetic "Protestant principle" that Paul Tillich juxtaposed to "the Catholic substance" still has enough life-force to matter.[5] If, that is, it can do more than turn against itself in an endless and often politically progressive critique, if it heals its own habits of ambivalent exploitation of the material universe, and thus discovers a certain sacramental cat/holicity of its own. We will finally stir up some biblical metaphors as one Protestant theologian's hints and pleas for the future of her tradition.

III

In order to sidestep temporarily the debate that Lynn White[6] in 1967 prophetically inaugurated but that Christians, either defensively or guiltily, cannot let go of (the debate as to just how culpable biblical religion is for the destruction of the environment), I begin with a hopeful if self-critical Protestant position. It presumes, as any bibliographic essay on environmental theology or a sociological study such as *The Greening of Protestant Thought*,[7] that there are enough Protestants who have undertaken the needed "conversion of the mind to the earth"[8] and linked it to the clearly biblical social justice tradition, that the discussion itself can motivate wider activism.[9] It would be good if it could.

Protestants, who constitute a significant mass of the Euro-American majority of that 20 percent of the global population consuming 80 percent of the planet's resources, are a force to be reckoned with. Growing numbers of them belong to fundamentalist movements that downplay the material needs of the poor and aggressively oppose the Christian progressivism that has staked out those needs as its terrain. To the extent that fundamentalist and other conservative Protestants deploy a literalist apocalypticism anticipating the near end of "this creation," they associate environmentalism with futility—individual souls, not their social or natural content, need to be saved—and indeed with paganism, for its sense of the immanence of the divine in nature.

I do not imagine that this particular born-again population constitutes a likely constituency for rebirth to the eco-ecumenism of this consultation. Yet among self-designated evangelical Protestants there does exist a movement for stewardship of the earth's resources and for the economics of sustainability.[10] Also African American evangelicals, conservative on the theological spectrum but not regarding social justice, potentially mobilize a strong public, though perhaps one that will need to be accessed through its own style of argument. But the old-line denominations still maintain a presence, deeply rooted if diminished and diluted, among the European and North American affluent classes. In these various nonfundamentalist Protestant publics live certain tendencies worthy of hope. However, my hopefulness is not optimism. That unavoidable twentieth-century Protestant Karl Barth has neatly distinguished "Christian hope" from any sentiment that gets caught in worldly cycles of optimism and pessimism—like social movements in their cycles of messianism and despair.

IV

However, Barth's neo-orthodox theology also enacts the classic gesture of denaturalization. "Nature" for him could only refer to the fallen creation, which is but for the (only) Incarnation empty of God's presence and in need of God's sovereign act of salvation. For Barth "natural theology" became the catchphrase for not only the "liberal theology" he opposed but all forms of arrogant human rationalisms, all projects of human self-glorification. The typical Christocentrism of Barth's definition of natural theology bodes well neither for ecology nor ecumenism: "Natural theology is the doctrine of a union of man [sic] with God existing outside God's revelation in Jesus Christ."[11] In other words, the "natural" pertains to that realm of knowledge presumed to be given independently of the special revelation of Christianity, thus available to scientists and non-Christians, and so irrelevant to what *matters*, that is, to the knowledge of God.

"If it was admissible and right and perhaps even orthodox to combine the knowability of God in Jesus Christ with His knowability in nature, reason and history, the proclamation of the Gospel with all kinds of other proclamations . . . it is hard to see why the German Church should not be allowed to make its own particular use of the procedure."[12] The "German Church" refers to the Protestants who saw God's will revealed in Hitler. With this particular gesture of rhetorical self-indulgence, Barth associated nature with Nazism, thus attaching the postwar prestige of the Barmen Declaration to a polemic against his old bogey, natural theology. In this he builds on the tradition of Protestant repudiation of Roman Catholic scholasticism, in which "general revelation" through natural law, reason, and science played a close second fiddle to "special revelation." This anti-Catholic animus infuses the cultures of Protestantism with antagonism toward any holism, cosmology, and, by implication, ecological vision.

Intriguingly, we may note the trend in secular critical theory to recapitulate this protest against holism as well, adopting unknowingly this Protestant anti-universalism and antinaturalism. Thus postmodern theories easily associate any notion of "nature" or "whole" with totalism or fascism. Certainly this continuum of protest against "nature," stretching from the Reformation to the postmodern, provides important correctives to both static natural law theism and mechanistic scientific atheism.[13] The totalism of the antinaturalist continuum should itself be critically examined, however. The critique of postmodern antinaturalism lies beyond the bounds of the present essay, though I will be elsewhere eager to analyze its unreflective continuity with Protestantism.

To note the totalizing origins of the Protestant nature discourse, let us call on Calvin. "The manifestation of God in nature speaks to us in vain," according to Calvin's doctrine of Creation—unless our eyes "be illumined by the inner revelation of God through faith."[14] There is truth there. This manifestation is acknowledged, as is the possibility that at least the elect may read it as knowledge of God. Yet the point is that since "we lack the natural ability to mount up unto the pure and clear knowledge of God, all excuse is cut off because the fault of dullness is within us."[15] So our nature in its fallenness proves unable, without a special dispensation of grace, to perceive the revelation of God in nature. In terms of his notion of double predestination, no excuse means no exit: the system is closed, total. Yet the collective alienation from God, "original sin," entails for him a depravity that does "not spring from nature, but rather from the corruption of nature."[16] An analogous ambiguity as to "nature"—what Calvin insightfully calls the "natural" corruption of the "nature" created by God—persists in current theory, in which "natural" can refer either to that which always precedes human manipulation or to that which has become culturally habituated (like gender roles) to seem "natural."

From an ecological point of view, the spectacle of a planet upon which all creatures share in the depravation, and most in the deprivation, wrought by a minority of human creatures, lends a certain credibility to the doctrine of original sin: but, of course, only if, after acknowledging that none of us are finally excused, we insist on a more Hebraic differentiation of degrees of responsibility—and perhaps, therefore, desist in corrupting the concept of "nature" along with its ecology. For within the claustrophobic Calvinist universe, even a prelapsarian nature in its goodness remains inherently void of the spirit—"the spirit comes, not from nature, but regeneration." Whatever we have from nature, therefore, is "flesh"[17]—that is, carnal, incapable of and indeed oppositional to "spirit." God's absolute transcendence of all nature—*finitum non est capax infiniti*—secured a gulf that fleshly experience could not cross. The persistent modern reproduction of this dualism itself prevents the regeneration that, we might say, the *spirit* of Calvinism so sternly envisioned.

V

Protestantism has not yet as a public mass or an intellectual tradition outgrown its ambivalence toward "nature"—that of other species and our own, that which can be considered by science, philosophy, and economics, that which may be constructed in terms of static "natural law" or reified substance, or, alternatively, in terms of our entirely fluid and aching planetary process. But how did such indifference on a spiritual front provide the basis for the successful metabolism of the Reformation with the "New World" of modernity? Protestantism, at the least, did not intrude on the new scientific quest for power through knowledge; at most it provided the spiritual impetus for the genocidal and ecocidal conquest of North America. With such wariness toward the corrupt cravings of the flesh, such disinterest in the material world, how did Protestant cultures not merely permit but give rise to the most powerful capitalist consumer economies in the world?

Max Weber may provide the missing link: the notion of "Protestant Asceticism." Before actually reading *The Protestant Ethic and the Spirit of Capitalism*, one might wonder how Weber could yoke the work ethic so formative of modern bourgeois Protestant capitalism with the anti-works, *sola gratia* polemics of the Reformation. One might presume that economic rather than religious factors must have drawn Protestants into their successful pursuit of profit. Weber, however, leads us back to Luther's invention of the *Beruf*, the calling.[18] Previously referring exclusively to religious vocations, it purveys for Luther the equality in the sight of God of all honorable work and, then, in his later, socially conservative writings, the fulfillment of one's assigned worldly duties, under all circumstances, as the only way to live acceptably to God. Already this vocationalism cut against the New Testament "give us this day our daily bread," but compared to Catholicism, with the symbiosis of its culture with traditional feudal and agrarian economies, it dramatically enhanced the religious sanction for organized worldly activity.

Weber argues that it was especially through the Calvinist tradition that this world-wary worldliness, focused by its new mundane asceticism, put the disciplines of the monastery to work in businesses. Add to this the actual unliveability of Calvin's *decretum horribile*, that closed system doubly predestining lonely souls, who—unless certain of their election—can get no true help or solace from the community or from nature, and one has a formula for the future of capitalist individualism. Calvinism, having established the incapacity of the flesh for the infinite, turns to the evidence of salvation in the "effective faith," *fides efficax*, of the Savoy Declaration.[19] This efficaciousness shows itself in "a life of good works combined into a unified system."[20] From this follows the seventeenth-century Puritan and then eighteenth-century Methodist sense of the rationally conducted life (hence the epithet "methodist"), free of the worldly spontaneities of the flesh and of the soul, yet called to perform this rational asceticism within the terms of worldly business. As Wesley would put it so clearly, in a certain presolidarity with Weber's analysis: "I do not see how it is possible, in the nature of things, for any revival of true religion to continue long. For religion must necessarily produce both industry and frugality, and these cannot but produce riches. But as riches increases, so will pride, anger, and love of the world in all its branches."[21]

Weber traces the movement of this logic of ascetic enrichment from the Puritan ethicist Baxter, who preaches hard, continuous bodily or mental labor as ascetic practice and proof against the flesh, to Benjamin Franklin, who recapitulates the same ascetic devotion to work as inherently salubrious but free now of religious constraints or motivations. With Franklin, turning a profit becomes not just a fringe benefit but a cheerful duty: "Remember, that *time* is money. He that can earn ten shillings a day by his labour, and goes abroad, or sits idle, one half of that day, though he spends but sixpence during his diversion or idleness, ought not to reckon *that* the only expense; he has really spent, or rather thrown away, five shillings besides."[22] Here we see the gospel of capitalism, a spirit that does not just proclaim the foolishness of wasted earning opportunities but the *ethics* of profit. The net result was prophetically described by Weber at the turn of the last century: "In the field of the United States, the pursuit of wealth, stripped of its religious and ethical meaning, tends to become associated with purely mundane passions, which often actually give it the character of sport."[23]

I hope the foregoing account of Weber's eminent thesis helps to illumine the operative paradox of Protestant rationality: its worldly asceticism, enabling it to join its indifference to nature with the rationalized control and exploitation of nature. If we add to his cultural history the *Wirkungsgeschichte* of the Puritanized myth of apocalypse in the conquest and development of North America, the "city on a hill" that situated itself amidst a "waste and howling wilderness," the lack of interest in the past of the earth and its indigenous dwellers, as well as in its long-term future, begins to make a certain sense.[24] The future is the site of the kingdom of God, but *this* world is never long with us. . . . We glimpse how the formidable spiritual energies of reformation could be channeled so profitably—and with such unjust and unsustainable effect. Without this religious base, it is impossible to grasp the peculiar North American dynamic of cheerful capitalist optimism spliced with messianic righteousness on the one hand and on the other, a blithely apocalyptic willingness to destroy the material matrix of life itself.

VI

"I do not wish to be reminded of my relation to her; she has lost the fragrance." This dissociation that Kierkegaard attributes to the seducer—the naturalist, who finds signs and portents in the nonhuman environment—we may also let characterize mainstream Protestant disconnection from nature itself—*herself*. Returning to *Either/Or*, seeking less dualistic paths than that title implies will allow us to incorporate a dimension that has heretofore been notably lacking in the present analysis of sex and gender. For Kierkegaard the "natural" is engulfed in his examination of the aesthetic as manifest in the "immediacy" of "romantic love." "Romantic love shows that it is immediate by the fact that it follows a natural necessity. . . . The sensual seeks instant gratification, and the more refined it is, the better it knows how to make the instant of enjoyment a little eternity."[25]

Thus sensuous enjoyment of nature symptomatizes the province of seduction, of what he calls immediacy. In his later *Concluding Unscientific Postscript* he elaborates upon the theological association of nature-love with instant gratification. "The immediate relationship to God is paganism, and only after the breach has taken place can there be any question of a true God-relationship."[26] In other words, any sense of direct or "natural" connection to God in the world perceivable by the senses is idolatrous, is a confusion of the infinite with the finite, of the Creator with the creation. "Paganism" usually was code for Catholicism, and indeed Kierkegaard disdains "the astonishing, the shrieking superlatives of a southern people" that "constitute a retreat to idolatry, in comparison with the spiritual relationship of inwardness."[27] Thus he shuns the superficial emotion associated with "astonishment over the vastness of nature and the countless forms of animal life" as lacking "the true understanding."[28] Certainly contemporary inter-Christian ecumenism, let alone environmental spirituality, would be undermined by such Protestant stereotypes of those sensuous, southern peoples, emotional, outward, and "natural" in their expressions of wonder. Such disdain, ever recognizable just beneath the surface of northern cultures, has proved a receptive ground for breeding the wildly materialistic projects of white colonialism against all manner of southern peoples and their material milieux.

Yet I think it serves little good to perform a converse reduction of Protestantism or even of Kierkegaard to their baser elements. "But this breach," he continues in his thought about overcoming the illusion of immediacy, "is precisely the first act of inwardness in the direction of determining the truth as inwardness. Nature is, indeed, the work of God, but only the handiwork is directly present, not God."[29] Theologically speaking, such protest against seeking the divine in the immediate need not discourage that creaturely love of the creation upon which Christian environmentalism must depend. Certainly the contemporary ecological movement includes a kind of elite nature mysticism, which circulates in the sphere of mere aestheticism, which operates from a kind of seduction, a hope for a consummatory experience, and which proves itself too narcissistic to provoke either respect for the intrinsic worth of other creatures or ethical action on their behalf. Such nature-aestheticism, if it does rise to the environmental occasion, rarely pursues the painful analyses required to put ecological concern into economic and social focus. A faith in the invisible God hidden from immediate view may, conversely, motivate a more embracing sense of commitment, able to include but transcend, Kierkegaardian fashion, the aesthetic and the ethical.

"Nature, the totality of created things, is the work of God. And yet God is not there; but within the individual man [sic] there is a potentiality (man is potentially spirit) which is awakened in inwardness to become a God-relationship, and then it becomes possible to see God everywhere."[30] "Not there" in what sense? As in any sense immanent to nature, or as identifiable with it? The Creator for any Protestant will be unidentifiable with any piece or combination of pieces of the creation—especially construed a closed totality of already done deeds. The internalization of Hebrew iconoclasm and its deconstruction of idolatry—of, in Tillich's words, any identification of the finite with the Ultimate—beats the heart of Protestantism. Ecojustice Protestants may or may not find God "there." I would only want to ask where the Spirit is, if not animating the Creation itself. To draw Protestants into care for that "everywhere," one will need to respect some version of Kierkegaardian indirectness, a certain non-Cartesian inwardness of spirit. But the trick will be to affirm that spirit-potential without surrendering to the dissociative lull of the private pietism into which Protestantism, after its radical moments and its Kierkegaardian leaps of faith, so easily falls.

Of course, the disengaged inwardness through which Protestantism abstracts itself from its material matrix is not at all abstract in its effects. As noted earlier, it practices specific economics: such as those involved in the transmutation of the early Puritan frugality into the industrial capitalism of the northeastern United States, or the suppression of liberation theology by the growing evangelical presence in Latin America, imported from North America with the blessing of the national security dictatorships. In its gestures of denaturalization such privatizing piety offers freedom from the passion of involvement in the material realities of the human and nonhuman species of the creation. Such passion, in its pain and in its eros, becomes itself subtly associated with the illicit sensuality of a dumb voyeurism, of animal instinct, of all that remains deaf to the "Word of God." And so love for the world, even the biblical love of stranger, neighbor, and enemy, the "and God so loved the world" sort of passion, leaks out through the plumbing of transcendence, that system of practices and beliefs through which the patriarchal divinity is so readily drained from "His" Creation.

I have suggested that Christianity can perhaps only be cured of its systematic association of nature with seduction, illicit sex, the female, and the superficial, in other words with the depravity of the "things of the flesh," to the extent that it experiences a Kierkegaard-like enhancement of "subjectivity"—but not within the terms of his own opposition of its inwardness to the external world. That enhancement of subjectivity would need to recognize itself in the act of drawing its own energy precisely from the material matrix of its "nature."

VII

The argument might run like this: the wider our relationship to the material world and its suffering and beauty, the more profound the impact on our spirit, that is, the more outward our attention, the more it resonates inward. Social justice movements within and beyond Christianity need a refreshing sense of inwardness in order to survive burnout, and it may be precisely the sense of renewal of our creatureliness, the connection of our exhausted spirits to the fragrant (if only sometimes flowery) life of nature that enables the healing "leap" beyond the dualism of spirit and nature and thus the rejuvenation of ecumenical Protestantism itself. Not as what Protestantism has been, or what it is "essentially"—we can join Barth in rejecting the naturalism of any given. Certainly a feminist—and Barth was more or less the opposite—can only deconstruct the "natures" we are supposed to conform to, as assigned to us not by nature but by culture disguising itself as nature. (But then I would call them pseudonatures; or more accurately, deformed second natures.) Any core or nature of Protestantism is rotten with the modern diseases of nation-state and New World imperialism it acquired so early, and the patriarchy it unquestioningly absorbed. But perhaps we can prevail upon a Protestantism understanding itself as heir of what it might have been—already a tragic set of abreactions to the distortions of the Constantinian Christianity of empire, and as ancestor of what might yet be, requiring a—Kierkegaardian—leap across the canyon lying between this millennium and the next.

It may seem that by assuming that Protestantism can be aligned with the global alliance—cat/holic in the most holistic sense—working for a sustainable world I have put cart before horse. Perhaps this is so, given my eagerness to liberate the wealth of that cart's cargo. But at the present millennial moment, I doubt that the question of whether Christianity in general or Protestantism in particular is merely guilty or merely innocent advances either discourse or action. In fact, Christendom, as the social form of the religion, has been the carrying culture for the colonization of the planet. To this end it has interpreted its theological sources, its manly mandates to populate, dominate, use, and convert the world. If I do Christian theology, I do it in penance for the effects of Christendom. Yet at the same time, many of the most marginalized of the planet, with scriptural legitimacy, claim Christianity as theirs—and as their inspiration for liberation and decolonization.

"Christianity" designates in other words an immense, multilayered, self-contradicting, and—contrary to the secularization doctrine of the sixties—*unfinished* field of mythic habits, political justifications, and cultural presumptions. One can hardly, after all, designate internal dissent against its own colonizing tactics as any less "Christian"—let alone Protestant—than that against which it protests. Perhaps the same must be said of any major world religion, wrapped as each will remain in the vicissitudes and visions of its culture. The point is to work with those specific cultural codes and live communities that signal some openness within the religion to the humanly needed, radically ecumenical, global task.

VIII

If not *sola scriptura*, Protestant theology today will certainly require a scriptural soul. So let us in closing have recourse both to the biblical Wisdom, who, like all ancient wisdom teachers, warned of destruction by avarice; and to her male embodiment in one who did not send us to our jobs on time, but rather—back to the fragrant lilies. Not to ogle nature, but to emulate it. The more fundamentalizing forms of Protestantism always prefer those parts of the New Testament—such as the epistles—that make much of Jesus' status and little of his narrated teachings. Those words and acts, as remembered in the synoptic gospels, strike one as much more . . . material. Jesus the Nazarene seems to focus so much on what by later Christian standards seems subspiritual: feed the hungry, clothe the naked, visit the imprisoned, heal the sick. Yet his vantage point, at once keyed to frugality and abundance, reflected in parables drawn from the matter of nature and daily life, does not reduce spirit to matter, but points to the transfigural potential of these material natures. Figured as the "kingdom of God," its work cannot be accomplished by heroic, pious, or enterprising individuals. This is a radically social, transnational, transracial, transgendering task.

Of course, no matter how indispensable to any mobilization of Protestant energies, biblical appeal cannot rest upon a fallacy of representation, as though a program or a model had been set forth two millennia ago, only waiting for our enlightened reappropriation of its flawless wisdom. Yet theological reconstruction not only legitimates what might otherwise seem alien and irrelevant to those most needful of conversion to the earth. It also performs a sociolinguistic analogy to environmental recycling: it filters out poisons, produces sustainable forms for energies captured in wasteful ones, inhibits fresh exploitation, and privileges an aesthetic of limits. So if we recycle the code of the kingdom, we may then highlight the asceticism of the synoptic gospels for precisely its lack of sex-negative withdrawal from the world. The choice not to procreate, which then meant celibacy, with the textual silence of any fertility blessing, must be read in tandem with the attention to material necessity and judgment against accumulation running through the Sermons on Mount and Plain. It signals the option of another priority: that spiritual discipline of the *basileia,* or kingdom, which entailed redistribution of present resources, sufferings, and pleasures for the nurture of already living lives within a circumstance felt as crisis and last chance. Literally the End never came. But the enhancement of the subjectivities of the community suggests that the benefits of new creation accrue to the participants no matter what happens and what they can accomplish around them.

Yet while this basileia stretched into an "eternal life" gathering all times into itself, it does not function within its originary code as a nature-discarding apocalypse ahead or heaven overhead. The eschatology of the Jesus-movement may be evocative today—inasmuch as crisis is felt, indeed interiorized, as a crisis of the creation itself—of a *green asceticism* that admits of application to Korten's three categories of consumers: it can teach us Protestant "overconsumers" the low-impact pleasures of nature and community as a substitute for our world-devouring habits; it can embolden the "marginals" to claim the abundance that is theirs by the right of the basileia; it can vitalize the "sustainers" to train themselves as models of spiritual-material practices for the rest of us. Because the sustainers according to Korten already constitute 60 percent of the population, such a hope grounds itself in real possibility. Yet it requires an expansion of subjectivity beyond the bourgeois bounds of *homo economicus,* into something that takes the preciousness of "I" into something like Harold Coward's "we-self." Scripture inscribes in our "nature" as Protestants a spiritualization of the flesh in its holy, honest confluences with the self, the neighbor, the stranger, the other. With these beings who *matter,* in relation to whose infinite need and newness my finitude is called to its capacity. *Finitum capax infiniti.* Only with them do I matter. And today, knowing of our hitherto undreamed of capacity to commit apocalypse upon all creatures, reading the omens of nonhuman nature not as cues for seduction but as cries of beauty in protest, we add—with the lilies of the field and the birds of the air.

NOTES

1. Søren Kierkegaard, *Either/Or,* vol. 1, trans. David F. and Lillian Marvin Swenson (Princeton: Princeton University Press, 1944), p. 439 (orig. pub. 1843).

2. Søren Kierkegaard, "Fear and Trembling," *A Kierkegaard Anthology,* ed. Robert Bretall (Princeton: Princeton University Press, 1947), p. 118.

3. John B. Cobb Jr. and Herman Daly, *For the Common Good: Redirecting the Economy toward Community, the Environment and a Sustainable Future* (Boston: Beacon Press, 1989).

4. For a positive, postmodern deployment of the term "denaturing," indicative of an alternative feminist stance toward "nature," cf. Judith Butler, *Gender Trouble: Feminism and the Subversion of Identity* (New York: Routledge, 1990).

5. Paul Tillich, *Systematic Theology,* vol. 1 (Chicago: University of Chicago Press, 1951), p. 37.

6. Lynn White, "The Historical Roots of Our Ecological Crisis," *Science* 155.10 (1967): 1203–7.

7. Robert Booth Fowler, *The Greening of Protestant Thought* (Chapel Hill: University of North Carolina Press, 1995).

8. Rosemary Radford Ruether, "Toward an Ecological-Feminist Theology of Nature," *Healing the Wounds: The Promise of Ecofeminism,* ed. Judith Plant (Philadelphia and Santa Cruz, Calif.: New Society Publishers), p. 149.

9. So this chapter works in solidarity with such contemporary works in Protestantism as: John B. Cobb and Herman Daly's *For the Common Good* (Boston: Beacon Press, 1989), Dieter Hessel's *Theology for EarthCommunity*

(Maryknoll, N.Y.: Orbis Books, 1996), Jay McDaniel's *With Roots and Wings* (Maryknoll, N.Y.: Orbis Books, 1995), Sallie McFague's *The Body of God* (Minneapolis: Fortress Press, 1993), James Nash's *Loving Nature* (Nashville: Abingdon Press, 1991), Larry Rasmussen's *Earth Community, Earth Ethics* (Maryknoll, N.Y.: Orbis Books, 1996), and George Tinker's "Ecojustice and Justice," in *Theology for Earth Community*, ed. Hessel (1996).

10. Robert Booth Fowler, *The Greening of Protestant Thought*.

11. Karl Barth, *Church Dogmatics: A Selection*, trans. and ed. G. W. Bromiley (New York: Harper and Brothers, 1961), p. 51.

12. Ibid., p. 57.

13. Michael Welker, *Schöpfung und Wirklichkeit* (Neukirchen-Vluyn: Neukirchener Verlag, 1995).

14. Jean Calvin, *Institutes of the Christian Religion*, vol. 1, ed. John T. McNeil, trans. F. L. Battles (Philadelphia: The Westminster Press, 1975), p. 68 (orig. Pub. 1559).

15. Ibid.

16. Ibid., p. 163.

17. Ibid., p. 287.

18. Max Weber, *The Protestant Ethic and the Spirit of Capitalism*, trans. Talcott Parsons (New York: Charles Scribner's Sons, 1930), p. 79 (orig. pub. 1904–5).

19. Ibid., p. 114.

20. Ibid., p. 117.

21. Ibid. (Weber quoting Wesley), p. 175.

22. Ibid. (Weber quoting Franklin), p. 48

23. Ibid., p. 182.

24. Cf. Catherine Keller, *Apocalypse Now and Then: A Feminist Guide to the End of the World* (Boston: Beacon Press, 1996), chap. 4; also Kirkpatrick Sale, *The Conquest of Paradise: Christopher Columbus and the Columbian Legacy* (New York: Knopf, 1990).

25. Søren Kierkegaard, *Either/Or*, vol. 2, trans. Walter Lowrie (Princeton: Princeton University Press, 1944), pp. 21–22 (orig. pub. 1843).

26. Søren Kierkegaard, *Concluding Unscientific Postscript*, trans. David F. Swenson (Princeton: Princeton University Press, 1944), p. 218 (orig. pub. 1846).

27. Ibid., p. 221.

28. Ibid.

29. Ibid., p. 218.

30. Ibid., pp. 220–21.

CHAPTER 7

The Promises of Exiles:
A Jewish Theology of Responsibility

Laurie Zoloth

At the heart of the vast and global crisis in the world's health, population, consumption, and the environment lies the persistent and tangible issue of meeting specific human and planetary needs in a deeply interconnected ecology. All of the crisis, all of the complex discourse about ecology ultimately comes down to the dilemmas of necessity and desire confronted in each family. As the world community struggles to justly harvest, distribute, and treasure the resources we share in common, meeting in conferences and committees, we each also turn to our neighbor and ask one another about the details of obligation and generosity. It is an act that is at once personal, spiritual, and enmeshed in the deepest complexities of political and economic citizenship. Those classics, called world religions, are of necessity, not by choice, enmeshed in the complex moral challenges in our global political economy presented by Korten and Loy in this volume.

The necessity for justice, for justice to attend to the vulnerable, and to speak to the powerful in an unjust world has long been central to the vision of many religions. It was a vision that ordered the social resistance, and existence, of communities for generations, but it is a vision that is now barely visible amidst the seductions of the marketplace, as we are reminded by David Loy in his discussion of the competing religiousness of the market ideology.

It is the contention of this book, of course, that this can be changed. It has been a measure of our collective failure that we have not offered a convincing language powerful enough to challenge the social organization of consumption and conservation, of population growth and environmental protection, to raise essential questions of the principle, purpose, and meaning of justice. It was with this in mind that a small group of "neighbors" in the disparate scholarships of our religions began to speak and write of a new language for this discourse. We asked both how our particular theological voices could address the highest level of international decision making, and how theology could transform daily life. As we struggled with the answers, the crisis of the planet became increasingly extreme: a series of interlocking catastrophes. We spoke of the severity of emerging micro-organisms, as new epidemics swept into the food and the air, the inexorability of shifts in climate, as the dead were taken from the Chicago heat. Colleagues came to our meetings as witnesses to the losses of entire fragile species, to the poisoning of whole regions. If religion is a response to the sacred, the religions of the world have been all too nonresponsive to the assault on earth life.

The task of my voice in this conversation, and my great privilege, was to consider how a careful application of Jewish theology, a (re)membering of texts, and a praxis of faith, might animate the vision of a just, abundant, and joyful world community, in which the shared earth sustains, protects, and nurtures the humanity that sustains, protects, and nurtures the earth. Jewish thought brings much to the discourse, and I was challenged to bring even more: holocaust, history, geopolitics, text, practice. This chapter is about one argument: that the central narrative and the spiritual metaphor of exile, and the methodology of exilic response, discursive debate, are critical to a new discussion about population, consumption, and the environment. It could be argued that the Jewish community, only 13 million people worldwide, have only the faintest of impacts. Even in American terms, Jews are only 2 percent of the population.[1]

Let me develop an alternative claim: "Not by might, and not by power, but by *ruach* alone" (Zech. 4:6), do the claims of Jewish history and thought take a place in this debate. This Hebrew word *ruach* means "spirit," and the verse is a reminder to us, the collective progeny of the slaves of Exodus, whose very victory was one of faithful opposition, a warning against overweening pride, or technological prowess militarism, chariots and horses. But *ruach* also means "breath," and, metaphorically, the breath of speech. If what is critical to new theology is not might, and not power, but narrative, then what Jewish thought brings to the discourse of a public policy informed by theological considerations is the particular, resistant, history, the particular language, the central narrative of Exodus and Exile that locates the Jews as central actors in the shared community of the moral imagination of the peoples of the world.

LIBERATION AND EXILE: EXODUS AND DIASPORA

Two thousand years of this narrative and history yield many moments in the biblical and rabbinic text that are critical to a search for theological language that supports rigorous ecological caution. Hence, many recent and important works have emerged in the last several years that describe Jewish thought by selecting one or another of these quotes: the injunction to protect the fruit trees of a city that one is waging war against,[2] for example, or the generally applicable call to seek justice,[3] the calls for a Jubilee, or the mystical prayers for *Tu b'Shevat*, a celebration of the new year for trees.

In fact, there has been a renaissance of theology and deeply felt correspondent grassroots practice around the issue of ecology. Shromrei Adamah, for example, a national organization within the Jewish Renewal Movement is devoted to teaching Jews to make the connection between tradition and the environment. They publish workbooks for families, run a camp in New York, and speak nationally on this topic. Arthur Waskow, among others, has long written of the connection between the agricultural basis for Jewish holidays, and a general sense of commitment to the protection and peace of the land. In Israel itself, strong environmental movements—among them, the Society for the Protection of Nature—have emerged. In religious yeshivoth, such as Pardes, attention is turned to texts of environmental protection. Like the Hindu and indigenous peoples described in this book, thousands of ordinary Jews hear the imperative of ecology, infusing holidays like *Tu b'Shevat* and *Sukkot* with new liturgy, new resolve, and concrete gestures: planting and habitat preservation.

EXILE AND RESISTANCE

But this is not a descriptive account of practice: of either the paradox of Jewish power, the frailty of Jewish survival, or the sweetness of these new efforts. In this chapter, I want to attempt something different from the usual accounting of disparate proof texts. I want to create a descriptor of a central theological stance, that while Jewishly derived, is metaphorically applicable to all peoples: the notion of an overreaching, existential Exile, a Galut, a journey in the world in which we are all—Jews and non-Jews alike—in a difficult diasporic condition that demands terrible obligation from each one of us to the community of sojourners and strangers of which we are a part. This is an agonistic account of the condition of human life, far from the assumption of harmony, or easy comradery. It assumes that the work of a human life and of a human community is serious, death-defying, and profound, that the goal is not simple happiness, or even simplicity (certainly not simplicity) but uprightness and courage on the Road.

Exile, hunger, the way closed behind you, and the future stony, difficult, and as yet unredeemed: this is the starkness of the world that we are given, and given again and again. Arnold Eisen has pointed out that the original banishment of Adam and Eve was metaphysical and existential, and was redoubled by the political and social Exile of Cain, banished from everywhere, and from all human society:

> Cain will suffer the fate of the alien denied the protection of his clan. "Anyone who meet me may kill me." God must therefore become Cain's sole protector—an eerie foreshadowing of the destiny of God's people Israel. They too will be made strangers, by God's will, in strange lands, and safeguarded only because God's blessing proves a shelter as well as a curse.[4]

Adamic exile is a nakedness beyond naming, a stripping of all but the scent of Paradise, carried on the animal skins of Adam and Eve, later in the skins of Esau that Jacob steals, later on the coat of Joseph, a scent that will reemerge again and again in the world of rabbinic midrash, and in the work of Emmanuel Levinas, as a hint of the infinite possibility of a world healed.

Eisen claims the exilic state as emblematic of the Jewish condition. I want to extend his insight to include that metaphor to a humanity that searches for home in a fragile modern world. We are both lost and at fault, at risk and accountable, bearers of the scent of Paradise and lovers of the pleasure of the desert, easily seduced by idols, losing track of the dangerous column of Fire in the night.

A WORLD OF LIMITS

The Exile into time, labor and grief, the deeper exile created by violence, is replicated by the tension between lostness and wandering. Abraham and Sarah, bearing their homelessness, nomadic, the flights from hunger into Egypt, the wandering in the desert—in fact, very little of the Torah narrative of their progeny takes place in the Promised Land. The great Exodus is to a new exile, not to the Land, forty years in the desert to burn out the slave in the bone. The Torah of exodus ends not with redemption, but on the shores of the Jordan, the home is in sight, but not entered.

The time that is spent in landedness is fraught with prophetic rebuke. It is clear in the understanding of the later rabbinic reflection about the last exile that God is also seen as a wanderer, "like a King without his retinue" in the desert.[5] The Talmud and the Responsa literature struggles with the realities held in tension, exile, and the possibility of redemption. The intellectual problem of the leadership is to make meaning of the wandering into Babylon and then beyond, into Spain, renewed expulsion, Western Europe, again expulsion and finally exile from the Enlightenment, from science and rationality of modernity itself, into the splintered postmodern new landscape—a landscape where, once again, the explanatory story is riveted and must be retold, where the mark of chance and of escape from death is born, like Cain's sign, a trace of numbers on the forearm.

It is my contention that the way chosenness is to be understood in this story is not through a pitying distance, but as a clarifying light that illuminates the Exile of all of humanity, in a world of uncertainty. The meaning of chosenness that I explore here is unitive, not separative. The symbols of all great religions have universal, not merely sectarian, application.

Making and rediscovering theological meaning is just the start. We are heirs to the rabbinic tradition of practical prophecy. The work of faith was to provide tools for the details of daily life in the Exilic present. It is to the specificity of response to the condition of Galut that we now turn.

Jewish tradition does not support a completely unbridled autonomy nor is it based in a cynical consequentialism. Both of these points not only create a specificity of response to the use of technology and the problems of how to best order society, but create a stance about the notion of limits that questions the very premise of the use of the natural world itself. Since in Jewish thought, human creatures, human families live in exile both in an existential and in a literal sense, we need to understand the promises of exiles, the obligations of sojourners. Our collective human exile, marked by our exit from an Edenic reality, is to a world of limits: of temporality and specificity. There is, after Eden, the terrible temporality of each human life, of the seasons of harvest and of growth, of lunar cycles. For each event ordered by the natural world, rabbinic law prescribes detailed human restraints. Acquisition, consumption, sexuality, all seen as robustly good acts, are not unregulated acts. Limits are not tragedies, but social realities. Desire, seen as infinite, is not rebuked, but refined; expected, but contained, by collective necessity—moral finitude.

WILDERNESS AND CULTIVATION

In much of the literature of the ecological movement, the needs of the natural world, left as untouched as possible, are set at odds with the needs of human persons. We are urged toward "fewer people and more bears."[6] This view of the natural world as essentially wild and untamed is a quintessentially unJewish construct. The world of Exile is a world that needs to be cultivated. Hence the mitzvah, given early in Genesis, "leshev et ha'aretz," "to settle the land." It is precisely this insight that allows for a middle way between the intensely debated arguments for productive development and for preservation that marks so much of the literature, scholarly and popular, on ecology.

The *golah*, the exiled population, lives in the "testing ground"[7] of Sinai and Babylon and make for themselves an order. And what tames and cultivates the earth is not violence or submission, but justice. The rules of encampment in the desert and the rules of agronomy, worked out carefully far from the facticity of the Land of Israel, are theologies of how we exiles are obligated to (re)member the physical world by remembering the social fact of our own estrangement. Enjoined to know the heart of the stranger and to see that he can live by your side, the *golah* is thundered at by prophets and reasoned to by teachers: the wealth and resources into which you walk are not yours, they are transient gifts in a world that is not fully yours. This uneasiness, homelessness, alienation, and nakedness is mediated only with careful attention to the most fundamental needs of the poor.

What laboriously transforms the curse of wakefulness and wariness, of danger and chanciness into a blessing of community is the structure of sociability, the necessity of vulnerability that mutual and universal estrangement brings. Embodiment is a condition of the creature, first cause and structure. The labor of birth to which Eve's daughters are given is the work of loving newborns, the terribly weak, whose vulnerability requires human community.

Further, the rabbinic structure of elaboration of laws about the Land of Israel is a complex theological gesture. Why is it that large sections of the Talmud might be devoted to an agricultural order that at least some must have suspected was far beyond their grasp? Even more curious, why did the rabbis continue to debate the details of the Jubilee year long after its enactment was a possibility? I suggest that this gesture was the moral equivalent to the clothing of the nakedness of Exile itself. The garment of consideration is shaped by a meticulous attention to the problem of limits. It is the correlation between limitedness and law that allows for enormous industry, vision, and productivity with a limit to prideful acquisition.

This theological approach is promising: now we begin to envision a cultivation that is a partnership between God and human, between physical necessity and spiritual task, and everywhere in Jewish texts this partnership within the exilic state is referenced. It is a rabbinic truism and a later constant in the work of mystics Isaac Luria and Abraham Isaac Kook, theorists Buber, Rosensweig, Heschel, and Soleveitchik, and political leaders Theodor Hertzl and Henrietta Szold, that both spiritual and physical homecoming requires a partnership in the process of Tikkun Olam, world repair.

And it is promising as well, in a world so full of lost chances, when Jews remember to understand the world as fundamentally unredeemed but redeemable. To discuss the details of the renewed Temple, commits one to a homecoming that is absolute, no matter how dark the broken world or how remote the vision, how impractical.

PERSONAL ACTION IN A PUBLIC WORLD

Yet how, specifically, does such an exilic philosophy compel substantially different behavior from a world leadership that organizes consumption and commodity exchange? Such a task is, for each of us, of course, personal as it is political. Consider: My own grandfather, Nathan Cohen, who saw his village burned to the ground in the pogroms of 1905, never saw Yosemite, nor much of wilderness, and walked on the beach in shoes. He made his small living, happily painting the hundreds of new houses of immigrant Los Angeles that filled up and destroyed the fragile California desert. He liked crowds, studying Talmud inside rooms. He planted his backyard carefully, gloried in his grape vines—that was the natural world, something he could tend. He loved progress, the fact of airplanes, the endless fecundity of American grocery stores. How does this life fit into the tragedy of the loss of the commons?

It is at once maddening and compelling to think that the catastrophe in the climate, and the destruction of vast ecosystems, have anything to do with his, or my, paltry choices, whether the granddaughter of that urban working class Jew decides to use her car or take a bus to work. After all, I can reason, vast forces far outside of my control actually govern the world economy, an economy at an absurdly far remove from my moral gestures. Consider David Korten's insight that "the globalizing economic system is reconstructing itself in a way that makes it almost impossible for even highly socially conscious and committed managers to operate a corporation responsibly in the public interest."[8]

Almost impossible, in a world governed solely by economics or scientific theory. But not impossible in a world also moved by considerations of faith and human community, a force, despite falling on skeptical times in the late twentieth century, that has historically and contemporaneously reorganized the odds of the fixed and given order more than once.

For Jews, it is the method of *halachah* that offers us a way to talk about the relationship between small personal acts of daily life and the largest possible social order. A Jew responds to her world with attention to every detail. Faith depends on habits of order that surround and encompass a human life to render the secular world holy. At all times, the minutia of the moral gesture is important: exactly thirty-nine acts prohibited on the Sabbath, the animal killed in precisely this way and no other, articles counted, measured, weighed, compared precisely, with the exactitude of consumption and commerce all watchfully addressed in the rabbinic literature. The Jew is aware of the vastness of God, and of the vastness of the cosmos, and of the impossibility of control. But the covenantal relationship, the promises of exiles to God-in-exile, are to live in a commanded world of use. It is not that individual acts change the world, any more than habits of recycling change how the Pepsi corporation uses world resources. It is that to live a fully human life, a moral life, one must act as though it does. The messiah is brought, not to perfect the world, but the day after the world is perfected by the cumulative weight of such acts.

THE PROCESS OF DISCOURSE AS CITIZENSHIP: A POSTMODERN VIEW

And more is gained from the textual turn: it is the methodology of the discursive community, a disparate collection of arguments and additions, redactors and disputers that form a reflective canon that is the critical aspect of *halachah*[9] The central claim of Jewish ethics is that truth is found in the house of discursive study—the *bet midrash*.[10] Such a public discourse is created when we argue, face to face, about the meaning and relevance of the narrative, symbols and referents. [11]

This is not merely a postmodernist insight about the fluidity and mutability of text (although it is in part that). It is a historical-literary observation that anyone can make upon opening a page of the Talmud, the literal record of the oral tradition of proof text, argument, and counter text that circles and circles virtually any truth claim. Revelation is given to the imperfect world, to nomads and recently freed slaves, to the rabbinic decisors of the Talmudic and post-Talmudic period, who were shoemakers and tenant farmers alike, to Polish shtetl wise men, and to me and to you, any listening reader.

You might wonder why we need the disagreements of *halachah* at all. Why not just start with a general discussion of ethics and values? But Jewish ethical reasoning cannot be fully separated from this religious legal system. It is this carefully preserved dispute, and the tradition of dispute itself that is preserved. It is the nature of justice that it must be proven in the specifics of the actual.

There is an assumption of reversibility in the text, a recollection of a concrete moment of human gesture, an internal logic based on the effort to identify the hearer of the story or *midrash*, with the players in the narrative. The story makes sense of the textual quote, itself a sign of the argument about the original query. The text, the example, and the explanatory narrative serve to create a tension that places the hearer of the argument in the position of the subject and thus the hearer is given the opportunity for reflexive analysis. The problem, the narrative and the textual fragment exist at different historical moments, allowing the contemporary account the same privilege as earlier commentary. The text is reversible in a variety of circumstances each slightly unlike the other, linked by an analogy that places index and subject against context, conversational.[12] The multivocity of the form itself insists on the questioning of the solidity of the text. For many of the proof texts there are strong countervailing premises and correspondent inimicable truths, and rabbinic decisors who defend differing positions: the proof texts are not a narrative, but a dialogic notation.

Why is all of this of importance? It is the first task of Jewish ethics to create the possibility of a discursive venue for wildly difficult and fiercely contentious ethical debate. Beginning in this way allows for us to confront each other, and one another's premises face to face, and to disagree in full public voice. Argument is not the roadblock to but the first premise of social citizenship. It is this attention to the argument that makes exilic journey possible, a journey in which both your story, and my story, and the dispute matter terribly.

Walking in Exile means that one walks on a continent not of one's making, on a land soaked first with the blood of Abel (Gen. 14:11) and then with the blood of so many other brothers and sisters. A possible stance would be to abandon the actions of the self entirely, to surrender to inevitability. But this choice is to be animal, not human. To be human and to have a profoundly human task is to understand that the condition of exile can be, must be, altered by a myriad of human choices.

Jews do not offer a theology of return to Eden, not a time when plants or animals are animated with equal moral worth. The very blessing of humanism is the ability to work, and to rest, to tame, subdue, harvest, alter, co-create nature. The environment, in Jewish texts, is not Paradise, it is the actual world, and it more than needs us—it would be a restless wilderness without our hands, a place for beasts, not children, not learning, not *avodah*, the word for both service, and the word for faith.

Hence, parking lots, neonatal ventilators, PCR machines, plastic legos, spaceships, and electron microscopes are a necessary part of what it is that humans do, and their beauty and their compromises are the reverse side of the appreciation that both dolphins and roaches, redwoods and kudzu are part of creation. It is foolish to waste or ruin the land, to poison or to strip it, but in Jewish thought, it is not morally incorrect to manipulate it. It is our work, as much as anything about us, that makes us holy. Yet long prior to the modern environmental movement, the limits of work was the subject of careful theological reflection. It is exactly the paradox of work that makes it clear that our ability to stop is critical to understanding God sovereignty.

Samuel Raphael Hirsch, the nineteenth-century founder of modern Orthodoxy, saw the triumph of rationality and modernity in every Jewish law and custom. But even he, speaking from a classically patriarchal, hierarchal frame saw the structure of Shabbat as the organizing principle of Jewish practice: a practice that called for a constancy of attention to place, task, and limits for the marketplace.[13]

It is this deep biblical structure of cessation, of voluntary retreat from the endless possibility of production and consumption that is found in every agricultural law. We are enjoined always to take less than we could, to wait longer to harvest the first fruits, to let the land rest every seven years, in an entire year of Shabbat, and finally to declare a year of Jubilee every fifty years, when not only the land rests, but the marketplace and social hierarchy itself is restored to its point of origin. This original position is the position not only of John Rawls, but of the moment of origin of Exile itself: when the Land was only a theory, a promise, a consequence of the choice for goodness and of Torah, and the tribes stood, in full and public view of one another, receiving their location of the Land, and their responsibility.

This moment, of identity, accountability, and promise, is the moment that is redolent of the scent of paradise—of the possible. It is a moment at once both intensely personal—your commandedness and your responsibility, your choice for good and evil itself—and public— your witness of the acceptance of responsibility of your community. Emmanuel Levinas reminds us that this act, the first act of a people liberated from slavery, was into the service of mutual responsibility, a taking on of the other's responsibility.[14] It is not only the minutia of consumption and production and social life that is both taken and witness, it is the commitment to witness itself, the interlocking network of deeds and debt that will hold the exilic community together. It is the obligation toward the stranger that is at your side, and hers to the one at her side, that will make the time in the desert bearable.

The moral agent in Jewish thought is corporate, communal, and infinitely, ceaseless, "sleeplessly responsible" for the other.[15] It is a truism in much of new theology, and communitarian philosophy, but it is an absolute organizing principle in Judaism that the community has a stronger appeal than the autonomous individual. The *golah* is a collective noun—an exilic population, and the diaspora is a shared fate of peoplehood. To act only for oneself, even to act only on behalf of one's family is not only proscribed, it would be shortsighted to the point of folly. The community must act on behalf of the promises made in order to expect a world in which the minimal promises of natural order are returned. To break the oaths of justice and fair dealing is to literally stop the rain.[16]

But what of the powerful traveler whose actions threaten the welfare of the entire fragile diasporic community? What of the careless, the selfish ones? Evil, sinfulness, and idolatry are hardly new theological problems. Hubric destruction of the planet, ravaging the land, and excessive and greedy use of the resources held in common was in fact quite possible in antiquity. Biblical accounts speak of the ability to utterly waste the land we travel in. The option to husband the wealth of the world for the benefit of the most powerful, or to distribute the social goods of the whole unfairly has long been an option.[17]

And the essential Jewish narrative stands as testimony to what can happen when the evil is unchallenged. What is possible is extinction, the ultimate extremity of the Holocaust. For example, while any debate about justice and ecology begins with an acknowledgment of the impact of the growth of the population in a world described as "full,"[18] Jews have a history that is at decided odds with this surge in growth. It was at precisely the moment of rapid population increase that Jews were counting their losses, 30 percent of the total population, dead after 1948. In a real and specific sense, European Jews[19] had already experienced life in a period of total environmental collapse, a near species extinction.[20]

It is not only the lessons of recent history that cast a tragic light on the question of population control and ecological justice, but the entire textual account of biblical history as well. Despite the injunction from God to be fruitful, and despite the promises to Abraham that "your descendants will as numerous as the stars" (Gen. 15:5), the account of Jewish history is framed by narrow escapes from total annihilation. The Exodus story is an account of the outwitting of the decree to destroy all male children, the subversion of the midwives (who are the textual representors of fertility itself) at the heart of the drama. The skirmishes in Canaan always have complete annihilation at stake.

The rabbinic commentators themselves, a remnant after the Roman victories, struggle with the problem of whether to restrict the birth of children into so dangerous and devastated a world, its fields sown into barrenness with salt, its cites ravaged by plague, its fundamental social, economic and religious structures destroyed.[21] The answer was not to order a restriction on bearing children, an answer that was replicated in Responsa that emerged throughout the long centuries of confinement in ghettos, the persecutions and pogroms. Rome controlled and defined the entire world known to the scholars writing under its yoke. Their ability to dominate the environment must have seemed as total as the enormity of the multinational economy does to us today. Nothing has particularly changed about the gesture of accumulation, what has changed is the quickening of the pace and the broadening of the scope of the actions. Yet in the face of this, the theological account was not only to critique the problem, to stand outside of the persuasive ideological stance it offered but to outline exactly the task necessary to restore the human scales of justice, one by one.[22]

Any new theology, then, must do at least two difficult things. If it does not, theology will be no more than sweet and peripheral, a sort of moral muzak. The first is for each person in the exilic community to act according to her promises of accountability—daily, habitually, and against the sense of futility that envelopes such acts. The template is the system of discipline in religion, but the moral boundaries, the limits to total and individual personal action, can exist without reference to the specificity of any view of God. Each self will have to extend her boundaries, understanding herself as self-in-community, self in full view of the other. Because of the near hegemony of the assumption and power of autonomy in both ethics and in the discourse of public policy, it is important for Jewish ethics to offer some reflection on the tenuousness of that claim. Jewish thought struggles not only with the nature of the self relative to the other, and the self relative to the community, but whether the embodied self has what post-Enlightenment thinkers describe as rights at all. The notion of the good in this formulation rests not on the promise of voluntariness, but on the promise of obligation. The commitment of daily action simply because it is the right act and because it is demanded of you because of your moral location on the planet confronts directly the post-Enlightenment model of the unencumbered disconnected trader in the open and "free" marketplace. Such an approach insists on the community of others that are dependent on, and dependable upon, and questions whether unconstrained accumulation itself is either possible or the ground for human freedom.

The second task for any new theology is to speak truth to power. How difficult an act! It is tempting to only rail against the powerful Other, or to yearn for a retreat to Eden, or Egypt, or the shtetl—wherever the last expulsion was from. But the rabbinic turn takes us from this. We are enjoined to go beyond complaint, far beyond nostalgia. We need to see the other, and the choices of the other, as our responsibility and our business. We need to find clarity in the religious voice and claim its power, rather than acceding to its privatization. The prophets of the Hebrew Bible, and the leadership of the Jewish communities consistently spoke to the necessity of justice: to the vulnerable, to the laborer, to the land. But of all of these prophetic rebukes, the most compelling is to the powerful, to leadership itself. Jewish communities must reflect on their alliances: when the poor tell their stories, will they speak of the solidarity of the Jewish community or of its silence? We must insist that all of us strangers in the exile have the courage to name evil. The stakes for such engagement are high. But if persons of faith do not call the ethical question, if we too are lulled into a somnambulant despair by the pursuit of commodities, the coolness of the silk on our cheeks, the pleasure of the company we keep, and that company's proximity to power, then who will?

Calling the ethical question in the marketplace that orders so much of the largest environmental decision making is, of necessity, very difficult. The one who brings moral imperative, much less God, into the equation will be told, patiently, that the tangible, the tough, and the actual way the world works is by the fulfillment of desire, by the call of the marketplace. Yet the prophetic tradition can tell us much about the imperative of the outsider who can see an alternate vision. Challenging the "is" with the "ought" leads us to fruitful understandings about the role of the alternate claim, leads us to challenge the givenness of the relationships as presented, and leads to an ironic view of diagnostic certainty. Such language is neither safe nor endearing. That the historical place of the philosopher as well as the theologian was to remain the outsider can easily be forgotten. The first task of any theology is to remember that it is the brokenness of the world itself that calls us to the work of repair. It is not a new call: Jeremiah (22:13) reminds us that long after the ceders were stripped from Lebanon, we have a chance to reflect and reconsider what we mean by wealth. It is a task for each to insist on, a performative as well as a theoretical commitment.

Jeremiah, the prophet of exile, speaks to the exiled people, and they remember and carry his words to read every year on Tisha b'Av, the day that mourns the drama of exile itself. The paradox that the holyday of midsummer comes one half year after Tu b'Shevat, the midwinter holiday of trees, land, promise of harvest. Rebuke in August abundance, assurance in January barrenness, the world a place that is capable of anything. It is, say Jewish sources, not a world in harmony, but a world in which promises can be made to struggle toward harmony, where justice and true wellness are linked.

New theological conversations, more than they allow us to agree, allow us to argue. The work of Jewish thought has always been to make ordinary meaning out of extraordinary moments of revelation, to answer the question, "now how are we to live?" as we stumble out of the last place we have left. The promises of the *golah*, all of us, are to enable the vision of homecoming to lead the daily work of the journey.

NOTES

1. In the discussions about earlier drafts, this sentence was followed by extended debate. In it, several of my colleagues challenged me, frankly, with the paradox of their experiential perceptions of Jewish economic power. I am not a political scientist, but a theologian and an ethicist, so I can attest only to the certainty that the concept of Jewish monetary control of international finance is the oldest of tropes of accusation. The scope of response is far beyond the work of this chapter.

2. Deut. 20:19.

3. See, for example, Deut. 16:20: "Justice, justice shall you pursue."

4. Arnold Eisen, "Exile," *Contemporary Jewish Religious thought*, ed. Arthur A. Cohen and Paul Mendes-Flor (New York: The Free Press, 1972), p. 220.

5. *Sifre: A Tannaitic Commentary on the Book of Deuteronomy*, ed. and trans. Reuven Hammer (New Haven, Conn.: Yale University Press, 1986).

6. J. Baird Caldicott, "The Search for an Environmental Ethic," in *Matters of Life and Death*, 2nd ed., ed. Tom Regan (New York: Random House, 1980).

7. Eisen, "Exile," p. 223.

8. Korten, p. 10.

9. Laurie Zoloth, "Face to Face but Not Eye to Eye," *The Journal of Clinical Ethics* (Winter 1995).

10. Herb Basser, as noted on the Post-Modern Jewish Philosophy Network.

11. John Puddefoot, from a discussion on the Post-Modern Jewish Philosophy Network. In this posting, Puddefoot reminds us that authoritative texts ought to be regarded as living texts carried along by a tradition that simultaneously qualifies them and is itself qualified by them.

12. It is this vagueness that Peter Ochs claims is another name for multivocity. Internet posting, Thursday, 18 May 1995, Post-Modern Jewish Philosophy Network.

13. Consider: 11 August 1996, marked the total collapse of the Western Grid Power System in six of fifty states for several hours. This event shut down all uses of electrical power for four hours. No matter how wealthy, or how close to the trillion dollar marketplace one was, the electricity that worked the world was absent. That day was Shabbat. And on that day, my family, in my community, was oblivious to the event that dominated the front page of every Western state newspaper. We walked to synagogue, ate a shared meal, sang, prayed, read the Torah, studied together, walked home, slept, played with the children, shared another meal with friends, sang. That night we noticed the clocks had

stopped. We had, as a community, stepped out of the crisis itself—a model for what a conscious community might be able to do, a metaphor.

14. Emmanuel Levinas, *Difficult Freedom: Essays on Judaism* (Baltimore: Johns Hopkins University Press, 1990).

15. Levinas.

16. Deut. 11:13–22, as said twice a day in the Sh'ma.

17. Consider the following from *Pesikta 'd Rav Kahana 9:1*

> When R. Joshua ben Levi went to Rome, he saw marble pillars there which had been carefully covered with wrappings to keep them from cracking during the heat and freezing in the cold. At the same he saw a poor man who had no more than a reed mat under him and a reed mat over him to protect him from the elements.

18. David Korten, "Sustainability and the Global Economy" in *No Place for People : The Global Economy on a Finite Planet* (West Hartford, Conn.: Kumarian Press, 1995), p. 3

19. And native populations in the Americas.

20. Consequently, many Jews in the immediate generation post-Shoah feel a obligation to restore the terrible losses to Jewish population that occurred at the hands of the Nazis. Moshe Tendler, *Pardes Rimonim* (New York: The Judaica Press, 1982).

In the United States, the population has dropped from 4 percent to 2.3 percent a result of a consistently low birthrate and an intermarriage rate of 50 percent, with 75 percent of those families not raising their children as Jews, resulting in an unprecedented loss of identification and affiliation. "State of the Jewish World," A Report of the World Jewish Congress, as reported in *The New York Times*, 12 February 1996, pp. A1–B4.

21. Talmud Balvi, Bava Batra 60b; P'nai Shlomo, ad loc.; Talmud Balvi, Yevamot 90b; Taz, Shulcan Aruck, Orah Hayyim, end of 588; Biur ha-Gra to Shulchan Aruch, Even Ha-Ezer, chapter 1, section 10. See Rabbi Herschel Schater, "Halachic Aspects of Family Planning," *Halacha and Contemporary Society*, ed. Rabbi A. Cohen (New York: Ktav, 1983), pp. 15–17. See also Sharon Joseph Levy, "Judaism and the Environment," in *Population , Consumption and the Environment*, ed. Howard Coward (Albany: State University of New York Press, 1996), p. 75.

23. Barry Holtz, *Finding Our Way* (New York: Schoken Books, 1990), p. 243. Holtz notes a midrash from *Ecclesiastes Rabbah 9:7* about how the rabbi violated Shabbat to help a beggar. "When the people of the city pointed out this surprising violation of the law by such a pious man, God miraculously caused the sun to shine (thus extending the secular time in which the work of carrying is permitted), thus preserving Abba Tahnah's saintliness both in matters of *tzedakah* and in punctiliousness about ritual law. The commandment to concretely address injustice, when a life is at stake, overrides even the prohibitions on the Shabbat.

CHAPTER 8

"One Tree Is Equal to Ten Sons": Some Hindu Responses to the Problems of Ecology, Population, and Consumerism

Vasudha Narayanan

The Epics and Puranas, revered books within the many Hindu traditions, give detailed narratives of the periodic destruction of the world. The epic *Mahabharata* (c. 500–200 B.C.E.) is graphic in the portrayal of the events at the end of the fourth—and worst—on and what happens after a thousand such ages. The population increases, trees do not bear fruit; a drought prevails, people destroy parks and trees and the lives of the living will be ruined in the world.[1] The texts also speak of a close relationship between *dharma* (righteousness, duty, justice) and the ravaging of earth. When *dharma* declines, human beings take it out on nature. There is, however, no Hindu text focussing on *dharma* or this worldly righteousness that advises us to be passive and accept the end of the world scenario with a life-negating philosophy. Many Hindu texts are firm in their view that human beings be committed to, indeed be proactive in the enhancement of the quality of life. In this chapter, we will look at the resources and limitations within the many Hindu traditions to see how the interconnected problems of overpopulation, ecology, and consumption/consumerism can be addressed. The challenge of this will be to see how these ancient symbols and ideas speak with power to the problems outlined by Loy and Korten at the beginning of this volume.

TEXTS ON DHARMA AND TEXTS ON THEOLOGY:
BIMORPHIC WORLDVIEWS

Classical Hindu texts in the beginning of the Common Era enumerate the goals—or matters of value—of a human being. These are *dharma* (righteousness, ethics, duty), *artha* (wealth, power), *kama* (sensual pleasure), and *moksha* or liberation from the circle of life and death.[2] While *dharma*, wealth, and sensual pleasure are usually seen as this-worldly, *moksha* is liberation from this world and the repeated rebirths of a soul. The multiple Hindu traditions do differ from other world religions in having this variety of goals and array of texts to go with them. What all this translates to is that there are several competing conceptual systems, intersecting but distinct, that inform human behavior.

The texts that deal with *moksha* or liberation include discussions on the nature of reality, that is, the relationship between the supreme being and the human soul. Generally, the nature of reality/supreme being is called *tattva* (truth) and corresponds with the term "theology." These texts do not focus much on ethics or righteous behavior in this world; that is the province of *dharma* texts. It is important to keep this taxonomy in mind, because *theological doctrines do not necessarily trickle down into dharmic or ethical injunctions; in many Hindu traditions, in fact, there is a disjunction between dharma and moksha. Dharma* texts promote righteous behavior on earth and *moksha* texts encourage one to be detached from such concerns. A few texts like the *Bhagavad Gita* (c. 200 B.C.E.) have tried to bridge *dharma* and *moksha* paradigms.

Theological Resources for Social Problems

The many Hindu theological texts do contain engaging accounts of reality, which, if understood and acted upon directly, could serve as resources for several social and moral problems. However, the *tattva* discourses and the knowledge embedded in them were hardly available to the general public until the advent of mass media in this century. In the Hindu tradition, epic stories and narratives, devotional and folk songs, as well as dharmic practices and rituals, are the elements most accessible to the people.

To a certain extent this situation has changed in recent years. The advent of mass media, the dissemination of books and tapes to an educated elite of middle-class Hindus in India and in the diaspora has resulted in a popularization of these philosophies. Particularly popular in many parts of India is the *Bhagavad Gita*, a text that domesticates many of the principles of asceticism, and that deals with both the realms of *dharma* and liberation.

Central to the *Bhagavad Gita* is the vision of the universe as the body of Krishna (Vishnu). While the immediate context of the vision is to convince Arjuna of the supremacy of God, many theologians including Ramanuja (traditional dates 1017–1137) equally emphasize the immanence and transcendence of the supreme being. According to Ramanuja, the universe, composed of sentient (*chit*) and nonsentient stuff (*achit*) forms the body (*sharira*) of the Vishnu.[3] Just as a human soul (*chit*) pervades a nonsentient body (*achit*), so too, does Vishnu pervade the souls, the material universe, and Time. The name Vishnu, in fact, means "all pervasive." Vishnu-Narayana is inseparable from Shri-Lakshmi, the Goddess. According to the Shri Vaishnava theologian Vedanta Deshika (1268–1368), both Vishnu and Shri pervade the universe together; the universe is their body. It is important to note that in this philosophy, it is *not* the case that the material universe is female and the transcendent god is male; together, the male and female deities create and pervade the universe, and yet, transcend it. What the body-soul metaphor translates to in devotional praxis for Ramanuja and Vedanta Deshika is that we—as part of the universe—are the body of Vishnu and Shri, are owned by them and are supported by them. Vishnu and Shri are also seen through personal metaphors: Vishnu is the master, father, support, beloved one, lover. Shri is the mother of the universe. The proper response of the human being is to be devoted to, worship, and surrender him/herself to Vishnu and Shri. However, while the devotional songs emphasize the drama and engagement of interpersonal relationships, the philosophical underpinnings of the universe as the body of the deities has been practically unknown, except among a few philosophically learned followers of Ramanuja.

Thus, although some *tattva* texts such as those of Ramanuja's contain rich resources for the problems of ecology, population, and consumerism, regrettably, in the Hindu contexts they have limited power over ethical behavior. Mumme senses this point in her elaborate and sensitive account of the theological eco-resources within the Hindu tradition and thinks the discussion may be little more than rearranging the deck chairs of the Titanic. Despite this caveat, Mumme proceeds to give an excellent account of the theological richness of the Shri Vaishnava (followers of Shri and Vishnu) tradition of Ramanuja, which emphasizes panentheism, that is, the transcendence and immanence of God.[4]

While logically the theological/*tattva* texts *ought* to eventually translate to human action, the time frame for such connections would probably be rather large since it would be seen as too idealistic. I suspect it would be analogous to having "thou shalt not kill" emblazoned over every doorway of the Pentagon and "turn the other cheek" printed on all its stationery and expecting the workers to adopt nonviolence and vegetarianism. What I am urging is a shift in our perspective from the *tattva/ moksha* texts to the resources that have a more direct relevance to this-worldly behavior. These are the religious/*dharma* texts *and* popular practice embodied in the dharmic cumulative tradition. My chapter will focus on several proactive attempts taken already by Hindus in responding—on the basis of *dharma*—to the problems of ecology, population, and consumption/consumerism.

DHARMA AND ARTHA TEXTS AND PRACTICES AS RESOURCES FOR ECOLOGY

The texts that focus explicitly on *dharma* were composed in the first few centuries of the Common Era. In addition to these, many sections of the epics *Ramayana* and *Mahabharata* and the *Puranas* also focussed on *dharma*. Other scriptures have encouraged the planting of trees, condemned the destruction of plants and forests, and said that trees are like children. In this context, a passage from the *Matsya Puranam* is instructive. The goddess Parvati planted a sapling of the Asoka tree and took good care of it. The divine beings and sages came and told her: "O [Goddess] . . . almost everyone wants children. . . . What do you achieve by creating and rearing trees like sons?" Parvati replied: "One who digs a well where there is little water lives in heaven for as many years as there are drops of water in it. One large reservoir of water is worth ten wells. One son is like ten reservoirs and *one tree is equal to ten sons.*"[5]

The words of Parvati are relevant today. Trees offer more than aesthetic pleasure, shade, and fruits. The main *Puranas*, texts of myth and lore, (ca. fifth to tenth centuries C.E.) have wonderful resources on trees. The *Varaha Purana* says that one who plants five mango trees does not go to hell and the *Vishnu Dharmottara* (3.297.13) claims that one who plants a tree will never fall into hell. Just as the planting of trees was recommended and celebrated, cutting them was condemned by almost all the *dharma* shastras. Despite these exhortations, the twentieth century has seen a massive destruction of trees. In the deforestation that has occurred in the Himalayas and in the Narmada basin, there has been a tragic transgression of *dharma* in the destruction of national health and wealth. Temples are now in the forefront of the "afforestation" movements, urging devotees to plant saplings.

The Tirumala Tirupati Initiative

"Vriksho rakshati: rakshatah"   "A tree protects: Let us protect it" or "A tree, when protected, protects us." Billboards with statements like this greet visitors to the sacred pilgrimage town of Tirumala-Tirupati, in

Andhra Pradesh, South India. The statement is obviously adapted from the Laws of Manu, which say that *dharma* when protected, protects us. In response to the ecological crisis in India, the Venkateswara ("Lord of Venkata Hills"; a manifestation of Lord Vishnu) temple at Tirumala-Tirupati began what is called the *Vriksha* (tree) *Prasada* scheme. Whenever a pilgrim visits a temple in India, s/he is given a piece of blessed fruit or food to take home. This is called a *prasada* or "favor" of the deity. Some temples in India are known for their preparation of sweets; the Tirupati temple, for instance, is well known for its making and selling of *laddus*, a confection in the shape and size of a tennis ball. Although small quantities of *prasada* in most temples are free, *laddus* are also sold for a small fee. Approximately 80,000 to 125,000 are sold *daily* by the temple kitchens.[6] Ingesting *prasada* is a devotional and mandatory ritual; by eating what is favored and blessed by the deity, divine grace is said to course through one's body.

The Tirumala-Tirupati temple, which is located on an elevation of three thousand feet and was once surrounded by heavy forests, has now established a large nursery on the hills and encourages the pilgrims to take home tree saplings as *prasada*. This temple is the richest shrine in India and carries with it a great deal of dharmic and financial clout both in India and with the "NRI" ("non-Resident-Indian") temples of Hindus in the diaspora. The wealth of the temple is legendary; in 1996, the reported annual income was upward of U.S. $35.6 million a year. This does not include the gold and silver contributions (around three hundred kg. of gold and 1880 kg. of silver in 1996) or the income from the fixed assets. This temple has about twelve major temples under its care and initiatives launched here are taken up in other places.

The plants sold as *prasada* are inexpensive—in December 1995 they were only about two rupees (a little more than five cents) each. The saplings cultivated are suitable for the soil in various parts of India, and by planting them at home one can have a real piece of the sacred place of Tirumala wherever one lives. Apart from this public-relations initiative that one may call an ecology-consciousness-raising venture for the pilgrims, the Tirumala-Tirupati Devasthanam (TTD, the official bureaucracy of the temple) has also started the Shri Venkateswara Vanabhivriddhi Schemes. The Forestry Department of the TTD began this scheme in 1981 and it was initially called the "Bioaesthetic Plan." The donation made by the devotee is used for the purchase and planting of trees and plants. The donor is honored by being granted special *darshan* (viewing of the deity in the inner shrine), accommodations on Tirumala, (normally very hard to get), and by having his/her name displayed by the tree that has been planted. Boards, placed at strategic places, announce the names of the donors and the amount of donations to the afforestation scheme. From all accounts this initiative has been very successful and over 2,500,000 indigenous trees are said to have been planted on the hills and the plains.[7] The temple quotes some relevant texts on the importance of trees, builds on the traditional structures of endowments and distribution of *prasada*, and, most important, on the distribution system of honors for devotees in mounting this thriving program. As an added incentive, large billboards in the temple nursery also list the medicinal value—as per some medical texts within the larger Hindu religiocultural tradition and popular practice—of many plants and trees in an effort to encourage the pilgrims to grow the trees.

Sacred Trees in Temples

While the texts praised the planting of trees, temples tried to exemplify the practice of venerating them. Almost every temple in South India dedicated to the gods Shiva or Vishnu, or to a manifestation of the Goddess, has a *sthala vriksha* ("the tree of a [sacred] place"), a particular tree that was sacred to that area. This is the "official" tree of the temple and is usually a grand old specimen that is surrounded by a beaten path used for circumambulation by pilgrims and devotees. This *sthala vriksha* is only a symbol of all other trees that are worthy of respect. Now, in the light of extensive destruction of trees, many temples in south India have vivified the custom of planting trees within their precincts. The Marudeeswaar temple in Tiruvanmiyur (Madras), for instance, actively encouraged its devotees to contribute to the tree-planting program in 1994–95.

It is not just trees, but the mighty rivers of India that are considered to be sacred.

Rivers: Physically Polluted Moral Purifiers

By bathing in the great rivers of India, one is said to be morally cleansed of sins *and* to acquire merit or auspiciousness. One not only gets physically cleansed by the rivers, one is morally purified and one's sins (*papa*) are destroyed. A story popular in oral tradition makes the point:

> A king goes to sleep on the banks of the River Ganga. When he wakes up in the middle of the night, he sees some women covered in filth taking a dip in the holy river. They emerge from the river cleansed and then disappear. The king returns on several nights and sees the same thing. Eventually he asks them who they are; they reply that they are the embodiments of the rivers of India. Everyday, they tell him, human beings bathe in the rivers and their sins are absolved by that act. The rivers—embodied as women—absorb the moral dirt and then come to the Ganga, the grand purifier, to purify themselves.

Variations on the story say where the Ganga goes to get herself purified although it is generally assumed that she needs no purification.[8]

The generic version of the story distinguishes between two kinds of dirt—moral dirt or sin, known as *papa* in Sanskrit, which is perceptible as physical dirt in the bodies of the river. The story, therefore, makes a direct connection between morality and physical pollution. In addition to moral purity, and physical purity, one may also note that in other Hindu contexts there is a third kind of purity: ritual purity. When one bathes in them, rivers and other bodies of water may bestow the pilgrim and his/her clothes with ritual purity. Ritual purity encompasses physical purity, but all that is physically clean is not ritually pure. Even if a person is physically and ritually clean, the mere association with people and garb that are deemed ritually unclean or impure may be contagious enough to "pollute" him or her.

In light of recent destruction of the ecology, the story of the rivers' need to purify themselves is particularly poignant. The need for consumer goods and the need for quick profit has led to a rapid industrialization and release of toxic waste in the rivers that is most dangerous and scandalous. With overpopulation and lack of basic sanitary facilities, the sacred rivers are being used as latrines, despite the injunctions in the *dharma* texts against this. The rivers that are supposed to physically, morally, and ritually purify us stand stagnant, reflecting the rancid countenance of *adharma*, unrighteous behavior. The ecologically insensitive values of market capitalism have reached our rivers; competing definitions of the sacred have undone gentler Hindu valuations.

One may also reflect briefly on the gender of the rivers. Though there are some exceptions, most of the rivers of India are considered to be female and mountains are generically male. Rivers are perceived to be nurturing (and sometimes judgmental) mothers, feeding, nourishing, quenching, and when angered, flooding the Earth. Rivers are also personified as deities; Ganga is sometimes portrayed as a consort of Lord Shiva. In the plains of Tamilnadu, Kaveri Amman (Mother Kaveri) is seen as a devotee and sometimes the consort of Lord Vishnu, and several temples (like Terazhundur, near Kumbakonam) have a striking image of this personified river in the innermost shrine. In the pre-eighth-century Vishnu temple at Tirucherai, a small village near Kumbakonam, River Kaveri is seen as in a maternal posture with a child on her lap. When the Kaveri was swollen after the early monsoon rains, I have heard the residents of Srirangam (a large temple town on an island in the midst of the river) say she was pregnant. This was a wonderful celebration of her life-giving potential; the surging river, rich with the monsoon waters swept into the plains, watering the newly planted crops in the Thanjavur delta, giving birth to the food that would nourish the population. On the feast of *patinettam perukku*, the eighteenth day in the Tamil month of *Adi* (15 July–14 Aug), all those who lived on the banks of the Kaveri in Tamilnadu, would celebrate the river's "pregnancy food cravings." They would (and still do when there is water) take a picnic to the banks of the river and eat there; Kaveri Amman was the guest at every picnic. Just as the food cravings of pregnant women were indulged by the family, Kaveri Amman's extended family celebrated her life-giving potential by frolicking and picnicking with her. In some families, the oldest woman of the family "led the festival and threw a handful of colored rices to satisfy the *macakkai* [food cravings during pregnancy] of the swiftly flowing Kaveri . . . as she hastened to the Lord's house."⁹ According to local *sthala puranams* (pamphlets that glorify a sacred place), bathing in the river Kaveri during a specific month of the year (generally held to be the Tamil month of Aippasi, 15 Oct.–14 Nov.) will wash away one's sins and give a human being supreme liberation. Thus, according to some Hindu traditions, only Lord Vishnu or Mother Kaveri can give one both nourishment and salvation. It is this river, this mother, who is now bound and gagged in Karnataka, the state of her birth, a hostage to political ambitions. The damming of River Kaveri in Karnataka state deprives the crops of Tamilnadu of all water. The rice fields of Tamilnadu dry and die as the Kaveri is held up in Karnataka by politicians who do not share the water as per the rulings of the water tribunal and instead hold the river and the dry earth of Tamilnadu hostage to election aspirations.

The denigration of the rivers in recent years is comparable to the denigration of women at various times in the Hindu civilizations. Historically the situation is complicated; there have been powerful women whose names are known as poets, patrons, performers, and philosophers; on the other hand, there have also been some androcentric texts where trees seem to have had a better deal than some women. Although one cannot make a general statement that women have been dominated by men in the history of the Hindu tradition and that this corresponds to man's domination of nature, one can say that the assaults on nature in India and the assaults on women through the new greed-crime of dowry deaths in the last decade has been unprecedented in the religious tradition. The rivers, flowing though India and personified as women in the story quoted at the beginning of this section, have absorbed the sins and follies of human beings and the slime, sludge, and excreta of human greed and consumption. It is hard not to draw a comparison between the rivers and the plight of women who are now the target of crimes of greed and power. We will be discussing this issue shortly under consumption/consumerism.

Although some women caught in families with patriarchal structures are controlled and abused, in recent years, other women have also been proactive in ecological issues. It is not surprising that women in the Chipko ("hugging trees") movement and in many parts of India are involved in protecting trees.[10] Women are also involved in communicating the tragedy of ecological disasters, sometimes using traditional religious art forms.

Classical Dance and Ecology

Awareness of ecological concerns has been heightened through the medium of traditional Indian dance, the Bharata Natyam. The theory and practice of classical dance in India (*natya shastra*) is seen as a religious activity. In other words, dance—indeed, most performing arts—are ways to salvation within some Hindu traditions. Mallika Sarabhai, a noted dancer and feminist communicator, presents the story of Chipko ("tree-hugging") movement in her *Shakti: the Power of Women*. Instead of performances where the central piece highlights the pining of the individual soul for God, some women performers now portray ecologically sensitive messages. Sujatha Vijayaraghavan's compositions on ecology are choreographed by Rhadha and regularly performed by Suchitra Nitin and Sunanda Narayanan. One of these songs/dances is particularly striking in its visual-mythic impact. The song refers to a myth in which the God Shiva drank poison to save the universe. When the gods and the demons were churning the ocean of milk, using the serpent Vasuki as a rope, the snake spit out poisonous fumes that overwhelmed the participants. Shiva saved them by consuming the poison and his neck turned blue. He is known as Nilakantha—the blue-throated one. The following song is set in the pattern of Karnatic music in the raga *Begada*: "O Nilakantha, lord, come here/ You have your work cut out for you/ I understand you consumed poison that day/ but will it do to just to sip a tiny bit of poison in your palm?/ We have spread potent poison / all over this earth, / the waters of the sea, the air, everywhere./ O Shiva, be a sport, O Shiva, be a sport/—if you suck this poison out/ you too will turn blue all over like Vishnu!"[11]

Notice that the references here are not to philosophical texts, but to a story from the *Purana*s that many Hindus would know. The tone of the song is teasing—a mood adopted in many classical Bharatanatyam songs, in which the young girl teases God, frequently in a romantic situation. Here, Shiva is told that the sipping of a little poison at the time of the churning of the ocean is not enough; he is to suck out the poison from the whole world. The traditional dance context is adopted but the message has been changed to draw attention to the poison that we have spread through our earth, waters, and air. The aesthetic and mythic context of the message also enables the writer to use the strong word "poison," which catches one's attention, rather than a more muted, often used word like "pollution."

The audience for these dances is diverse. Most of the audience would be the very government workers, industrialists, and management executives who would be connected directly or indirectly with the programs, organizations, and industries that regulate pollution and the clean-up operations. Mallika Sarabhai dances in urban and rural areas and is able to get the attention of multiple audiences. The particular strength of the medium of dance is that it is nonconfrontational, yet the music and the expressions convey a powerful message that lingers long after the performance is over. To a large extent, I would argue, this takes the place of the textual theological framework that shapes, reshapes, and molds attitudes and perspectives in the Abrahamic religions. These intellectualistic religions have much to learn of ritual and symbol as motivating and instructional powers.

The philosophic insights of Hinduism were not strong enough to prevent the disasters, but the dharmic resources have proved rich enough to commence several initiatives to help make the subcontinent green and toxic free. Are these resources equally rich to help the problems of population and consumerism?

POPULATION

Parvati, the Goddess, may have said that ten reservoirs of water are equal to one son and ten sons are equal to one tree, but the message has still not reached the teeming millions of Hindus in the subcontinent. The population is high and water resources low. India's population stands around 950 million in 1996. Obviously this adds significantly to the burden of stripping Earth of her resources. The increased need for housing and consumer goods leads to the felling of trees. With lack of proper housing and sanitary facilities, people use rivers and tanks for bodily excreta, polluting further. As India is poised to well repeat the mistakes of the Western world in buying into the convenience of synthetic disposables, we realize that more people translates to more demands on and disposal of plastics and synthetics, further polluting the environment. How did it get to be this way and what can be done?

Almost all dharmic texts of Hinduism praise the joys of having children, especially sons. The Laws of Vasishta say that nonviolence (*ahimsa*) and procreation are the common duties of members of all castes.[12] The texts are also proactive in giving religious rituals and charms that will facilitate the birth of children. The epic *Ramayana* and several other stories include the performance of rituals to beget children. However, we must note that these injunctions to beget children were made in specific population contexts. The mortality rate for children was high and life expectancy was low. Epidemics and famines drastically decimated population levels. Further, there were many days (some phases of the moon, some sacred months) when cohabitation between husband and wife was prohibited. Thus, during the entire Tamil month of Adi (15 July–14 Aug.), women in Tamilnadu returned to their natal homes. This was a month sacred for Amman, the mother goddess, and almost all castes prohibited sexual relations between married people. This is still practiced in many families in Tamilnadu. As late as early this century many of these cultural and health factors controlled population levels in South Asia. Unfortunately, the late-twentieth-century version of the plague haunts us in the form of the AIDS epidemic. It is estimated that in India alone about three and a half million people are infected with the AIDS virus and that most of them are ignorant of the fact. The toll on India's population will be costly and drastic, and will cut the numbers in less than felicitous ways.

One must also consider fertility levels in India. Birth rates have, apparently, dropped quite dramatically in developing countries from 6 to 3.6 children per woman. The birth rate in India is 3.4 children. An average of 2.1 children per woman is said to be replacement level, that is, zero growth. In the state of Kerala, where women's literacy is extremely high, and where most castes accept a matrilineal system, the level is down to 2.2 children, close to zero growth. While the birth rate is going down steadily in India, life expectancy has grown, as elsewhere in the world. Although lower than other countries such as the United States and China, India's life expectancy has grown from 32 in 1947 to 61–62 years. Manzur says quite succinctly: "It is declining mortality, not rising fertility, that is causing the current population surge."[13]

Obviously, the solution to population control lies not in lowering life expectancy or hoping for a plague to strike (it already has). The infant mortality rate in India is one of the highest—some sources put it around eighty per thousand live births.[14] Unless this primary problem can be addressed with better health care facilities and nutrition, people will produce many children hoping at least a few survive, and the population problem will only be aggravated.

A further tragic and unique wrinkle in India's population problem is the sex ratio of children. The Hindu traditions have not been averse to technology; they have harnessed it for their own ends. The technology of amniocentesis has been adopted with tragic consequences; the sex of the child is determined and female children are aborted. While female fetuses are aborted the world over, India seems to regrettably have a specially leading role. Female infanticide is also practiced in some rural communities of India. With combined abortion and infanticide, the sex ratio in many states is low. In 1901, there were 972 women to 1,000 men; by 1991, it had dropped to 927 to 1,000 men.

On the birth of girls, the parents sometimes continue to have children until they get a boy. Both through dharmic texts as well as practice and convention Hindus have prized sons. Although the reasons for a patriarchal society preferring sons may not be very complex, textual sources usually focus on the salvific value of having male progeny. Androcentric texts say that a son is supposed to save his father from hell. Physical and spiritual immortality, power, and pulchritude is promised to the patriarchs through the procreation of male progeny. These texts are chosen selectively to ratify practice and custom.

The ethical limitations of the texts on *dharma*, seen from a late-twentieth-century perspective, include their pronouncements about the hierarchical relationships based on gender and caste. However, we must note that females do not seem to have been discriminated against in other periods of Hindu history; the Upanishads, philosophical texts composed around the sixth century B.C.E., describe rituals to ensure the birth of a "learned daughter" (*pandita*). One may also note that some *dharma* texts like the *Narada Smirti*[15] recognize the value of women and give them rights, for instance, to divorce. To balance the misogynistic statements of some dharmic texts, I think it is entirely appropriate, indeed necessary now, to highlight powerful women from the dharmic narratives in the epics and Puranas. We should also revive texts from the *dharma* shastras that favor women (there are a few of these), and to highlight historical women who did not let a patriarchal society or androcentric texts cramp their styles (names like Lalla, Akka Mahadevi, Andal, Tarigonda Venkamamba, and others come to mind). The popularizing of such women and texts of strength, disseminating their stories, will empower women and lead to the valuing of women and girls. Such valuing of girls is bound to have an effect on population growth and the gender ratio.

The real solution to India's population problem lies in accomplishing the most difficult task in about two thousand years of cultural history: the systematic and steady (not sporadic) valuing and education of girls and women. If women are perceived as contributors to the finances of the home, their births will not be feared and prevented. Education of women results in better prenatal and neonatal care. With confidence in child survival, the anxiety for a large family will be diminished.

Contraception, Abortion, and Adoption

The Indian government's aggressive plans to limit family size is based on contraceptive measures. While the many texts on *dharma* as well as

Hindu customs encourage the birth of live children, resistance to contraception is based on issues of child mortality and survival, rather than religious concerns. Family planning is promoted through street plays, billboards, slogans on public transportation, puppet shows, radio and TV commercials, and even toys. The most massively deployed form of contraception is sterilization; 72 percent of all contraception is through this method. Health care officials promote this form of preventing births because it needs the least amount of follow-up care. In many rural and urban areas, there is also a nascent fear that vasectomies may impair a man's virility and so, again, it is the woman who is hit hard. Many of the government's quota and target-oriented family planning programs have no time for educating a woman, giving her choices, or caring about overall reproductive health.

Adoption would be an obvious solution to some of the population problems, but would not be popular in the Hindu communities, unless the biological and caste origin of the child is known. In the so-called higher castes, there is a notion of keeping the purity of one's caste, and clan (*gotra*) and adoption of an unknown child would be unacceptable for many Hindus.

Population, Hunger, and Traditional Values of Sharing

While we aggressively work for the population figures to steady, we have to make the best of the resources. It is estimated that the per capita consumption of grain is less than 180 kilograms a year. (The famine commission appointed by the British government in 1880 had estimated that 200 kilograms would be the bare minimum to ward off starvation deaths.) If one includes the potatoes, fish, and meat consumed, the total is about 200 kilograms a year. This is to be compared with 860 kilograms of grain consumption in the United States and 974 kilograms of grain per person in Canada.[16] In India, the problem is not just lack of food, but uneven distribution and sharing.

Bajaj and Srinivas draw upon traditional resources of *dharma* to argue that we ought to work for multiplying our grain and then sharing it with our brothers and sisters. The title of their book is *Annam Bahu Kurvita*, a phrase from the Taittiriya Upanishad (ca. sixth century B.C.E.). This phrase can be translated as "multiply food manyfold." It is when talking about the *dharma* of sharing that the authors draw on a rich lore of traditional texts and practices. On the domestic level, they point out, the norm was for the householders (man and woman) to eat only after the other members of the family and all others who seek food at their house have been fed. In the past, individuals and kings took these dharmic narratives seriously and endowed money to free boarding and feeding houses. According to the authors, the British who believed in the work ethic, discouraged such forms of religious distribution and charity.

As David Loy correctly states, consumerism overlooks the superior joy of giving to others. A revival of some of these virtues at the grass-roots level and a propagation of them in organized and regularized form can be achieved with the promotion of institutions such as the Tirumala-Tirupati temple, which is already in the business of churning the millions dropped into its offerings container into universities, hospitals, free accommodations for the poor and food for pilgrims. Hindu temples in the diaspora regularly collect funds to help with disasters in India. Unfortunately, the virus of consumerism is in the Indian market and the anemic country is selling its blood for a few cheap thrills.

CONSUMPTION/CONSUMERISM

With increased population, low economic growth (dubbed as the "Hindu" rate of growth in former years), the government of India is now eager for aggressive growth in the market and economy. Unfortunately, in terms of the national interest there is an exploitation of water, land, and forest resources for quick economic growth of the country. While consumption is not high in India, the sheer numbers of the population will increase its levels in a few years. The more immediate problem is consumerism, which obviously leads to higher consumption levels than in the past. Consumer goods such as refrigerators and insulation add to the process of the thinning of the ozone layer.

Continuous growth resulting from strong market demand would have been an economic dream of many societies. But this growth has necessarily involved the rape of the earth of all her resources and a destruction of the environment for short-term goals. Rapid industrialization has led to greenhouse gases, mainly carbon dioxide, leading to global warming. Fast growth demanded by an increasing population and a clamor for quick profits has led to the contamination of rivers by industries—the very rivers that human beings are depending upon for water resources. By cutting down the forests we deprive the planet of its capacity to clean the air we breathe. India is now on the fast track to repeat the mistakes of the West. A burgeoning middle class in India is now hungry for the consumer bonbons of comfortable and luxurious living. The rich in India can easily surpass the middle class and the rich of the industrialized nations in their opulent lifestyles. There is no sense of *dama*, the restraint advocated by *dharma shastra*; unbridled greed reigns.

When In-laws Are Outlaws

This greed for consumerism is probably most notoriously displayed in the phenomenon of dowry deaths. A new bride is in some families seen as a blank check for a car, a scooter, a refrigerator, and the most in demand now, a VCR-TV combination. The bride's family, frequently viewing her as a burden, is anxious to unload her and pay several times their annual income on the wedding dowry. The demands may go on after the wedding; sometimes, when unable to meet demands, the newly married woman may be sent back in "shame" to her natal home. To avoid the social stigma, the bride's family may try to keep the bridegroom's family gorged with the consumer goods they demand. As Gargi Chakravarty of the National Federation of Indian Women says: "Modernization has not changed general views on women, whose status remains low and devalued . . . but at the same time, consumerism has brought increasing greed. The dowry system has become a convenient way of fulfilling greed for luxury items."[17]

Dowry, a custom that in part is meant to rectify financial inequality between male and female children, is now the showcase of greed and murder. According to traditional Hindu law, a woman could not inherit property and therefore could not get a share of the immovable property of her ancestors. Gift giving with jewels and precious metals was one way of compensation, and of providing financial security to the daughter. Dowry giving and taking is a crime, but gifts to the daughter, made in affection, are exempt. When a new bride cannot get any more consumer goods from her family, she may be harassed by her in-laws. Sometimes she commits suicide, and sometimes she is deliberately set on fire by her mother-in-law. In many cases, women perpetrate the crime; women are also victims of the crime. Some women activists in India point out that the perpetrator herself is usually a woman who has been abused by the system. The basic problem is the devaluation of women and greed for the newer consumer goods. While gifts of jewelry and modest cash dowries have always been prevalent in India, it is only since the 1970s—perhaps coinciding with the arrival of television programming in India—that the demand for consumer goods for dowries and the dowry-related crimes have come into prominence.

Educating women and providing job opportunities for them, educating men to tell them that women are capable of learning, working, and contributing to the economy as intelligent human beings, and providing jobs for men so they do not react adversely to the special opportunities provided for women would seem to be the key to addressing the problem of the devaluation of women. It is obviously easier said than done, because the creation of jobs frequently leads to rapid industrialization and unsustainable development, which in turn leads to the destruction of environment. Despite these caveats, the education for women must accelerate if we are to crack the problem.

The theological texts of the Hindu tradition are replete with the dangers and futility of possessions, but that is not the operating myth for the family that is plotting to get a refrigerator from the daughter-in-law's family or the politician who is hoarding gold bars. Unlike the issue of ecology where moral outrage is expressed by the middle class, consumerism frequently creeps in under the name of Westernization and modernization. Commercials push the bliss of owning designer jeans, fast motor bikes, and larger televisions; these images are beamed into village community television sets to people who barely have enough to eat.

The dharmic texts, I believe, do not have much muscle against this heavy seduction. The *tattva/moksha* texts do have glorious examples of renunciation, or the value of salvific knowledge over possessions. Given the compulsive nature of consumerism, the strategy is not in eliminating it, but containing it. The answer may be in the dharmic dictum of sharing and giving.

REFLECTIONS

There is no question that Hinduism has enjoyed the advantage of flexible *dharma* through the centuries; with selective highlighting, interpretations, and balances between text and custom, dharmic injunctions change in value and resonance. While textual *dharma* is frequently androcentric, in practice things have been different. Thus, while dharmic texts said a woman should have no independence and be subject to her male relatives, many women poets like Andal (8th cent.), Akka Mahadevi (11th–12th cent.), Tarigonda Venkamamba (18th cent.) and dozens of others have subjected their lives only to God, and certainly not to human men. The lives of these women have to be highlighted through the mass media if women today are to have powerful role models.

The flexibility of some of these *dharmic* rules come from generic statements on the essence of *dharma*. The texts have what is known as common *dharma*, which is applicable to all human beings, and specific *dharma*, which is incumbent on one by way of caste, gender, and station in life. The literature on common *dharma* is, for instance, vociferous on the importance of giving; the *Mahabharata* (Shanti Parvan 162.21) summarizes dozens of statements when it says: "Non-malice to all beings in thought, word, and deed; compassion and giving; these are the eternal *dharma* of the good."[18] The *Ramayana* (Sundara Kanda 1.23) says that remembrance of good deeds, that is, thanksgiving, is the eternal *dharma*. According to *The Laws of Manu* (10.63) the *dharma*s common to all human beings are *ahimsa* (nonviolence or noninjury), truthfulness, no wrongful taking of another's possessions, purity, and restraint of senses. We clearly have the building blocks here for a creative *dharma* relevant to our times.

When the guiding principles are clearly there, it is indeed the *dharma* of religious institutions and leaders to be proactive and promote the concept of sharing resources, and valuing female lives. The religious sector should share the responsibility in churning out the monies poured into the temples into humanitarian projects and mounting an alluring campaign to attract the youth toward these goals. The Tirumala-Tirupati Devasthanam has taken the initiative of the "tree *prasada*" and educational institutions for women. Clearly more is called for—more from the institution itself, and more from other temple complexes. Education of women through universities (as the Tirumala-Tirupati Devasthanam does) is a great step in plowing the monetary receipts of ardent devotees back to the community; but education of women in rural areas, especially in overall health is essential to give them access to the traditional Hindu blessing given by all elders to younger people: "*Ayushman bhava/Ayushmati bhava*" "May you have a long life."

The value of sharing is underscored by the T.T. Devasthanam; like the tree *prasada* scheme, they also have "gift of food" (*anna danam*) scheme. The payment of a fixed sum to a local sponsoring bank pays for the free distribution of food to poor pilgrims and devotees. As in the tree planting scheme, here too, the names of major donors are given prominence and projected on billboards. The advantage of this is the flattery of seeing one's name so advertised in a positive way—not unlike hearing one's name announced by Big Bird on public television as a high-level donor. To some extent, this sense of self esteem may replace the selfish happiness of consumerism.

The outreach done by Tirumala-Tirupati Devasthanam is seen in few religious organizations in India. There are many rich temples, and even more important, rich gurus. The disciples of Sathya Sai Baba are also engaged in major humanitarian efforts. Several religious organizations like the Arya Samaj, Ramakrishna Mission, and so forth, have spun off affiliates that are engaged in the formal education of women. While this is laudable, it should extend to rural areas and the urban slums with a focus on health care. If the guru entourages and temples assemble their resources, the first priority now should be education and valuing of women. Thus, the religious institutions will be involved in the creation of *panditas*, learned women that the Upanishads spoke about, as well as be instrumental in giving them the long life (*dirgha ayus*) that

Hindu blessings emphasize. Health-care education will give women knowledge to make informed decisions about their own bodies, and to take care of themselves and their children, so child and maternal mortality rates will be down. With education, women may insist on other life-preserving forms of contraception like condoms and not submit to sterilization against their will or knowledge.

Perhaps what Hindus should focus on is the notion of *dharma* given in the laws of Manu—there should be *no wrongful taking of what belongs to others*. The earth belongs to us only in our egos and avaricious hands. In reality, as Chief Seattle said, it is we who belong to earth, and by wrongfully usurping what is not ours, and what should be shared with the future generations of human beings, we are indulging in *adharmic*, unrighteous behavior. While accepting the importance of *dharma*, wealth, and sensual pleasure, the texts and customs on *dharma*, through injunctions and narratives, advocate restraint and control on all fronts. If, as Daniel Maguire says in the introduction, religion is a response to the sacred, then culturally powerful religions such as Hinduism must respond to the false sacreds proffered by the increasingly dominant religion of consumerism. The implementing of Vasistha's exhortations on *dharma* would provide the Hindu tradition the best guidelines for its future:

> Practice *dharma*, and not *adharma*.
> Speak the truth and not untruth.
> *Look far ahead, not near*
> *Look at the highest, not at what is not high.*[19]

NOTES

1. J.A.B. van Buitenen, trans., *The Mahabharata*, bk. 3, *The Book of the Forest* (Chicago: University of Chicago Press, 1978), pp. 586–89, 595–96.

2. Pandurang Vaman Kane, *History of Dharmasastra (Ancient and Mediaeval Religious and Civil Law)*, vol. 2, part 1, second edition (Poona, India: Bhandarkar Oriental Research Institute, 1974) pp. 8–9.

3. John B. Carman, *The Theology of Ramanuja* (New Haven, Conn.: Yale University Press, 1974), pp. 124–33.

4. Patricia Y. Mumme, "Models and Images for a Vaisnava Environmental Theology: The Potential Contribution of Srivaisnavism," edited by Lance Nelson. (Albany: State University of New York Press, 1998).

5. Adapted from "A Taluqdar of Oudh," trans., *Matsya Puranam*, pt. 2 (Allahabad: Surendra Natha Vasu of Bhuvaneswari Asrama, Bahadurganj, 1917), pp. 506–12.

6. Choodie Shivaram, "Court Decree Retires Tirupati Temple's Hereditary Priests." *Hinduism Today* 18.6 (1996): 1.

7. Pamphlet of T.T. Devasthanam n.d. available in the information office of T.T. Devasthanam.

8. Professor Diana Eck, Harvard University, personal communication.

9. V. Sadagopan, personal communication.

10. Vandana Shiva, *Staying Alive: Women, Ecology, and Development* (London: Zed Books, 1988); J. Baird Callicott, *Earth's Insights: A Survey of Ecological Ethics from the Mediterranean Basin to the Australian Outback* (Berkeley: University of California Press, 1994), pp. 220–21; Bart Gruzalski, "The Chipko Movement: A Gandhian Approach to Ecological Sustainability and Liberation from Economic Colonisation," *Ethical and Political Dilemmas of Modern India*, ed. Ninian Smart and Shivesh Thakur (New York: St. Martin's Press, 1993), pp. 100–25.

11. Sujatha Vijayaraghavan, "Neelakanthare Varum Ayya," Song in Begada raga, unpublished, personal communication.

12. Kane, *History of Dharmasastra*, p. 10.

13. Quoted in Wright, "World-view: The Fuse Still Sizzles on World Population Bomb," 1994.

14. *World Development Report*, 1994.

15. Richard Lariviere, "Matrimonial Remedies for Women in Classical Hindu Law: Alternatives to Divorce," *Rules and Remedies in Classical Hindu Law*, ed. Julia Leslie (Leiden: E.J. Brill, 1991), pp. 37–44.

16. *India's Demographics* [http://www.earlham.edu/earlhamcollege/ polisci/ globalprobs/ population/indiademos.html].

17. "Till Death do us Part," *Time*, special issue, Fall 1990, p. 39.

18. Kane, *History of Dharmasastra*, vol. 2, pt. 1, p. 6.

19. *Apastamba Dharma Sutra*, adapted from Kane, *History of Dharmasastra*, pp. 6–7.

CHAPTER 9

An Islamic Response to the Manifest Ecological Crisis: Issues of Justice

Nawal H. Ammar

INTRODUCTION

The crisis of an earth bleeding and burning to accommodate a fivefold economic expansion in just the last forty years is, by definition, global, and not specific to Muslims per se. Nonetheless, the manifestations of the crisis in Muslim communities and countries are as alarming as anywhere else in the world and illustrate some of the problems that afflict other religions. Some argue that the ecological crisis is the divine will of God as revealed by the Qur'an denoting the nearing of the end of life on earth. As such all this discussion about avoiding an ecological crisis is futile since it is predestined. The collective human disapproval of the crisis is of no consequence and it is actually discredited as a standard of value by some in Islam.[1] This view of predestination in Islam is not, however, maintained by all believers, although it dominates today. Islam also includes a progressive view wherein humans impact and change the world in ways that are not predestined. This debate between predestination and human free will in Islam is known as the *naql* (knowledge transmitted from revelation and tradition) versus *aqal* (knowledge transmitted from independent reason) debate. The proponents of *naql* see morality and values as not subject to human free will because only God can know what is good and what is bad.[2] The *aqal* view proponents, on the other hand, maintain that reason, guided by revelation, can provide the basis for a progressive Islamic vision of human action. Evidence supporting this progressive view can be found as early as the seventh century. The party of Unity and Justice, or the *Mu'tazilites*, insisted that God gave humans intellect to "choose conduct to decide and even to create their own acts free from predestination."[3] Reason guides in accordance with general principles and revelation gives particular parables of such principles.[4] The Qur'an emphasizes rationalism for example "Say (unto them Muhammad): Are those who know equal to those who know not? It is those who are endued with understanding that receive admonition."[5] Hence, humans, according to this school, when punished in the hereafter will be punished for sins they could have avoided. This chapter will be framed by arguments proposed by *ahl al-aqal* (the rationalists) with revelation guiding the general principles of reason.

A MUSLIM RESPONSE TO THE ECOLOGICAL CRISIS

Framing the Issues

It is not difficult to understand the ecological crisis in its apparent manifestations as polluted air, radiation, contamination of water, and the eradication of entire species of animals and plants. It is, however, more difficult to ascertain that the processes that lead to environmental depletion and thus an ecological crisis of the magnitude we are experiencing on our earth today are the result of human injustices and greed. This type of correlation between behavior and the resulting ecological crisis is particularly difficult for a group of people, such as the Muslims in the world, who view themselves as victims of postcolonialism, racism, poverty, enslavement, and an unfair demonization. In this chapter, I am proposing, based on a rational basis, a retrieval of an Islamic response to the ecological crisis that has been long forgotten. This response assumes a confident and responsible world community of Muslims that sees itself engaged in the problems on this earth as active contributors to a global solution. This response views the reasons underlying human crisis (including the ecological one) to be behaviors of greed, lack of moderation, inequity, and disrespect (or, as Loy says in his chapter, believing in the religion of the market). Islamic history is full of examples of how such behavior has lead to losing battles against the pagans, making bad judgements, and losing the Islamic empire and hence, the Islamic identity altogether in the nineteenth century. Contemporary behavior of Muslims is also full of examples of greed, lack of moderation, and hence nonreverence to God's creation. In recent years Muslims have extracted eightfold their level of consumption of oil for export to the United States, Western Europe, and Japan.[6] The extraction of oil and its byproducts is undertaken with minimal controls on toxic emissions and hazards. The Muslim world owns 800 billion barrels of oil in future reserves.[7] To keep the price of oil at a competitive level for global consumption, stringent pollution controls are not likely to be introduced. Muslims must join other world religions in recovering the sense of the sacred, which, as Daniel Maguire says, is at the heart of all religion. The false sacreds of the market religion are invading and pervading all cultures and are the modern idols challenging all world religions today.

The polluting effect of oil reaches far beyond its production. We were all reminded of this in 1990 by the "Desert Shield/Desert Storm" war. The Iraqi invasion of Kuwait meant a loss of 25 percent of world oil reserves and a future threat to 54 percent of the world's oil reserves held by Saudi Arabia and the Emirates (Tanzer 1991, 271–72). In a war that the British press dubbed "the real estate war," 93 percent of the "precision" bombs dropped were misguided and 75 percent missed their target. At least two hundred thousand people were killed and injured. More than ten thousand Kurds were displaced. Today, a large number of U.S. Desert Storm veterans suffer from what is feared to be the consequences of a germ warfare.[8]

The setting ablaze of over six hundred oil wells on 22 February 1991 exemplifies the environmental impact of war. Toukani and Barnaby, two British scientists, summarized the global environmental effects by stating "Close to Kuwait, the plume could cause a considerable reduction in daylight; the obstruction of sunlight might significantly reduce the surface temperature locally. This in turn could reduce the rainfall over parts of South East Asia during the period of summer monsoon. If the smoke reaches the ozone layer, the smoke could lead to small reductions in ozone concentrations within the northern hemisphere."[9] Once again, the maldistribution of resources and the desire to maintain or extend access to them is directly implicated in this "real estate" war.

More than thirty Muslim nations were directly involved in this war that environmentalists are calling the "Nuclear Winter," because the effects of the oil burning has reduced sunlight and temperatures throughout the region. The future does not look any brighter for Muslims. In the last world Arms Proliferation Treaty (1995), two among the countries that refused to sign the treaty were Muslim, Pakistan and Turkey.

War, however, is not the only polluting factor in Muslim countries and communities. Water is also polluted in Muslim countries. Waste dumping into rivers, seas, or nearest streams is common and the state apparatus cannot control it. Explosives are also used to fish, thus eradicating the symbiotic environment in the habitat. Air pollution results from unregulated industrial waste disposal, the use of leaded gasoline, and the overcrowding in cities. A recent study conducted by the U.S.

Agency of International Development (AID) in Egypt shows that air in Cairo is ten times more polluted than a city equal to its size in the United States. Industries discharge 1,350 tons of lead yearly into the air in Egypt. Drinking water has at its lowest estimate 9.3 milligrams more lead than the average acceptable rate globally.[10]

The behaviors illustrated above that lead to human crisis can be understood through the Arabic word *hay'a*. The word is virtually untranslatable to English. It actually denotes behaviors that reflect shyness out of respect and reverence rather than out of fear. It is behavior that reflects balance, honorable manners, and protection of God's glory including his creatures and other creation. For the purpose of this chapter I will translate the word as "dignified reserve." I am proposing that we revive this conceptual framework of *hay'a* as a guiding theological principle that could avert an ecological crisis. I suggest that the absence of *hay'a* has contributed to a livelihood among Muslims that is causing the ecological crisis. This is reflected in the disparity between the poor and the rich, a production system that is entirely dependent on the monopolies and big corporations, which in turn leads to maldistribution of resources and overconsumption, authoritarian leadership, wars, disrespect of human diversity, and finally a way of life that depletes natural and human resources. In this livelihood that lacks dignified reserve Muslims have also dehumanized women, which in turn has contributed to reducing their status to reproductive apparatuses only, hence causing the overpopulation that Muslim communities experience today. This overpopulation in turn has led to the manifest results of environmental depletion in the forms of pollution, disease, infant mortality, and crime.

In the balance of this chapter I will look at how the behaviors that lack *hay'a* in production and consumption, and toward women have contributed to the manifestations of ecological depletion. I will suggest throughout some ethical responses that are Islamic in principle and hope that their retrieval provides a solid response to averting the doomsday approach that some Muslims believe is beyond human free will and reason.

The Issues in Detail: Muslims' Economic and
Political Livelihood and the Ecological Crisis

Islamic teachings from the Qur'an, Hadith, Sunna, and history all emphasize the need for moderation and modesty in a Muslim's life. The integration of Muslim countries and communities into the larger market economy as a consequence of national modernization, development, and desegregation have left them with maldeveloped patterns of production and consumption that do not function by moderation principles. Although Muslim countries and communities are considered as peripheral in terms of their production capacity—that is, they are marginal contributors to manufacturing markets—the way Muslim countries produce and consume creates glaring disparities between the poor and the rich, makes them dependent on monopolies, leads to authoritarian leadership, and creates an elite class that overconsumes and overproduces and, hence, contributes to depleting the environment. By and large the forty-six Muslim countries mainly extract raw materials, oil being the most important (56 percent of the world's oil export). Although Muslim countries have some manufacturing industries such as cement, textile, and light armaments, it is not at a level to move them into a competitive advantage within the global market.[11] Hence, most of the trade (95 percent) that occurs is with non-Muslim countries. The oil industry, although nationalized, is heavily dependent on foreign technology, expertise, and security (as the Gulf War lately showed), and the maintenance of an elite group with which foreign heads of state can interact.

Robert Reich notes this structure of elites benefitting from the global economies wherever they are by stating, "the economic globalization . . . has served to delink the interests of the wealthy classes from a sense of national interest and thereby from a sense of concern for an obligation to their less fortunate neighbors. . . . It is no longer meaningful to speak about this delinking in terms of a North-South divide. . . . It is class."[12]

For Muslim countries, the problem involves the uneven development in the global capitalist system that has led to extreme disparities between the elites and nonelites both among and within nations. Understood in terms of disparity between the poor and the rich, Islam has a very clear response to how Muslims should produce and consume. Hourani, a famous scholar of Islam writes "Islam could also be a basis of economic life . . . and if accepted that will ensure social justice and liberate humans from servitude."[13] The Islamic economic system has been set forth as a "third way" that differs from both "laissez-faire capitalism and Marxist socialism."[14] The basis of the system is set out in general terms in the Qur'an, but the details have been worked out by legal scholars. The system, ideally, creates a society of private ownership and enterprise without the vast accumulation and concentration of wealth. Two principles summarize the Islamic economic system. The first sees that income, exchange, and trade should be based on just transaction and not claims on natural or market resources. The second is similar to the ideas presented in Coward's chapter in this volume, and sees that the community has an overriding priority over individuals. Adherence to these principles would serve to constrain the unequal distribution of resources and, hence, the overconsumption and overproduction of resources among the few. The following outlines these principles.

Principle One: Income, exchange, and trade should be based on just transaction and not claims on natural or market resources. Just interaction in the Islamic perspective should not be confused with the Buddhist concept of eliminating desire as mentioned in Gross's chapter. Actually Islam sees desire as a source of happiness, but what is problematic with desire is its attainment. In Islam individual desires should be attained in ways that permit everyone in the community to fulfill his/her individual desires and individual desires take a lower priority over community desires. Hence, there are conditions that regulate individual and communal fulfillment of desire.

Work is one of the conditions of just interaction. The Qur'an is very clear about issues of reward and revenues. For example it states "Humans shall have nothing but what they strive for."[15] People who work are not equal to those who do not in Islam.[16] Work in the Islamic tradition includes more than a "job," and the word would translate as "labor."

Equal, exact, and honest exchange is another condition of the just transaction in Islam. The Qur'an emphasizes "O my people give full measure and full weight with equity, and wrong not people in respect of their things, and act not corruptly in the land making mischief."[17] This concept becomes clearer to many of us living in the West when we consider the madness of Christmastime and the desire to buy toys for children during this time. In 1996 in the United States, a toy called 'Tickle Me Elmo' from the *Sesame Street* children's show that sells normally for $26 became so rare in the market that some people were auctioning it for over $1,500. This kind of exchange that is based on creating an artificial need and crazed desire is not permitted in the Islamic system. All exchange in the Islamic system ought to be of *use value*—that is, a good, or service for another equivalent in value. Exchange should never be of *surplus value*—i.e., a commodity with a value altered for some humanly imposed reason. Surplus-value exchanges (i.e., values determined not by the real use value of the good or service, but by the value imposed by supply/demand forces of the market) are considered usury.

Usury, *riba*, is forbidden in Islam. The rule governing *riba* in Islam states that any profit or interest accrued without working for it, or without being a full partner in the risks of gain and loss makes the transaction unjust. *Riba*, thus, is defined as "asking something for nothing in an interaction . . . it is not equal for equal."[18] As such the Qur'an warns "that they used usury though it was forbidden and that they usurped human wealth with falsehood."[19]

Interest accrued from Western-style banking is considered *riba*. The client in Western-style banking, according to Islamic interpretation, is at a disadvantage. As a depositor his/her money is used to create more money under false guarantees of delivery. As a borrower, she/he pays interest on imaginary assets that the banks do not have. The imaginary money that banks have creates artificial wealth by exploiting the hard-working depositor and the needy borrower. In addition this artificial wealth is not redistributed equitably, but remains concentrated in the hands of a small minority of financiers. The Qur'an refers to such practices by saying "That which you lay out for increase through the property of [other] people, will have no increase with God: but that which you lay out for charity seeking the countenance of God, [will increase], it is these who will get a recompense multiplied."[20]

Cummings, Askari, and Mustafa note that the Islamic banking system operates on the principle of equity ownership not interest.[21] Money invested in a bank as though it were a business venture without guarantees of profit or loss would be Islamic. Hence, the investor gains interest only if the business produces profit. This kind of investment guarantees more conservative risk-taking ventures and thereby reduces creation of vast sums of artificial wealth and its concentration in few hands.

Principle Two: The right of the community over individuals.   Islam emphasizes the concept of communal good and duties to the community in a way that is similar to Coward's suggestion in his chapter on the we-self. This community of believers has a collective ethos of goodness: "let there arise out of you a band of people inviting to all that is good, enjoining what is right and forbidding what is wrong."[22] It is a community where Muslims protect each other, hold together tightly, and cooperate on generosity and righteousness.[23] Islam's emphasis on the right of the community over the individual is demonstrated through its position on issues of distributive justice in general. The particularities of this position can be best illustrated in Islam's treatment of the three issues of: (*a*) taxation, (*b*) community leadership, and (*c*) its vision of the "other" in the community.

a. Taxation.   Islam outlines three tax structures: one for Muslims, one for non-Muslims, and one that is universal and applies to all regardless of religion. All taxes aim to redistribute the wealth and power of the rich to the poor. *Zakat* is a tax that all Muslims should pay. It is a tax that has become a religious obligation and it is particularly intended for the rich to fulfill the needs of the poor in the community. This fulfillment is not charity in the Western sense but a community obligation. The state, *dar al-Islam*, oversees the collection of *zakat*. The exact levy of the *zakat* varies in accordance with different legal schools of thought. Generally, a 2.5 percent tax on one's wealth is applied. Some Islamic jurists include taxation on mines as part of the *zakat*, others assess it as a separate tax. Regardless all Muslims must pay a tax for extracting the land's wealth.

Some jurists also argue that if *zakat* is inadequate to meet the demands of the needy, then the state can impose additional taxes.

Muslims also pay taxes on agricultural land, *ushur*. The levy on land is applied to the gross production before deduction of production costs.[24] The Qur'anic injunction recommending this tax states: "O you who have attained to faith spend on theirs out of the good things which you may have acquired and out of that which we bring forth for you from the earth."[25] Non-Muslims living in an Islamic state pay a poll tax (*jiziyah*). This tax is paid as compensation for being defended by and included in the state. The tax rate is based on a community consensus (*ijma'*) and should be assessed on the ability to pay.[26] Finally, all citizens of the Islamic state must pay a land tax (*kharaj*). The tax is levied on two bases. The first is assessed on a fixed rate regardless of the output, and the second is paid only if there is output from the land.

Islam's prescriptions on taxation offer an economic mechanism for limiting the disparities in access to resources the economic system otherwise generates. Nonetheless, two noneconomic prescriptions concerning community leadership and respect for human diversity are also critically important for an Islamic economic system and further serve to diminish inequities in the Islamic community.

b. Distributive Justice beyond Utilitarian Economies: Leadership Qualities.   The Imam, Caliph, or Sultan is the person who leads the Islamic community and who would be responsible to facilitate and promote distribution within it. The quality of the leader is a very important element in securing a just community. Mernissi writes: "It is difficult to imagine a weaker political leader than a Muslim one. The ideal leader is modest, trembling with fear before his God and terrified before those he/she governs for making an unjust decision will lead him directly to hell."[27] The legitimacy of the Muslim leader is based on the will of the community (*ummah*) according to Islamic jurisprudence.[28] In Islam the leader has no divine powers.[29] The leader of the Islamic state ought to guarantee freedom for the subjects.[30] The leader ought to treat subjects equitably, and consult the community on the affairs of the state. The Qur'an states clearly the issue of justice as the working ideology of the leader in many verses.[31] Ibn Taymiya, a famous Muslim thinker who based his interpretations on reason, stated that "people have never disagreed on the negative consequences of injustice and the positive impact of justice. As such God will render a just nation victorious even if its citizens were non-believers, while the unjust state will be defeated even if its citizens were believers."[32]

The above-mentioned characteristics of the Islamic leader have disappeared in our modern day. Most leaders today in the Islamic world exercise some kind of authoritarianism. According to Mernissi: "The vulnerability has disappeared from the scene through the combined effect of the separation of Muslim memory from the rationalist tradition and the modern media that have created an unchallenged leader."[33] As such the issue of disparity between the poor and the rich in Islamic countries that are the result of maldevelopment requires the restoration of a just leader who is accountable to the community he/she rules. Once the leaders are ruling under Islamic precepts—justice, equality, and humility—rather than manipulating them, economic policies aimed at distributive justice could work and the ecological crisis resulting from the lack of distributive justice could be checked.

The above response, however, partially disregards the fact that Muslims do not live alone in this world. The relationship between Muslims and non-Muslims is very important to ensure equitable distribution of resources. Since I am writing an Islamic response I will focus on Islam's position toward non-Muslims. (Others in this volume have considered the other side of this relationship, see especially Keller and Múnera.)

c. Distributive Justice beyond Utilitarian Economies: The Vision Of the "Other" in Islam.   In addition to the need of having a just leader, Islam enjoins Muslims to treat others peacefully and kindly if distributive justice is to be a characteristic of their community. There is some confusion about what Islam says concerning the relationship of Muslims to non-Muslims. Visions of the "other" are often tainted by three verses of Surah 9, Al Tawbah in the Qur'an.[34] The three verses enjoin Muslims to fight those who do not believe in Allah. Chapter 9 of the Qur'an is among the last that was revealed to the Prophet Muhammad. Sayed Qutb, a well-known Egyptian Islamist and a prominent thinker among the Muslim Brotherhood, argues that this chapter provides a final and absolute injunction. He argues that all other verses enjoining mercy, justice, tolerance toward non-Muslims were voided by this revelation.[35] This interpretation leads a number of Muslims to believe that Islam is the religion of the sword in its relationship to the non-Muslims. Numerous Muslim scholars (Abdu, Rida, Shaltout), however, disagree strongly with Qutb's interpretation. They argue that this chapter was revealed to address one specific historic instance. Al-Ghazzali notes that the Qur'an contains 120 verses related to respecting the non-Muslims including pagans, and that three verses cannot void so many injunctions.[36]

Difference and diversity in Islam must be understood as God's will.[37] This will of God for diversity among humans has to be respected: "We have indeed created humans in the best mold."

The Prophet's tradition and Islamic history are also full of stories about respect for non-Muslims. "Upon the passing of a funeral procession near where the Prophet gathered with some of his friends, he stood up in respect and so did the rest of the gathered. After the procession passed, one person in the crowd said: O Messenger of God did you know that this was the funeral of a Jew? The Prophet replied: Wasn't he human and had a human soul? Was he not a human created and made by God? Wasn't he a being with dignity?"[38] Another well-known story in Islamic history about the fourth Orthodox Caliph Ali is indicative of respect of the "other." Ali told the ruler he sent to Egypt, Malik al-Ashtar: "fill your heart with mercy and love to your subjects since they are two kinds: A sibling in belief or a human created by God the same way you were."

Islam not only prescribes respect of the "other," but urges cooperation with all peoples and nations.[39] Muslims are very clearly ordered to befriend the "other." The Qur'an states: "If one amongst the pagans sought asylum or refuge grant it to him."[40]

To summarize, the maldevelopment in the economic systems of Muslim communities that led to maldistribution of resources, overconsumption, disparity between the rich and the poor, dependency, authoritarianism among leaders, and disrespect of human diversity are at the basis of the ecological crisis. Islam prescribes an economic system that constrains the extent of the maldistribution of resources through its principles of taxation and distributive justice. Once Muslims practice these principles of equity in distribution of resources and treatment of others, which are at the heart of Islamic teachings, we will be moving one more step toward averting the ecological crisis.

The economic and political principle of *hay'a* (dignified reserve) has implications for other social and cultural relationships that pertain to the ecological crisis, namely the relationship between men and women. It is to this that I now turn.

Absence of Hay'a toward Women and the Ecological Crisis

Scientists have ascertained that overpopulation is a major contributing factor in the ecological crisis. The population growth rate in Muslim countries is among the highest in the world. The crude birth rate of the forty-six Muslim countries is 1 percent higher than that of the developing world as a whole.[41] In the mid-1980s even countries that adopted family planning programs (with the exception of Indonesia) in the early 1960s had very high natural increase rates of the population. For example, Pakistan's rate of increase was 2.8%, Egypt's rate was 2.6%, while the rate of increase in non-Muslim countries such as India and Colombia was 2.3% and 2.1%.[42]

Islam is indisputably a pronatal religion.[43] Nonetheless, family planning programs have also used Islamic teachings to convince people to use contraception. Various verses from the Qur'an that favor family planning outcomes were stressed. These included injunctions concerned with leaving heirs in good conditions, educating children to be useful, the quality and not the quantity of children, and how children are an enormous responsibility for parents.[44] Other interpretations based on reason were reiterated. For instance, in the Arab Muslim world distinctions between lifetime family planning (*Tahdid al-nasl*) versus family planning as the spacing of children (*Tanzim al-nasl*) were made to sanction the use of contraception.

Although Islam sanctions the use of various methods of family planning and many Muslim countries and communities have adopted family planning as a state policy, only one country, Indonesia, has succeeded in curtailing its population increase significantly. What accounts for the limited success of these attempts to reduce population growth through the adoption of family planning programs and hence reduce the pressure on environmental resources?

The root of the reproductive problems for most Muslim women lies in the fact that they live either in the less developed world or the less affluent parts of the developed world. As such their social and material conditions inhibit following family planning programs successfully. While women are the target of most family planning programs, seldom do they participate directly in their design and implementation (i.e., they remain "invisible"). The human context of women in the programs ought to be emphasized and brought to the forefront. Data has shown that the empowerment of women through higher education, active involvement in the labor force, legislative policies, and increased access to health services oftern serve to delay marriage, reduce the number of offspring, and diminish the incidence of polygamy.[45] In Egypt, for example, 60% of women who cannot read and write had at least one co-wife, while the incidence of polygamy was reduced to 0.01% among women who had university degrees.[46] In most Muslim countries the patriarchal, misogynist local cultures favor interpretations of the Qur'an that debase women. Islam, however, sees women as equal to men and deserving of the same treatment; and both men and women will be judged on equal grounds before God.[47]

The equity that Islam grants women is not reflected in popular culture, economic opportunities, or formal substantive law. For instance, popular culture, as reflected in some Arabic proverbs, encourages violence against women ("if you break a girl's rib, twenty-four other ribs will grow"), glorifies male offspring ("those who bear boys never die"), and encourages women's dependence on men ("a straw husband is better than none").

Women's participation in the paid labor force still remains marginal in most Muslim countries and the jobs they do take typically offer little power, prestige, or income. According to statistics from the 1990 UN report on the Situation of Women, women constituted only 6% of the labor force in the United Arab Emirates (one of the wealthiest Muslim countries) and 62% of women above the age of fifteen were illiterate. Similarly, women made up only 10% of the labor force in Egypt (one of the poorest Muslim countries), and of these 20% worked in agriculture (a low-paying job) and 41 percent were self-employed (a less secure job).

Legal codes in Muslim countries, whether totally dependent on divine law (Shari'a) or partially dependent at the level of personal status codes, very clearly debase women. In all these countries, codes are legislated to favor men over women even if the punishment was un-Islamic. For example, in fornication cases, women are punished more severely than men, a practice that goes against the letter of the Qur'an. In cases where the texts are silent, the codes derived from the spirit of the text also favor men. Hence, a Muslim woman from an Islamic country cannot give her citizenship to her children if she is married to a foreign man. A man from a Muslim country, however, can give his children his citizenship even if his wife is foreign and he does not live in his native country. Women cannot divorce their husbands except in court, while men can declare a wife divorced by verbally uttering the words "I divorce you" three times. In many Muslim countries a Muslim man can divorce his wife or take a co-wife without any legal requirements to inform the concerned wife.

The empowerment of Muslim women as humans is central to the discussion about population increase and its impact on the ecology. Unless we improve the conditions of Muslim women according to Islamic teachings, the discussion of family planning would be as relevant as talking to an incubator. This means including women as active participants in family, economic, and political decision making. This can only be made possible by improving the conditions under which they live and bringing equity and dignity to women.

The improvement of Muslim women's status applies to both the rich and the poor. Islam has its own share of powerful women both in its history and in the contemporary world. Consequently, a return to Islamic teachings about women is essential to make family planning successful. Muslims, hence, need to remember how the Qur'an emphasizes the dignity of women by stating "Never will I suffer to be lost the work of any of you be he male or female ye are members of one of another" and behave with hay'a toward them.[48]

In sum, Islam offers much in response to the manifest ecological crisis of population growth. This response, however, focuses on a behavior toward women as humans rather than simply permitting a techno-logical fix such as family planning. While Islam leaves open several avenues for family planning, traditional approaches using education about contraception have achieved limited success in most Muslim countries. This suggests that the population problem runs deeper than merely extending the knowledge about and availability of contraceptive devices. Rather, the empowerment of women (or lack thereof) lies at the core of the population problem, and hence, the ecological crisis. Islam views women and men as equal participants in the Muslim community, even if, in most Muslim (and, I might add, non-Muslim) countries this equity has not been realized. The population problem, then, appears to stem from un-Islamic behaviors and attitudes that lead to inequity between men and women. I am thus suggesting a revival of the Islamic behaviors of dignified respect toward women as mentioned in the Qur'an and Hadith.

CONCLUSION

Progressive Islam has several effective responses toward the ecological crisis. These responses have action-oriented components toward avert-ing evil and promoting the good. Hence, the Qur'an emphasizes: "Ver-ily never will Allah change the condition of a people until they change themselves."[49] The orientation of action in progressive Islam toward averting the ecological doom is one of dignified reserve: *hay'a*.

In relation to distributive justice between the poor and the rich that creates an elite that overconsumes and overproduces, and hence con-tributes to the ecological crisis by depleting the environment *hay'a* is reflected in the ethic of hard work. *Hay'a* is also reflected in the eco-nomic system of exchange that is based solely on use value versus sur-plus value of a good. Such an exchange value would bring equity among community members, reduce concentration of wealth and diminish the maldistribution of resources. The leader's humility and consultative duties with the community also bring forth the issue of respect of the leader to his/her subjects, which would eventually promote distributive justice. Further, Islam advises the respect for human diversity, something that is necessary for averting wars and for ensuring distributive justice within and outside the community.

In relation to population increase that also puts pressure on the ecol-ogy, *hay'a* requires action toward empowering women to have family planning programs, which would contribute to a reduction in natural growth rates in population.

Islam has a very clear and unequivocal response to the depletion and destruction of the environment and nature. Nature was created by God in an orderly fashion.[50] This nature is given to humans as a trust (*ammanah*). Thus, the Qur'anic injunction says "I am setting on earth a vice-regent."[51]

This vice-regent is a manager of the trust and not an owner. Depending on how humans manage this trust, they will be judged in the hereafter. Hence, there is a direct relationship between the utilization of nature and rewards on the day of judgment. The relationship not only emphasizes a "no-harm" principle to nature, but insists on the doing of good. The Prophet, for example, said: "anyone who witnesses evil should remonstrate upon it by hand, mouth or heart, the last is the weakest of faith."

Islam counsels Muslims to use of environmental resources in accordance with five rules:[52]

1. The use of nature and its resources in a balanced, not excessive manner;
2. Treat nature and its resources with kindness;
3. Do not damage, abuse or distort nature in any way;
4. Share natural resources with others living in the habitat; and
5. Conserve.

These rules are set forth by jurors to ensure that nature and its resources are managed well by humans who are the executors of God's trust. Balance, admonitions against excess, justice, and the sharing of resources are, once more, found at the core of the Islamic attitude toward the environment. *Hay'a* of God's creation requires that Muslims use earth's resources in moderation and conserve it.

The dignified reserve prescribed by Islam toward life on earth is not only the responsibility of some people, but it is every Muslim's duty. Muslim jurists have set forth a rule stating that "the executor is a guarantor even if the act is not deliberate or intentional." On account of this rule, every Muslim and every community claiming the faith ought to listen. Regardless of one's ethical preference to human free will or predestination, given the state of the earth's warming climate, increasing pollution, rates of deforestation, state of war, and disease due to the ecological imbalance, Muslims will be and are responsible on the day of judgment for this crisis.

NOTES

1. The following format will be utilized to denote reference to Qur'anic chapters and verses: Fatir: 8.
2. Al Ra'd: 17

3. G. F. Hourani, 1985, *Reason and Tradition in Islamic Ethics* (Cambridge, England: Cambridge University Press) p. 7.

4. M. Khadduri, 1984, *The Islamic Conception of Peace* (Baltimore, MD: John's Hopkins University Press), p. 41–48.

5. Al Zumar: 9.

6. BP Statistical Review of World Energy, 1990, (London: British Petroleum Educational Service).

7. BP Statistical Review of World Energy, 1990.

8. The Presidential Gulf War Illnesses Commission Report has shown that a large number of U.S. Desert Storm Veterans have been exposed to germ warfare during combat.

9. Penny Kemp, 1991, "For Generations to Come: The Environmental Catastrophe", in: *Beyond the Storm: A Gulf Crisis Reader*, ed. P. Bennis and M. Moushabeck (New York: Olive Branch Press), p. 331.

10. "Al-Qahira Akhthar Mudin al'Alam Talwitha" (Cairo is the most polluted city in the world), *Al-Akhbar Daily News*, 6 June 1995, p. 8.

11. Quoted in Pervez Houdbhoy, 1991, *Islam and Science* (London: Zed Books Ltd), p. 30.

12. Quoted in David Korten, 1994, "Sustainability and the Global Economy: Beyond Bretton Woods" (Opening Plenary Presentation to Fall Retreat, 13–15 October 1994, The Environmental Grantmakers Association, Mount Washington Hotel & Resort, Bretton Woods, New Hampshire), p. 7.

13 Hourani, *Reason and Tradition in Islamic Ethics*, p. 372.

14. J. T. Cummings, H. Askari, and A. Mustafa, 1980, "Islam and Modern Economic Change", in *Islam and Development: Religion and Sociopolitical Change*, ed. John Espisito (Syracuse, NY: Syracuse University Press, pp. 25–48), p. 44.

15. Al Najm: 39.

16. Al Nisa':95.

17. Hud: 85.

18. Umar Vadillo and Fazlun Khalid, 1992, "Trade and Commerce in Islam", in: *Islam and Ecology* ed. Fazlun Khalid and Joanne O'Brien (New York, NY: Cassell) p. 73.

19. Al Baqarah: 161.

20. Al Rum: 39.

21. Cummings, Askari, and Mustafa, "Islam and Modern Economic Change".

22. Ali Imaran: 104.

23. Tawbah: 71; Ali Imran: 103; Al Mai'dah: 2.

24. Cummings, Askar, and Mustafa, "Islam and Modern Economic Change", p. 27–29.

25. Al Baqarah: 267.

26. Cummings, Askar, and Mustafa, "Islam and Modern Economic Change", p. 30.

27. Fatima Mernissi, 1992, *Islam and Democracy: Fear of the Modern World* (translated by Mary Jo Lakeland, New York: Addison-Wesley Publishing Co), p. 27.

28. Fahmi Houidi, *Al-Islam wa al-Democratiah* (Islam and democracy, Cairo: Markaz al-Ahram Llitargamah wa al-Nashr), p. 124.

29. Al Ghashiyah: 21–22.

30. Al Kahf: 29.

31. Al Nisa: 58; Al Mai'dah: 8; Al Nahl: 90; Al Shura: 15, 38; Al Hujurat: 9, 13.

32. Houidi, *Al-Islam wa al-Democratiah*, p. 122.

33. Mernissi, *Islam and Democracy*, p. 22–23.

34. Verses 5, 29, 36.

35. Houidi, *Al-Islam wa al-Democratiah*, p. 33–35.

36. Houidi, p. 24.

37. Yunus: 99; Hud: 18.

38. Houidi, p. 27.

39. Al Nahl: 92; Al Qasas: 18, 38.

40. Al Tawbah: 6.

41. I use the word *countries* because I can only obtain statistics from such geopolitical designations. It is essential to remember that Islam sees its adherents and those who live with them as a community (*ummah*).

42. Indonesia has had the most successful family planning programs in the developing world. See Hayim Adid, 1987, "Islamic Leaders' Attitudes Towards Family Planning in Indonesia 1950s–1980s," a master's thesis, Australian National University, Canberra.

43. Al Nahl: 72; Al Kahf: 46.

44. Al Nisa: 9; Al Tur: 21; Al Anfal: 28.

45. Hamed Abu Gamrah, 1980, "Fertility and Childhood Mortality by Mother's and Father's Education in Cairo", in *Population Bulletin of the Economic Commission of Western Asia* (Beirut, Lebanon), p. 81.

46. "Aqed al-Jawaz al-Jadid" (The new marriage contract), in *Nisf al-Dunia* (a weekly magazine), 15 June 1995, pp. 21–26.

47. Al Nisa: 1, 32.

48. Ali Imran: 195.

49. Al Ra'd: 11.

50. Al Ra'd: 8; Al Sajdah: 4; Al Mulk: 3, 4.

51. Al Baqarah: 30.

CHAPTER 10

Toward a Buddhist Environmental Ethic

Rita M. Gross

Whenever I think about issues of consumption and population, I think about the way I lived early in my life. For eighteen years I lived without central heating, indoor plumbing, pesticides, processed foods, packaging, or neighbors that could be seen from our home. We carried water from a spring, cut our own firewood, grew much of our own food, and used an outhouse, even in subzero temperatures. Dragonflies, butterflies, fireflies, and many other beautiful creatures that I never see in my city lot abounded. Traffic noise was a novelty. At night one could see a million stars in the black sky. Major environmental problems were nonexistent because we were few people (a family of three) living simply. Because we were so few living in a sparsely populated rural area, we could use simple technologies and renewable resources for heat and waste management without harming the land, water, or air, even though those same technologies become extremely problematic when people live in crowded conditions. This is one of many reasons why population growth is so environmentally devastating.

Though many would evaluate such a lifestyle as unacceptably primitive and uncomfortable, it was not particularly a deprivation. Even now when I return to my cabin for meditation retreats and writing time, I do not mind that lifestyle. Electricity for lights, the laptop computer, and a boombox that plays classical music is completely sufficient for a satisfying lifestyle with low environmental impact. Environmentally sensitive lifestyles and scaling back to live such lifestyles do not really deprive people once it becomes clear that the levels of reproduction and consumption indulged in by most people are not necessary to well-being.

But what does my religion of choice—Buddhism—say about this

vision? In this chapter, I shall be writing as both a scholar trained in comparative studies in religion and as a practicing Buddhist. My own Buddhist affiliation is with Tibetan Vajrayana Buddhism as taught by the late Chogyam Trungpa, but I will write about Buddhism in generic terms that could be accepted by most or all Buddhists.

BUDDHISM AND ECOLOGY

Currently, there is some debate about whether Buddhism can support an environmental ethic or the worldview of deep ecology and some Western scholar-observers are very skeptical of Buddhist efforts to derive an ecological ethic. As a scholar of religion familiar with both historical and constructive methods, I find that question somewhat beside the point. Historically, we know that all living religions have gone through major changes to remain relevant in altered circumstances. There is no reason that the same thing cannot happen in response to the ecological crisis. As a Buddhist feminist "theologian," I am more than familiar with the process of working within a traditional symbol system and worldview while doing reconstructive work to eliminate certain problematic conventions. The question is not what *has* Buddhism said about ecology and the environment, but what *could* Buddhism say about these subjects.

At the outset, I would suggest that Buddhism has not been especially oriented to an environmental ethic historically. In my view, other religious traditions, including the indigenous traditions so often praised for their reverence for nature have not historically focused on an environmental ethic either. I make this somewhat controversial statement because of a claim that I will make many times in this chapter. An *environmental* ethic must discourage excessive consumption and reproduction, even when such levels of consumption and reproduction are common in the culture and seem unproblematic to many people. By itself, a rhetoric of reverence for nature is insufficient as an environmental ethic. Too often a rhetoric of reverence for nature is combined with primitive technologies that limit human ability to destroy the environment, but when more sophisticated and destructive technology becomes available, it is readily adopted. To qualify as genuinely ecological, religious teachings and practices must entail *a choice* against excessive reproduction and consumption.

Environmental concerns are now so grave because humans have the technologies to consume and reproduce in ways that seem likely to destroy the ecological basis for human life. Therefore, the key question is what values and practices would convince people to consume and reproduce less when they have the technological ability to consume and reproduce more. The world's religions have not previously faced this situation, which explains why ecological ethics have not been in the forefront of religious thinking in any tradition. What we must do then, as constructive thinkers in our various traditions, is to place the inherited values and insights of our traditions in the light of the current ecological crisis to see what resources the tradition affords us and where we need to extrapolate new visions. The "religion of the market" has stepped up to supply what the classical religions are not supplying, a definition of what is truly sacred. The corporations are the primary teachers of values in this new arrangement and they are extraordinarily effective. Religions that ignore this are doomed to irrelevance.

When I am faced with a major intellectual puzzle, I usually contemplate it using a strategy that I learned from the oral traditions of Tibetan Buddhism—threefold logic. This strategy suggests that most problems can be fruitfully analyzed by locating a starting point, a process of change and development, and an end product. The task of articulating a Buddhist ethical response to the environmental crisis is daunting enough that I spent many hours going back to the basics of using a traditional threefold logic with which to think about what Buddhism might have to offer. The traditional system of threefold logic that offered the most insight is a system called "view, practice, and result." This particular system focuses first on the theoretical analysis appropriate to a specific issue—the view. Then, with the view well in hand, we turn to the question of what practices or spiritual disciplines will enable one to realize or internalize the view, so that it is no longer merely an intellectual theory. Finally, understanding the view and having practiced the appropriate contemplative and meditative exercises, what actions will one take when the view is fully internalized? In this chapter, I will apply the threefold logic of view, practice, and result to Buddhist teachings as they might be relevant to the ecological crisis.

My approach to developing a Buddhist environmental ethic will emphasize two things. First, I will appeal to simple pan-Buddhist teachings and practices for the most part, rather than to the doctrines of advanced Buddhist philosophy or the practices of esoteric forms of Buddhism. I do this so that Buddhists everywhere could find a Buddhist environmental ethic that is accessible and relevant. Second, I will emphasize practice over view. One of the reasons for working with the specific system of threefold logic that I chose is because the view—the theoretical analysis—is only the beginning of the discussion. I have been somewhat disappointed with the current small body of literature on Buddhist environmental ethics because most authors have focused on view or theory and have not sufficiently discussed practices promoting environmentally sound lifestyles.

In my view, Buddhism has many intellectual and spiritual resources that can easily support an environmental ethic. At the simplest level, because nonharming is so fundamental to Buddhism ethics, once one realizes that excessive consumption and reproduction are harmful, one is obliged to limit such activities. Such advice is also in accord with the most fundamental of all Buddhist guidelines—the Middle Path between extremes. This guideline is always applied to all questions, from questions about how much effort to put into one's meditation practice to how much luxury is appropriate to metaphysical questions about existence and nonexistence. It could perhaps be argued that these simple basics— nonharming and the Middle Way—which would automatically come to mind for any Buddhist could be a sufficient basis for an environmental ethic that would encourage limited consumption and reproduction.

THE VIEW ACCORDING TO BUDDHISM:
INTERDEPENDENCE

When one brings the vast collection of Buddhist teachings into conversation with environmental concerns, one basic teaching stands out above all others. That is the Buddhist teaching of interdependence, which is also one of the most basic aspects of the Buddhist worldview. This law of interdependence is said to have been discovered by the historical Buddha on the night of his enlightenment experience during the third watch of the night, the same time period during which the Four Noble Truths were discovered. Mythically, this story indicates how basic the teaching of interdependence is to Buddhism.

Simply put, interdependence means that nothing stands alone apart from the matrix of all else. Nothing is independent and everything is interdependent with everything else. Logically, the proof of interdependence is that nothing can exist apart from the causes and conditions that give rise to it. But those causes and conditions are also dependent on other causes and conditions. Therefore, linear causality and isolating a single cause for an event gives way to a more weblike understanding of causality in which everything affects everything else in some way because everything is interconnected.

Given interdependence, our very identity as isolated, separate entities is called into serious question and we are invited to forge a more inclusive and extensive identity. We do not simply stop at the borders of our skin if we are truly interdependent with our world. When we know ourselves to be fundamentally interdependent with everything else, rather than independent entities existing in our own right, our self-centered behaviors will be altered in very basic ways. Nothing that we do is irrelevant, without impact on the rest of our matrix.

The implications of this profound, thoroughgoing interdependence for ecology have already been articulated in a moving fashion by Joanna Macy and others.[1] In fact, interdependence is the most commonly invoked concept in Buddhist environmental ethics to date. Most often, it is celebrated as a view of our relationships with our world that invites and requires ecological concern and a view that is much more emotionally satisfying and realistic than the Western emphasis on the individual as the ultimately real and ultimately important entity. Western Buddhists especially seem to find immense relief in their discovery of what Harold Coward calls the "we-self" in another chapter. This joy is quite understandable, given the emotional burdens concomitant with modern Western individualism.

However, rather than emphasizing the lyrical beauty of interconnectedness, as others have already done very well, I wish to emphasize its more somber implications. First, given interdependence, we cannot intervene in or rearrange the ecosystem without affecting everything to some extent. Therefore, human interference in the ecosystem cannot be a glib pursuit of "progress" and "growth," two things that many view as ideals. The effects of growth and technological progress on the whole interconnected system are much more important and these effects are often not anticipated. For example, lowering the death rate, especially the infant mortality rate, through modern medicine seems like clear progress. But failure to see the link between the death rate and the birth rate, which sanctions the continuation of reproductive practices appropriate when the death rate is high, is an important factor in the current population explosion. Even when people have some awareness of the effects of human intervention into the ecosystem, stopping such intervention can be difficult. Even though many are thoroughly alarmed at the global consequences of destroying the Amazon rain forest, its destruction continues because of the overwhelming power of consumerism. The reality of interdependence is sobering, as well as poetic. Each of us feels the effects of actions taken far away by people whom we do not know and whom we cannot influence directly.

If pervasive interconnectedness is an accurate view, then nothing can be delinked from anything else. Taking interdependence seriously urges us to apply "both-and" solutions, rather that "either-or" arguments to knotty problems. This applies particularly to consumption and population. When discussing environmental ethics, one of the most important, but largely unrecognized moral agendas is the need to establish the fundamental similarity of the urge to consume more and the urge to reproduce more, rather than being lured into superficial arguments about whether excessive consumption or overpopulation is *the* major environmental problem, as so often happens in "North" versus "South" debates.

Not only are excessive consumption and excessive reproduction similar in their negative impact on the environment but also in the self-centered motivations from which they spring. The former similarity is somewhat recognized but the similarity of self-centered motivation has been completely overlooked. This is the case even for Buddhist environmental ethics, where, given Buddhism's especially developed critic of ego, one would expect to find such insights. This literature contains many denunciations, on Buddhist grounds, of personal, corporate, and national greed concerning consumable goods and many discussions of how such greed damages the interdependent ecosystem. But there are almost no discussions of the fact that excessive population growth is at least equally devastating environmentally and would make impossible the vision articulated in many Buddhist environmental writings of the value of the ecosystem, of wilderness, and of nonhuman sentient beings. More important, Buddhist ecological literature includes almost no discussions of the fact that much reproductive behavior is fueled by individual or communal greed and ego, and, therefore, on Buddhist grounds is just as suspect as greed for assets. Buddhist ecological literature ignores the reality that most frequently, physiological reproduction results because patrilineages or individuals desire physical immortality, or because of the many ways in which birth control fails, not because of altruistic, non-ego-based motives.

In this regard Buddhist ecological ethics follows a tendency common in religious or moral discussions—a predisposition to regard individual greed and excessive consumption as a moral failing, while excessive reproduction is not similarly regarded as a moral failing. In fact, reproduction is idealized and romanticized. Religions often promote large families, both through their discouragement of fertility control and their patriarchal tendency to view women primarily as reproducers, while governments implement pronatalist tax and social policies in an overpopulated world. Thus, to keep population and consumption properly linked, in religious discourse we may need to focus more on population issues. Because we can assume a moral condemnation of excessive consumption in religious ethics, such a focus will actually bring our attention to consumption and population into balance with each other.

Furthermore, if one accepts interdependence, then we must realize that many things that people regard as private individual choices, most especially choices regarding how much to consume and whether or how many children to bear, actually are not private matters because of their profound implications for all sentient beings. The "we-self," in Harold Coward's terminology, has very strong interest in individual practices regarding reproduction and consumption and its perspective needs to be taken seriously. Very strong ethical arguments that everyone must limit their consumption and reproduction follow. These arguments can be made both in terms of rights—the rights of other beings not to be infringed upon by our excessive reproduction and consumption—and in terms of responsibilities—our own responsibility not to harm other beings unnecessarily through our reproduction and consumption.

THE CORE PRACTICE:
BUDDHIST MEDITATIONS AND CONTEMPLATIONS
ON INDIVIDUAL DESIRE IN AN INTERDEPENDENT WORLD

An ecological ethic has been defined as a value system and set of practices through which people come to appreciate the entire matrix of life enough to limit their own consumption and reproduction for the well-being of that matrix. These limits are adopted despite technologies and economies that, by ignoring the big picture and the long run, foster the illusion that having more children and consuming more material goods are unproblematic. Buddhism, in my view, has some important, perhaps unique, insights to offer toward developing such an ethic.

Buddhism suggests that we look into our own desires when confronted with problems and misery and I believe such practices are quite relevant for developing the kind of environmental ethic defined above. The Four Noble Truths, often characterized as the Buddha's verbalization of his enlightenment experience, provide the basis for developing an ethic of adopting limits for the sake of the matrix of life. The First and Second Noble Truths foster especially fruitful contemplations relevant to ecological ethics. The First Noble Truth states that conventional lifestyles inevitably result in suffering; the Second Noble Truth states that suffering stems from desire rooted in ignorance. Translated into more ecological language, a conventional lifestyle of indulging in desired levels of consumption and reproduction results in the misery of an environmentally degraded and overpopulated planet.

The Second Noble Truth, with its emphasis on desire as the cause of suffering, is the key to a Buddhist environmental ethic. But before we can develop the implications of the Second Noble Truth for environmental ethics, it is necessary to clarify the meaning of the term "desire," since that term is widely misunderstood, with the result that Buddhism is often caricatured as a pessimistic, world-denying religion. The usually-chosen English word "desire" translates the Pali *tanha* and the Sanskrit *trishna*, but the connotations of the term "desire" are not strong enough to carry the meaning of Second Noble Truth. Most English-speaking people regard desire as inevitable and only a problem if it gets out of hand. But, in Buddhist psychology, *trishna* is always out of hand, inevitably out of control. Therefore, I believe more accurate connotative translations of *trishna* would be "addiction" or "compulsion," which more adequately convey its insatiable demands and counterproductivity. "Grasping," "attachment," "clinging," "craving," and "fixation" are also possible, more accurate translations; and the way the term "greed" is now used when discussing some multinationals also could translate *trishna*. All of these terms suggest that the object of desire is actually more powerful, more in control, than the desiring subject, which is precisely why *trishna* causes *duhkha*—misery.

Trishna is not about having lightly held plans or about preferring an adequate diet to malnourishment, as many people think when they try to refute Buddhism by saying that life without attachment is impossible. *Trishna* is about the extra weight we bring to our plans and preferences when they so control us that any change throws us into uncontrollable, heedless emotional turmoil. That is how *trishna* causes *duhkha*. *Trishna* is also about the mistaken view that getting something—wealth or a male child, for example—will bring happiness and satisfaction. Because of this view, such goals are pursued compulsively and, therefore, suffering results. Thus, it is clear that from a Buddhist point of view, *trishna* is at the root of both excessive consumption and overpopulation. Neither would occur if people did not think that more wealth or more children would satisfy an existential itch that only is cooled by equanimity. "I want . . ." are the two words that fuel the suffering of excessive consumption and overpopulation.

Because it is so counterintuitive to suggest that attachment is the cause of human miseries, let us perform a mental exercise. Buddhists, contrary to popular Western stereotypes about them, regard happiness as favorably as any other people. The First Noble Truth is not about preferring misery to happiness but about noting that conventional ways of pursuing happiness produce sorrow instead. Most people think that happiness results from getting what we crave, whereas Buddhists would say that happiness happens when *trishna* is renounced. Thus, craving and happiness are incompatible. Some reflection on one's last experience of unrelieved, intense longing will quickly confirm that it was not a pleasant experience. One endures the longing because of the pleasure that comes when cravings are satisfied. But the satisfaction is short-lived, quickly replaced by yet another longing. The satisfaction of our cravings is virtually impossible because of the insatiable, addictive nature of *trishna*, which always wants more. Since craving and happiness are incompatible, which one should be renounced?

The good news of Buddhism is that the mental attitude of grasping and fixation is not the only alternative. "I want . . ." can be replaced with simply noting what is. The enlightened alternative to *trishna* is detachment—equanimity and even-mindedness beyond the opposites of hope and fear, pleasure and pain. It is the unconditional joy that cannot be produced by the satisfaction of cravings, but that arises spontaneously when we truly experience unfabricated mind. Equanimity has nothing to do with getting what we want and everything to do with developing contentment with things as they are. It is the hard-won ability to be at least somewhat even-minded whether one gets one's heart-desire, or is denied it. It is the hard-won ability to put space around every experience, to realize that nothing lasts forever without feeling cheated, and to be at least somewhat cheerful no matter what is happening. Therefore, fundamentally, *trishna* and equanimity are states of mind; they have little to do with what we have or do not have. According to Buddhism, external factors, whether other people or material objects, are not the source of joy or suffering; rather *attitudes* toward people and things determine which we experience. Both rich and poor can be ridden by *trishna* and both can cultivate equanimity, though extreme poverty is not especially conducive to developing it. Those in poverty are often too consumed with survival to develop equanimity and enlightenment—strong arguments to work toward a small population living well, rather than a large population living in dire circumstances or the current extreme inequities between rich and poor.

On the other hand, greed is normal in people who live conventional lives, which is why it seems so counterintuitive to suggest that longings, such as those for more wealth or more children, are the cause of suffering. According to Buddhism, greed is normal in conventional people because of a pervasive and deep-seated erroneous view of the self. Craving for *more*, whether children or things, is rooted in ignorance. Ignorance of what? Classically, craving is rooted in ignorance and denial of our fundamental nature, which is the lack of a permanent individual self—*anatman*. But *anatman* is simply another name for interdependence. Because we are interdependent with everything else in the matrix of existence, we do not exist in the way we conventionally believe that we do—as self-existing, self-contained bundles of wants and needs that end with our skin, or, if we feel generous, with our immediate families. That imagined independent self that greedily consumes and reproduces itself is a fiction. It has never really existed and so giving up on it is not a loss but a homecoming. This is the aspect of Buddhism that has been so inspiring to deep ecologists, who have claimed that Asian worldviews are more conducive to ecological vision than Western emphases on the unique, independently existing, eternal individual.

Furthermore, when Buddhists discuss *trishna* as the cause of suffering, all compulsions are equally problematic because craving is incompatible with equanimity. Therefore, on other grounds than interdependence, one cannot delink population from consumption, or either from the environment. Frequently outsiders will ask whether it is not permissible to have "good" longings. The negative answer to this question is especially important in this context because it puts desire for too many things and desire for too many children on exactly the same footing. Both are equally problematic and destructive. The environmental crisis is not solved by arguing about whether overpopulation or excessive consumption is more serious but by "both-and" linkages between them.

These contemplations on individual longing in an interdependent world are rather steep, but they have many virtues in promoting a more radical way of linking consumption, reproduction, and the environment. The most important is that, while in terms of absolute truth individuals do not exist as independent entities, in terms of relative truth, a profound reorientation of consciousness to that fact, individual by individual, is necessary if the root causes of excessive consumption and reproduction are to be overcome. While I certainly favor governmental, economic, and social programs and policies that discourage excessive consumption and reproduction, I also think that, by themselves, such interventions at the macrolevel will be insufficient. Nor does Buddhism have a great deal to say about such policies. But, in addition to such policies, individual people need to realize and experience that their happiness does not require or depend on *more* of anything, and Buddhist practices have a great deal to offer in promoting such personal transformation. So long as limits, whether to consumption or fertility, are regarded as a dreary duty imposed from above and a personal loss, people will resent and try to evade them. But if one experiences such limits, not as personal loss but as normal, natural, and pleasant in an interdependent matrix, then they are not a problem.

WALKING THE MIDDLE PATH:
RESULTS OF BUDDHIST PRACTICE

A frequent complaint against religion in general and Buddhism in particular is that the profound ethical insights of the tradition have little practical impact on the world. In popular stereotypes, Buddhism, with its emphasis on silent, motionless meditation practices, is accused of being otherworldly. But this widespread evaluation is based on a serious misunderstanding of Buddhist ethics. Buddhism generally teaches that the first moral agenda is to develop clarity and equanimity oneself, before trying to intervene in or influence society at large. Thus, Buddhism's emphasis on practices promoting individual transformation is not antisocial or otherworldly in any way, but instead is aimed at avoiding the self-righteous excesses so common in religions that promote activism for all. According to Buddhist understandings of moral development, the meditative and contemplative practices discussed above result in the development of genuine compassion, said to be the only basis for a helpful program of social action.

Furthermore, stereotypes aside, the Buddhist record of personal transformation leading to social benefit is impressive. It must be remembered that Buddhism has been the dominant religion in very few societies; those societies, such as Tibet and Southeast Asia, are not especially overpopulated and have not been markedly aggressive since their conversion to Buddhism. Two of the most respected and effective recent winners of the Noble Peace Prize, the Dalai Lama and Aung San Suu Kyi, are Buddhists and base their social activism directly on Buddhist principles and their meditative discipline. The Dalai Lama has publicly advocated both population regulation and environmental protection as vital to the survival and well-being of the planet. Nor are these isolated examples. Twentieth-century Buddhism has developed a global movement called Engaged Buddhism, which some see as the Buddhist equivalent of liberation theology.

As already noted, thus far contemporary Buddhist ethical thought has not brought together the interrelated issues of population, consumption, and the environment. But certain conclusions regarding appropriate actions follow inevitably from the view of interdependence and the practice of replacing compulsion with equanimity. Within a finite matrix, it is not possible to have both all the material goods and all the fertility that people conventionally want. Some choices must be made. We could continue the current obscene distribution patterns, with a few people consuming most of the earth's resources and the majority of people pushing the margins of existence. If consumer goods are the ultimate concern, we could have a world in which most people have their personal automobile, though only with a significantly reduced population if breathing oxygen continues to be necessary for humans. If fertility and reproduction are the ultimate concern, we could reproduce until the entire earth is as crowded and impoverished as today's most crowded places, though I think the traditional controllers of population—violence, epidemic, and famine—would intervene well before such an apocalypse could occur. Or we could chart a middle course, balancing consumption and reproduction in ways that result in a world in which there are few enough people consuming moderately enough that all can be adequately cared for materially, emotionally, and spiritually.

I will conclude this chapter exploring the ways in which some traditional Buddhist ethical teachings might be applied to take action regarding issues of population, consumption, and the environment. I will work with Buddhist teachings that are specifically devoted to providing guidelines for compassionate action—the *paramita*-s ("transcendent virtues") discussed as part of the *bodhisattva* path in Mahayana Buddhism. I will also link my discussion of *paramita* practice with some Western ethical concepts relevant to issues of population and consumption, namely the language of rights and responsibilities. For Western Buddhists in particular, such linkages and cross-cultural conceptual translations are important, both for our understanding of Buddhism and for making Buddhist contributions to our Western cultural milieu.

In this context, it is helpful to focus on the first two *paramita*-s, generosity and discipline. Generosity is highly valued in Buddhism. Wealth is not inappropriate for a Buddhist, but wealth should be circulated rather than hoarded. Generosity is evaluated as the primary virtue of the *bodhisattva*, without which the other *paramita*-s cannot develop or will develop improperly. On the other hand, generosity by itself is meaningless and may well be counterproductive. It needs to be balanced and informed by the *paramita* immediately following generosity—discipline. If it is not so balanced and informed, generosity may well lead to what my teacher called "idiot compassion"—giving people things that are not helpful to them because one lacks disciple and *prajna* (discriminating awareness wisdom) in being generous. Instead, he often said, the *paramita* of discipline involves uttering "the giant NO" when the situation called for it. One could even talk of the gift of the "giant NO." (It should be pointed out that, ideally *paramita* practice is based on enough understanding of interdependence that the practice is nondualistic. Therefore, the question of giver and receiver of generosity or discipline does not arise, There is simply one spontaneous field of action.)

I suggest that it might be helpful to link this discussion of generosity and discipline to Western language about rights and responsibilities. Regarding such language, I agree with the widespread observation that it is a product of the European Enlightenment and individualism, and does not fit easily onto most Asian systems of thought, including Mahayana discussions of the *paramita*-s. This lack of fit is due to the fact that language of rights and responsibilities is extremely dualistic, based on assumptions of independently existing individuals who have rights and responsibilities vis-à-vis each other. I would also argue that in much contemporary Western discourse, rights and responsibilities have become dangerously delinked from one another. Claims for multiple rights abound, but very few wish to discuss the corresponding responsibilities, which often lends a tone of childish demand to claims about rights.

Nevertheless, despite lack of a perfect fit between the *paramita*-s of generosity and discipline with Western concepts of rights and responsibilities, some comparisons may be instructive. The example of the way generosity and discipline are linked in Mahayana thought may well prove a useful model for how to link rights and responsibilities in Western discussions. One could see generosity as roughly analogous to rights and discipline as analogous to responsibility. Those in need have rights to the generosity of those with more wealth but, to merit continued generosity, they have responsibilities to be disciplined in their own lives. Likewise, those with relative wealth have a responsibility to be generous with their consumables, but they also have both a right and a responsibility to exercise discipline in giving and to avoid "idiot compassion." Because generosity and discipline so balance and inform each other, the sharp line between rights and responsibilities is diminished. Those with wealth have something beyond responsibility to share it; sharing is a spontaneous discipline beyond rights and responsibility. Likewise, discipline undercuts the question of rights and responsibilities; whatever rights one may think one has, discipline is more integral to self-esteem and well-being. When discipline is well established, responsible and generous action is spontaneous and joyful, rather than onerous.

The way in which generosity and discipline balance and inform each other in this discussion suggests how to balance and link rights and responsibilities in Western discussions of population, consumption, and the environment. One frequently hears claims of rights to an adequate standard of living, as well as rights to reproduce as much as an individual chooses. But corresponding discussions of the effects of unlimited exercise of these "rights" on the ecosystem, corresponding discussions of the need for responsibility when exercising these rights is not always heard. The net effect is that these two rights are on a collision course with each other. Rather than discussing such rights as if they could be independent of each other, it is important to realize that the more seriously we take the claim of a right to a universal minimum standard of living, the more critical universal fertility regulation becomes. Only if we don't really think it is possible to divide the world's resources equitably can we afford to be casual about universal fertility regulations. And the more unrestricted fertility earth experiences, the more difficult it will become ever to achieve equitable distribution. Conversely, if unregulated wasteful consumption continues unabated, inequities of wealth and poverty can only grow; then the poor, whose only resource is their children, cannot possibly do without enough of them to put minimal food on the table and to provide minimal old-age care. The more that destructive patterns of growth and consumption increase, the more difficult it becomes to avoid excessive population growth. Only if it is thought that the wealthy can somehow insulate themselves from the negative environmental consequences of such growth can we afford to be casual about the need to forbid excessive and wasteful consumption.

Like generosity and discipline, rights exist only in interdependence with responsibilities. Those who refuse to meet their responsibilities lose their rights, which is why involuntary fertility regulation and involuntary limits to consumption are not always inappropriate. No one's rights to their consumables or their fertility are so absolute that they include destroying or damaging the environment in which we all live.

While writing this chapter, I returned to my childhood home, noting with sadness the negative effects of more people than ever before consuming at greater levels than ever before. The spring, the outhouse, and the woods to provide firewood are still there and all are still used. But traffic noise from long-distance eighteen-wheel trucks hauling consumables often interrupts the silence unpleasantly. My cabin is now on the first open land from town, and a nearby lake, wild and unsettled in my childhood, is now surrounded by houses as crowded together as if they were in a city. Year by year increased population increases the pressure to subdivide and sell my land; before I die, higher taxes due to these population pressures may force me to sell. One can still see more stars in the black sky than in a city, but those to the north are whited out by light pollution from the nearest town. Now I comment on dragonflies, butterflies, and fireflies because they are not as common as they once were.

To trade in this sacred, pristine environment to support more people consuming at unprecedented levels seems a poor bargain. I can see no way in which all this "more"—more people, more stuff—has improved the quality of life, except perhaps that I can now buy Chinese spices at the local grocery store! But surely we can figure out ways to increase quality without increasing quantity, and if not, I'd rather do without Chinese spices than without the spacious, untrammeled environment. More is not better, whether it is more people or more consumables. "Growth," the god we worship, is a false idol, needing to be replaced by "no growth," if not by "negative growth." "Growth" and "more" represent the unbridled reign of *trishna*, not appreciation and reverence for the interdependent matrix of the environment in which we live and upon which we depend unconditionally. But to be consumed by *trishna* is not human nature, not our inevitable lot or inescapable original sin. With enough meditation and contemplation of interdependence, *trishna* will give way to equanimity. Would that *trishna* give way to contentment and equanimity—speedily and in our time!

NOTE

1. Joanna Macy, *World as Lover, World as Self* (Berkeley, Calif.: Parallax Press, 1991).

CHAPTER 11

Chinese Religions on Population, Consumption, and Ecology

Chün-fang Yü

As we move toward the year 2000, humankind is facing unprecedented crises on many fronts. More than twenty years ago, environmental experts pointed out the intimate relationships between population, consumption, and environment by this formula: population × consumption × technology = environmental impact.[1] As a result of exponential population growth during the twentieth century, technological advances, and the ever increasing emphasis on consumption, we are now witnessing massive environmental degradation and ecological crisis. It is clear that humans are the culprits. "The planet's capacity to meet human demands for natural resources, and equally, its ability to absorb the wastes produced by human activities, is under attack."[2] What are we going to do in order to save ourselves and our planet from destruction? Natural and social scientists, governments, and United Nations conferences have discussed causes of the disaster and suggested guidelines and policies for remedy. Although scholars of religion have joined the common effort by writing books and teaching college courses on ecology, their opinions have generally not yet been incorporated into public debate. This is very unfortunate, for I believe that a fundamental reexamination of our values and beliefs is essential before we can change our lifestyles and ways of thinking conducive to a loving instead of injurious relationship with the earth and our fellow inhabitants (both human and nonhuman). It is time for each of us to go back to our religious traditions and discover or rediscover the spiritual resources to guide us in this critical moment of human history. Since most of world religions, including Chinese religions, appeared long before the population explosion, excessive consumption, and ecological degradation became problems, it is obvious that we will not find specific teachings on these topics. But they do have a lot of significant things to say about the nature of the world, human relationships, and humankind's attitude toward the world and other co-inhabitants of the world.

The great religions of the world were great because they were classic expressions of compassion and reverence for life. The religion of the market, described by David Loy, is not a classic of reverence. It is, rather, an illusion-filled and deviant worship of unlimited growth on a limited earth. The corporate missionaries of this religion, discussed by David Korten, are transforming life on earth, finding only profit and growth to be sacred. The classic religions of the world have never faced a challenge like this. These ancient repositories of wisdom must be tapped and their gentle ideals must be reenfranchised in the economics and politics of the next century.

FORMING ONE BODY WITH HEAVEN AND EARTH

The world in which human beings live is called in the Chinese language, "Heaven and Earth." Unlike most other religions, Chinese religion does not have a creator god. On the contrary, as seen in the *Book of Changes* (I Ching), one of the basic Confucian classics, and a divinatory handbook of great antiquity. The *Book of Changes* is divided into the texts and commentaries. The texts consist of sixty-four hexagrams and judgments on them. The hexagrams are based on the eight trigrams. There are also commentaries known as the ten appendices or the "ten wings." Tradition has ascribed the eight trigrams to the legendary sage emperor Fu-hsi, the sixty-four hexagrams to King Wen (r. 1171–1122 B.C.E.), the two texts to him or Duke Chou (d. 1094 B.C.E.) and the "ten wings" to Confucius. Most modern scholars have rejected this attributions, however, and most probably it is a product of many hands over a long period of time, from the fifth or sixth century B.C.E. to the third or fourth century B.C.E.[3] The universe, or "Heaven and Earth," is the origin of everything including human beings in the universe. This creating and sustaining force, otherwise known as *Tao* or the Way, is seen as good and the highest goal of the human life is to live in conformity to it. There is no God transcendent and separate from the world and there is no heaven outside of the universe to which human beings would want to go for refuge. The *Book of Changes* contains sixty-four hexagrams that are made up by the eight trigrams. The first and second trigrams, known as *ch'ien* and *k'un*, represent the two prime principles of *yang* and *yin* that constitute the *Tao*, and Heaven and Earth are the physical representations of these principles.

Chang Tsai (1020–77), a major thinker who contributed to the revival of the Confucian tradition known as Neo-Confucianism in medieval China, wrote a short essay called "The Western Inscription" that can be regarded as a Confucian credo. It reads in part:

> Heaven is my father and Earth is my mother, and even such a small creature as I find an intimate place in their midst. Therefore that which fills the universe I regard as my body and that which directs the universe I consider as my nature. All people are my brothers and sisters, and all things are my companions. The great ruler (the emperor) is the eldest son of my parents (Heaven and Earth), and the great ministers are his stewards. Respect the aged—that is the way to treat them as elders should be treated. Show deep love toward the orphaned and the weak—this is the way to treat them as the young should be treated. The sage identifies his character with that of Heaven and Earth, and the worthy is the most outstanding man. Even those who are tired, infirm, crippled, or sick; those who have no brothers or children, wives or husbands, are all my brothers who are in distress and have no one to turn to. . . . In life I honor and serve [Heaven and Earth]. In death I will be at peace.[4]

The basis for Chang's faith in the unity between humankind and the universe is *ch'i*, which has been translated as vital force, material force, or life force. *Ch'i* refers to *yin* and *yang*, and the five phases of wood, fire, earth, metal, and water evolving from the interaction of the two. All living and nonliving things in the universe are constituted of *ch'i*. This is the worldview shared by all Chinese religions, datable to the Chou (1111–249 B.C.E.) and formulated during the Han dynasty (206 B.C.E.–220 C.E.). Such a worldview has been described as "organic, vitalistic, and holistic" and the universe is seen as "a dynamic, ongoing process of continual transformation."[5] Because humans share the same substance with the universe, there is the possibility for communication between us and our environment. This belief is implied by the concepts of "mandate of Heaven" (*t'ien-ming*) and "stimulus and response" (*kan-yin*). Mandate of Heaven was originally used by the Chou founders to justify their rebellion against the previous Shang dynasty. According to them, the last two Shang rulers lost their mandate because they were deficient of virtue. The mandate went to the Chou founders because they were virtuous. That is why the *Book of History* says, "The Mandate of Heaven is not easily preserved. Heaven is hard to depend on. Those who have lost the mandate did so because they could not practice and carry on the reverence and the brilliant virtue of their forefathers."[6] Heaven not only gave and took away mandate, it also sent blessings or warnings before it did so. Thus the Chinese believed in omens and portents, taking them to mean Heaven's responses to the behavior of mankind. By the Han times, "the unity of men and Nature was turned into one of mutual influence, these influences were thought to be exerted through strange phenomena and calamities; Heaven, though not anthropomorphic, was purposive, asserting its will through prodigies as warning to men."[7] Tung Chung-shu (ca. 179–ca. 104 B.C.E.), the architect of Han Confucianism, was a firm believer of such ideas. "When a great ruler is about to arise, auspicious omens first appear; when a ruler is about to be destroyed, there are baleful ones beforehand. Things indeed summon each other, like to like, a dragon bringing rain, a fan driving away heat, the place where an army has been being thick with thorns. Things, whether lovely or repulsive, all have an origin."[8] If Tung were alive today, he would have definitely taken all the vital signs of the earth's travail as bad omens for humankind. The Han Chinese interest in observing natural phenomena was in fact related to the ruler's intense obsession with omens. Systematic notation of spots on the sun began in 28 B.C.E. and the first seismograph in the world was invented in 132 C.E. in order to pinpoint earthquakes, which were regarded as signs of disorder in nature.

The philosophical explanation for the mutual influence between nature and humans was explained by Tung Chung-shu thus, "Heaven possesses yin and yang and man also possesses yin and yang. When the universe's material force of yin arises, man's material force of yin arises in response. Conversely, when man's material force of yin arises, that of the universe also arise in response."[9] This provides the foundation for the Chinese belief in the correspondence between microcosm and macrocosm: a person is a small universe replicating the greater universe without. And the universe, in turn, could be envisioned as an image of God. Religious Taoism, which also flourished in the Han, deified Lao Tzu and talked mythologically of the universe being his cosmic body:

> Lao Tzu transformed his body. His left eye became the sun; his right eye, the moon, his head beame mount K'un-lun; his beard, the planets and constellations; his bones, dragons; his flesh, four-footed creatures; his intestines, snakes, his stomach, the sea; his fingers, the Five Peaks; his hair, trees and grasses; his heart, the flowery Dais; as to his two kidneys, they were united and became one, the Real and True Father and Mother.[10]

Although the Mandate of Heaven was originally used in a political context to justify the change of dynasties, very early on the Confucian thinkers understood it in a much broader sense of moral destiny, moral nature, or moral order. Confucius (551–479 B.C.E.) already used it in this sense when he said in the *Analects*, "At fifty I knew the Mandate of Heaven" (2:4), and "The superior man stands in awe of three things. He stands in awe of the Mandate of Heaven, he stands in awe of great men, and he stands in awe of the words of the sages. The inferior man is ignorant of the Mandate of Heaven and does not stand in awe of it" (16:8). Just as a ruler has to be vigilant in cultivating himself in order to keep his mandate to rule, for "the Mandate of Heaven is not fixed and unchangeable. The good ruler gets it and the bad ruler loses it."[11] Similarly, a morally sensitive person has to cultivate him/herself in order to live in accordance with the Way and in harmony with Nature and other human beings. The Neo-Confucians identified the Mandate of Heaven with the innate goodness of human nature that was first emphasized by Mencius. Human nature is good because it is bestowed by the Way, and according to the *Book of Changes*, "What issues from the Way is good and that which realizes it is the individual nature."[12] Ch'eng I (1033–1107) explained it this way:

> The fact that whatever issues from the Way is good may be compared to the fact that water always flows downward. Water as such is the same in all cases. Some water flows onward to the sea without becoming dirty. What human effort is needed here? Some flows only a short distance before becoming turbid. some travels a long distance before growing turbid, some becomes extremely turbid, some only slightly so. Although water differs in being clean or turbid, we cannot say that the turbid water (evil) ceases to be water (nature). This being the case, man must make an increasing effort at purification. With diligent and vigorous effort, water will become clear quickly. With slow and lazy effort, water will become clear slowly. When it is clear, it is then the original water. Not that clear water has been substituted for turbid water, nor that turbid water has been taken out and left in a corner. The original goodness of human nature is like the original clearness of water. Therefore it is not true that two distinct and opposing elements of good and evil exist in human nature and that each of them issues from it. This principle is the Mandate of Heaven. For anyone to obey and follow it is the Way. For anyone to follow it and cultivate it so that he attains his function [corresponding to his nature] is education. From the Mandate of Heaven to education, one can neither augment nor diminish [this function].[13]

The key to our forming one body with Heaven and Earth, as Ch'eng I stated above, is to follow our inborn moral nature and cultivate it to its fullest potential. In the Confucian tradition, the spiritual force that fueled this self-transformation and self-realization is called "sincerity" (*ch'eng*) or "humanity" (*jen*). Sincerity is the main theme in the *Doctrine of the Mean*, a chapter in the Confucian classic *Book of Rites*, but selected by Chu Hsi (1130–1200) to form, together with the *Great Learning*, the *Analects* and *Mencius*—the "Four Books" of Neo-Confucianism. When a person fully develops his/her nature through sincerity, he/she forms a trinity with Heavean and Earth. "Only those who are absolutely sincere can fully develop their nature. If they can fully develop their nature, they can then fully develop the nature of others. If they can fully develop the nature of others, they can then fully develop the nature of things. If they can fully develop the nature of things, they can then assist in the transforming and nourishing process of Heaven and Earth. If they can assist in the transforming and nourishing process of Heaven and Earth, they can thus form a trinity with Heaven and Earth."[14]

Sincerity is defined in the *Doctrine of the Mean* as "without any doubleness." Wing-tsit Chan explains it as "an active force that is always transforming things and completing things, and drawing man and Heaven together in the same current. If sincerity is to be true, it must involve strenuous effort at learning and earnest effort at practice."[15] The starting point for this practice, from the Confucian perspective, is the creation of true reciprocity in interpersonal relationships, which forms the fundamental meaning of "humanity." When Confucius was asked if there was one word that could serve as the guiding principle for conduct throughout life, he answered, "It is the word altruism. Do not do to others what you do not want them to do to you" (*Analects* 15.23). He expressed the same idea more positively elsewhere by saying, "The humane man, desiring to be established himself, seeks to establish others; desiring himself to succeed, he helps others to succeed. To judge others by what one knows of oneself is the method of achieving humanity" (*Analects* 6.28). Mencius uses the famous example of a person's feeling of alarm and distress when he sees a child about to fall into a well as evidence to prove that we all have the "mind which cannot bear to see the suffering of others" (*Mencius* 2A.6). Wang Yang-ming (1472–1529), a leading Neo-Confucian living more than a thousand years later, cites the same example to prove that we form one body with the child. He goes on to argue that a person of humanity not only identifies with his/her fellow humans but also with everything, both animate and inanimate, in the universe:

> The great man regards Heaven, Earth, and the myriad things as one body. He regards the world as one family and country as one person. As to those who make a cleavage between objects and distinguish between the self and others, they are small men. That the great man can regard Heaven, Earth, and the myriad things as one body is not because he deliberately wants to do so, but because it is natural to the humane nature of his mind that he do so. Forming one body with Heaven, Earth, and the myriad things is not only true of the great man. Even the mind of the small man is no different. Only he himself makes

it small. Therefore when he sees a child about to fall into a well, he cannot help a feeling of alarm and commiseration. This shows that his humanity forms one body with the child. It may be objected that the child belongs to the same species. Again, when he observes the pitiful cries and frightened appearance of birds and animals about to be slaughtered, he cannot help feeling an "inability to bear" their suffering. This shows that his humanity forms one body with birds and animals. It may be objected that birds and animals are sentient beings as he is, but when he sees plants broken and destroyed, he cannot help a feeling of pity. This shows that his humanity forms one body with plants. It many be said that plants are living things as he is. Yet, even when he sees tiles and stones shattered and crushed, he cannot help a feeling of regret. This shows that his humanity forms one body with tiles and stones. This means that even the mind of the small man necessarily has the humanity that forms one body with all.[16]

When I think what Chinese religions can offer us in dealing with our contemporary problems, I believe this insight that humankind forms one body with the universe to be most meaningful. We are one with the universe both because we are constituted of the same basic stuff (*ch'i*), and because this feeling of oneness is what we actually experience when we live authentically and humanely (*ch'eng, jen*). Since in this section I have so far quoted exclusively from the Confucian texts, perhaps I should offer a few words of explanation. It is common to say that there are three religions in China: Confucianism, Taoism, and Buddhism. It is also customary to speak of elite and popular religions. While such distinctions may make pedagogical sense when we teach a course, I do not think it will serve our purpose here to do so. For what we want to draw out from the traditional religions are the worldviews and practices that can teach us and guide us today. Although the worldview I have described above was formulated by Confucian philosophers, it has not been limited only to them, but rather has permeated throughout all social strata and met with approval among all Chinese people.

I offer now an example from the so-called popular religion to illustrate my point. In late medieval China, particularly during the Ming dynasty (1368–1644), pamphlets exhorting people to do good became very popular. Known as morality books, they were written by Confucian scholars, Taoist priests, and Buddhist monks in vernacular language to tell people what specific good acts to perform and what bad acts to avoid. The earliest prototype of this genre is *The Treatise of the Exalted One on Response and Retribution*, which dates from the latter part of the Northern Sung dynasty (960–1126), was first published in the Southern Sung (1127–1279), and apparently was in circulation after the beginning of the eleventh century. It is a brief essay that consists of some twelve hundred characters. It begins with a saying attributed to the Exalted One, a title given to the deified Lao Tzu: "The Exalted One says: 'Curses and blessing do not come through doors, but man himself invites their arrival. The reward of good and evil is like the shadow accompanying a body, and so it is apparent that heaven and earth are possessed of crime-recording spirits.'"[17] The expression "response and retribution" contained in the title is the same Chinese term that I have rendered as "stimulus and response" earlier, the belief that Heaven would respond to the behavior of humans by sending down either blessing or punishment. Both the Chou idea of Mandate of Heaven and the Han stress on omens and portents are related to this religious belief. The *Treatise* contains injunctions consisting of four or six characters. Their brevity and symmetry could have greatly facilitated their oral transmission and memorization. It has more to say about bad deeds to avoid than good deeds to perform. Aside from actions connected with people, we find the following prohibitions against harming animals and nature:

> Do not injure the multifarious insects, herbs, and trees.
> Do not shoot the flying, chase the running, expose the hiding, surprise nestlings, close up entrance holes, upset nests, injure the pregnant, and break the egg.
> Do not destroy the crops and fields of others.
> Do not scatter and waste the five cereals.
> Do not employ drugs to kill trees.
> Do not hunt with fire in the spring.
> Do not kill tortoises and snakes without a cause.

Kindness to living creatures and vegetation is argued here by an appeal to divine retribution. But the theological basis for this popular religiosity is ultimately the same as the Confucian spirituality of Mencius or Wang Yang-ming. Just as the latter believed in the existence of the human mind unable to bear the suffering of others because we form one body with everything, the writers of the morality books such as the *Treatise* share the same view. Some morality books assign points of merit and demerit aside from listing good and bad deeds. The authors recommend readers to keep a daily tally of the record and review their progress. The Buddhist master Chu-hung (1535–1615) wrote such a moral ledger called *The Record of Self-Knowledge*, in which we find the following actions singled out for sanction:

> To kill one animal or bird by poison counts as ten demerits.
> To kill a small animal intentionally counts as one demerit.
> To kill ten small animals by mistake counts as one demerit.

> To kill ten very small animals intentionally counts as one
> demerit.
> To kill twenty very small animals by mistake counts as one
> demerit.

In the case of disturbing a hibernating animal, surprising a nesting bird, filling up a hole in which animals live, upsetting a bird nest and breaking the eggs or harming a fetus, it is the same as killing animals with intent. To keep birds in a cage or to bind animals with strings for one day counts as one demerit.[18]

Such attitudes toward animals and nature can serve the cause of conservation. For someone who is deeply influenced by this way of thinking, it is conceivable that he/she will hesitate to kill animals, pollute water and soil with pesticide, or cut down the rain forest recklessly. There is another religious practice in China that I think shows even more strongly the belief in the unity between humankind and animals. This is the practice of redeeming captured animals and setting them free. The Chinese call it "release of life" (*fang-sheng*). It is closely connected with the related practices of refraining from killing animals and keeping a vegetarian diet. The theological justification is found in the Buddhist scripture *Sutra of Brama's Net*, which has exerted great influence on Chinese Buddhism. The passage that encourages the practice reads:

> All sons of Buddha, because of their compassionate hearts, practice the
> release of sentient beings. All men are my fathers and all women are my
> mothers. All rebirths of mine without any exception, from one rebirth
> to another, I receive from them. Therefore all the beings in the six paths
> of existence are my parents. If I should kill and eat them, it is the same
> as killing my own parents. It is also the same as killing my own self.
> For earth and water are my former body, while fire and wind are my
> original substance. Thus one should always release sentient beings.
> When we see that domestic animals are about to be killed, we ought to
> save them by the use of expedient means and spare them the suffering.[19]

Under the promotion of Buddhist proselytizers, the prohibitions against killing animals were made into governmental regulations. During the Sui dynasty (581–618), a regime favorable to Buddhism, it was legally stipulated in 583 that in the first, fifth, and ninth months of the year, as well as on the "six fast days" (eighth, fourteenth, fifteenth, twenty-fourth, twenty-ninth, and thirtieth days) of every month, no one should kill any living beings. The choice of these particular dates was based on the rule set down in the *Sutra of Brahma's Net*. It says that during these same three months and on these six days of every month a lay devotee should keep the eight precepts, including prohibitions against killing and theft, and the rule of not eating after the noon meal.

On the six fast days, the four Heavenly Kings would make an inspection of the world, observe the good and evil deeds of men, and make a record of these. Therefore, a person should be especially cautious on these days. During the T'ang dynasty (618–907), a decree was issued in 619 forbidding the slaughter of animals as well as fishing and hunting during the the the same three months of every year. Ponds for releasing life in which fish, shrimp, and crabs could be set free were also established. The earliest reference dates back to the reign of Emperor Yüan of the Liang dynasty (552–555), when a pavilion was constructed for this purpose. During the T'ang dynasty Emperor Su-tsung issued a decree in 759 setting up eighty-one ponds for releasing life in various parts of the empire.[20]

Known as "societies for the release of life," large associations with several hundred and even thousand members devoted to the collective practice became popular in the Sung dynasty. Buddhist masters active in the Pure Land and T'ien-tai traditions in the tenth and eleventh centuries were particularly successful in popularizing this movement.[21] In the late Ming dynasty in the sixteenth century, this practice received renewed emphasis from the leaders of the Buddhist revival. It was eventually no longer limited to Buddhist devotees. Even Confucian literati took up the cause of animal protection and argued for the restraint of meat consumption. Vegetarianism and release of life have remained the two distinctive Chinese religious practices. On major Buddhist holy days it is still possible to see people in Taiwan and Hong Kong get together and set birds or fish free. However, due to increasing concern for the environment, Buddhist masters in Taiwan have tried to persuade people to do things differently. They point out, rightly, that putting fish in rivers and ponds without knowing the environmental impact may be unwise. Since the main purpose of this practice is to show compassion to all forms of life, if one spends the money, energy, and time to clean up the environment or save endangered species, one would have fulfilled the same purpose. We are seeing the transformation of this traditional practice to serve the new goal of preserving the environment. Pure Land Buddhism has been one of the most influential Buddhist schools in China. The traditional goal of a Pure Land devotee is to be reborn in the Pure Land, a land of utmost bliss created by the vows of Amitabha Buddha for the faithful, upon death. Buddhist leaders in Taiwan and mainland China have in recent decades stressed the need to build a Pure Land on earth. They emphasize that Buddhism is for this world and the present life instead of the other world and nirvana. This "this-worldly Buddhism" (jen-chien fo-chiao) is a good example of how the Chinese Buddhists have drawn upon their spiritual resources to come up with creative new ways of solving contemporary problems.

There are a number of Taiwanese Buddhist leaders who are actively involved in this movement. I will introduce the work of Cheng-yen, a charismatic nun.[22] She is not an abbess of a great nunnery, but heads a grassroots organization called "Merit Association of Compassion and Relief" (*Tz'u-chi kung-te hui*). Together with four female disciples, Cheng-yen lived in a small temple in Hua-lien, a comparatively underdeveloped mountainous area on the east coast of the island, in 1963–64. They made their living by handicraft (baby shoes) and raising vegetables, refusing to augment their income by performing funeral services as was the custom. In 1966 when she went to visit a disciple who was staying in a hospital, she saw an indigenous woman being refused admission because the woman could not pay the required fee. Deeply distressed by the lack of medical facilities and the cold bureaucracy, Cheng-yen decided to establish the association to raise money to relieve the poor. She asked each of her disciples to make one extra pair of baby shoes and each of the thirty housewives who joined her and her disciples to save five cents each day from their grocery money as a contribution to the association. She was at that time not yet thirty years old. Twenty years later, she had received enough donations to establish the first Buddhist hospital, Tz'u-chi Hospital, in Hua-lien in 1986, which would treat any patient regardless of her/his ability to pay. Three years later, in 1989, Tz'u-chi Nursing College oppened its door. In 1994, the Tz'u-chi School of Medicine began to receive applicants. As her fame grew, the government and corporations also began to contribute, but her organization has retained its original characteristics of a grassroots and mass-oriented movement. There are now more than 3.5 million regular members, and more than four thousand executive members whom she praises as "thousand-eyed and thousand-armed [Kuan-yin]" members. Chapters of the Tz'u-chi Merit Association are not only scattered all over the island of Taiwan, but also found in Malaysia, Singapore, Hong Kong, Japan, Australia, England, Austria, South Africa, South America, Canada, and some twelve cities in the United States.

Cheng-yen is more interested in social action than Buddhist theory. She advocates linking the Buddhadharma with daily life and practicing the bodhisattva path in society. There are four areas to which the association dedicates its human and financial resources: philanthropy, medical cure, education, and culture. Women occupy roles of leadership in her organization. For instance, three quarters of the four thousand executive members are women. The same is true for the staff who manage the chapters. Moreover, they are not nuns but housewives coming from different walks of life and representing different strata of society. In fact, among Cheng-yen's followers, nuns occupy a tiny percentage. Her vision is to create a Pure Land on earth and she has successful mobilized lay women who have traditionally followed the Pure Land path to become her chief helpmates.

COSMIC FILIALITY

If humankind can love all forms of life, respect nature, and live simply and frugally, the adverse impact that we have made on ecology may have a chance to reverse itself. But what about the relentless rate of population explosion? What insights can we find in the Chinese religious traditions that we may use to lessen the trend? It is of course already well known that the Chinese government imposed the one-child policy to solve their population problem. As far as I know, the policy was not arrived at through any philosophical, not to mention religious, reasoning. The government uses primarily economic and utlilitarian arguments and sanctions to enforce it. What justifications for producing less children or even no children can be provided from within Chinese religious traditions?

The indigenous Chinese religions, both Confucianism and Taoism, are not ascetic. They do not regard sexuality as a problem, but on the contrary, as natural. In the *Book of Mencius*, the philosopher Kao Tzu says, "By nature we enjoy food and sex" (6A.4). Although this particular saying was attributed to a non-Confucian philosopher, there is no evidence that in the Confucian and Taoist traditions sex was ever condemned per se, but only its excessive and unrestrained indulgence. From the Chinese religions' perspective, therefore, it is possible to enjoy sexual pleasure in itself without always linking it to procreation. Taoism has particularly developed a long and rich tradition for both women and men to use sex not to procreate, but as a means of physiological and spiritual transformation.[23]

But Chinese religion is also a cult of ancestor worship. From ancient times, rituals performed by male descendants to their dead ancestors have formed central features of Chinese religion. The love and reverence to one's living and dead ancestors is called "filial piety." One of the most important ways to show this filial piety in traditional China was for a son to get married and have male children. Mencius made this very clear when he said, "There are three things which are unfilial, and to have no posterity is the greatest of them all" (4A.26). Buddhist monks were often accused of being unfilial because they observed celibacy and thus failed to produce children. Chinese Buddhist monks have defended themselves against this criticism by appealing to a new and expanded view of filial piety. Chung-feng Ming-pen (1263–1323), a famous Ch'an master, put it this way:

To inquire after one's parents morning and evening and dare not leave them for any length of time is what I call love with form. To engage in meditation effort whether walking or sitting, to vow to realize the Way with the span of this life and, with this, to repay the kindness of parents is what I call formless love. . . . Parents are the great foundation of my physical form. Yet is my physical form something I only have in this life? From innumerable kalpas until now, I have transmigrated in the three realms [of desire, form, and formlessness] and have received forms as numberless as the grains of sand. The so-called foundation of physical form fills the universe and pervades the cosmos. All that I see and hear could be the basis of my previous existences.[24]

Though using a different vocabulary, Ming-pen was saying something suprisingly similar to what Chang Tsai and other Neo-Confucians said earlier. Like they, he believed that the whole universe and he formed one body. The cosmos is our great parent. To realize this vision and live a transformed life is to be a filial child not only to one's physical parents, but to one's cosmic parent as well, even if one does not produce a physical heir.

It is never easy to change one's ways of thinking and one's lifestyle. But time for complacency is running out. Unless a new vision of the earth and human life is formed, the earth will be so damaged that life will not be worth living before too long. I have tried in this chapter to suggest a few insights from the Chinese religious traditions for our collective reflection. For the Chinese, the earth is our original home and we are a part of the living universe. To form a trinity with Heaven and Earth is to become fulfilled in one's destiny. To choose not to do so is to fail one's Mandate of Heaven. It is obvious what we should choose.

NOTES

1. Paul R. Ehrlich, Anne H. Ehrlich, and John P. Holden, *Human Ecology: Problems and Solutions* (San Francisco: W.F.H. Freeman, 1973), pp. 12–13, 206–7, cited by Ruether, *Gaia and God*, p. 88.

2. Anne Whyte, "The Human Context," in *Population, Consumption and the Environment*, ed. Harold Coward (Albany: State University of New York Press, 1995), p. 41.

3. Wing-tsit Chan, *A Source Book in Chinese Philosophy* (Princeton, N.J.: Princeton University Press, 1963), p. 262.

4. *A Source Book in Chinese Philosophy*, pp.497–98.

5. Mary Evelyn Tucker, "Ecological Themes in Confucianism and Taoism," in *Worldviews and Ecology: Religion, Philosophy and the Environment*, ed. Mary Evelyn Tucker and John A. Grim (Maryknoll, N.Y.: Orbis Books, 1994), p. 151. See also Joseph Needham, *Science and Civilisation in China*, vol. 2 (Cambridge: Cambridge University Press, 1969), p. 287; Frederick Mote,

Intellectual Foundations of China (New York: Knopf, 1971), chapter 2; Tu Wei-ming, "The Continuity of Being: Chinese Visions of Nature," in *Nature in Asian Traditions of Thought: Essays in Environmental Philosophy*, ed. J. Baird Callicott and Roger T. Ames (Albany: State University of New York Press, 1989), pp. 67–78.

6. *A Source Book in Chinese Philosophy*, p. 7.

7. Ibid., p. 292.

8. Needham, *Science and Civilisation in China* 2:282.

9. Ibid., p. 284.

10. Hsiao-tao lun, quoted in Kristofer Schipper, *The Taoist Body*, translated Karen C. Duval (Berkeley: University of California Press, 1982), p. 114.

11. This is found in chapter 10 of the *Great Learning*, which is one of the "four books" of the Neo-Confucian canon. It quotes from the "Announcement of K'ang" of the *Book of History*, one of the five Confuican classics. *A Source Book in Chinese Philosophy*, p. 93.

12. "Appended Remarks" (Hsi Tz'u, part 1) of *Book of Changes*. Ibid., p. 266.

13. Ibid., p. 528.

14. Ibid., p. 108.

15. Ibid., p. 96.

16. Wang Yang-ming, *Instruction for Practical Living*, trans. Wing-tsit Chan (New York: Columbia University Press, 1963), p. 272.

17. T'ai-Shang kan-yin p'ien, *Treatise of the Exalted One on Response and Retribution*, trans. Teitaro Suzuki and Paul Carus (La Salle, Ill.: Open Court, 1944), p. 51.

18. Chün-fang Yü, *The Renewal of Buddhism in China: Chu-hung and the Late Ming Synthesis* (New York: Columbia University Press, 1981), pp. 245–48.

19. Ibid., p. 68.

20. Ibid., p. 72.

21. Dan Getz, "Siming Zhili and Tiantai Pure Land in the Song Dynasty," 1994 Yale University dissertation.

22. I base my discussion on Cheng-yen's movement on personal interviews and fieldwork conducted in the summer of 1993. I am indebted to Dr. Lu Hui-hsin of the Academia Sinica for personal communications and unpublished articles that form portions of her ongoing study on the Tz'u-chi Association. For the life of Cheng-yen, see Yu-ing Ching, *Master of Love and Mercy: Cheng Yen* (Nevada City, Calif.: Blue Dolphin Publishing, 1995).

23. Douglas Wile, *Art of the Bedchamber: The Sexual Yoga Classics Including Women's Solo Meditation Texts* (Albany: State University of New York Press, 1992); R. H. Van Gulik, *Sexual Life in Ancient China: A Preliminary Survey of Chinese Sex and Society from ca. 1500 B.C. till 1644 A.D.* (Leiden: E.J. Brill, 1961); Henry Maspero, *Taoism and Chinese Religion*, trans. Frank A. Kierman Jr. (Boston: MIT Press, 1981), pp. 517–41.

24. Chün-fang Yü, "Chung-feng Ming-pen and Ch'an Buddhism in the Yüan," *Yüan Thought: Chinese Thought and Religion under the Mongols*, ed. Hok-lam Chan and Wm. Theodore de Bary (New York: Columbia University Press, 1982), p. 459.

CHAPTER 12

African Religions and the Global Issues of Population, Consumption, and Ecology

Jacob K. Olupona

INTRODUCTION

Contemporary Africa faces a myriad of moral, economic, and socio-political problems that call for sustained debate and urgent solution. But perhaps none are more urgent than the crises arising from ecological disaster, uncontrolled population, and overconsumption, especially as these relate to the overall growth and development of the continent. Undoubtedly, most African nations today are concerned with how to effect meaningful changes in their citizens' economic and social lives, especially at a period when their standard of living seems to have fallen below what it was at the time of independence in the 1960s. Some of these changes of course would involve harnessing the available natural resources into much-needed development projects. Paradoxically, it is becoming increasingly clear that no amount of development programs will usher in economic and social growth if the strategies adopted constitute the very source of other more serious social problems such as ecological degradation, overpopulation, and overconsumption, which inevitably inhibit sustained progress rather than promote growth. In the popular parlance, development then becomes forcing a square peg into a round hole. This sudden realization, observed a South African paper, is leading to "common perceptions that it [ecological crisis] constitutes perhaps the central moral and political issue of our time."[1]

Ecological, overpopulation, and overconsumption problems are as much moral and ethical issues as they are political and social. If Africa

175

is to respond adequately to these issues, it must do so primarily from the local resources emanating from its own belief systems and cultures. The problem must therefore be framed within the larger and central contexts of sustainable development, social and cultural transformations, and historical trajectory within which Africa exists in the world today. The impact of globalizing capitalism is not the same everywhere. The new cultural invasions of "the religion of the market" build on old invasions, and for Africa, they build on a history that is unique.

This chapter will focus on the problems of ecology, population, and consumption from the perspective of African religious traditions. First, I will examine the place of Africa today in the new world order, outlining the impact of this crisis on the continent, and the continent's response to it. Second, I will analyze how African religions and spiritual resources can provide a new indigenous theological and ethical response to this crisis. The sense of the sacred that is the mark of religion is always expressed through the specificity of a culture.

AFRICA AND THE NEW WORLD ORDER:
TOWARD UNDERSTANDING THE AFRICAN SITUATION

With the end of the cold war, it was assumed that a new wind of change of democratization and liberalization was blowing over the African continent. In reality nothing much had changed and indeed Africa's nation-states have gradually been sliding from the status of developing nations they enjoyed in the 1970s, to underdevelopment in the 1990s. Since I cannot deal with all the major problems responsible for the present situation in the amount of space available to me, I shall provide glimpses of Africa's present socioeconomic status and development to underscore the significance of these problems, which in the African situation derives from both internal and external factors.

The reality of the African situation today should be seen against the backdrop of its past and present; the precolonial, colonial, and postcolonial history would help us understand how Africa's present apparently looks so gloomy. First, African history within world history is unique. There are fewer other peoples, races, or cultures and societies that have been subjected to such a high degree of inhumane treatment as the people of this continent. As a result, the problem of overpopulation, disasters in the ecosystem, and poor health management are more acute in Africa than the rest of the world. Right from the time of its "discovery" by the Portuguese explorers in the fifteenth century, modern Africa has been subjected to foreign dominance and exploitation of its resources, laying bare its natural riches and human resources. Following several centuries of exploratory voyages to different parts of the continent, a large scale of human exportation of slaves to the New World began in the sixteenth century and continued until the late nineteenth century. By the time slavery was officially declared over, more than 20 million able-bodied men and women had been transported to the Caribbean and the Americas, where their descendants still continue to confront forms of racism and prejudice today. From the early nineteenth century to the early part of the twentieth century, under the pretext of emancipation, Africa entered a second phase of European dominance, as various colonial powers who had participated in the slave trade took charge of specific regions and territories where they had interests. With the Berlin Conference of 1884–85, Africa was hurriedly partitioned among the European powers without any considerations for the ethnic, linguistic, and cultural markers of the colonized people. The colonial economy that ensued was based primarily on the exploitation of the African resources for the development of the home countries. Tailored forms of education and social services were established in the colonies, new forms of village and township leadership systems were invented to replace the African traditional systems and to make the colonies easier and cheaper to govern. The result of these policies was that a new African elite group was created that continued to perpetuate the colonial legacy long after the independence of the colonies was won in the 1960s.

Shortly after independence, the euphoria that greeted self-rule quickly disappeared as the new African elite and neocolonial forces, instigated from outside the continent, combined to jettison the newly won freedom. In country after country, military rulers often backed by foreign governments were ushered in under the pretense of enforcing a corrective regime, as was the case in Zaire, where Mobutu Sese Seko seized power from a democratically elected government. By the 1970s, African countries began witnessing a gradual decline of their resources and natural wealth. The combined forces of internal problems of leadership and good governance and external influence of economic exploitation continue to place Africa in its unique unenviable situation.

This brief background of African political and economic history will explain why its own history and situation today differ from the rest of the world. Even though several other developing countries were once under colonial rule, Africa's recovery is different precisely because of the intensity of colonial economic exploitation and the role of its own political and military elite after colonial rule to further plunder the place. Reacting to the above situation a few years ago, Chief Abiola observed that asking why the African continent lags behind other regions of the world is like asking someone whose leg has been broken, "why can't you run, while others are running." Africa is unable to run while others are running the "development" race because her legs have been severely broken.

The New World Order that Africa and other developing countries thought would usher in a better life and a more peaceful relationship between them and the First World has not resolved any of the above crises. Rather it has deepened the great divide between the two regions. With no military or economic strategic interests to defend in sub-Saharan Africa, the amounts of aid and investment that were provided during the cold war era have dwindled. A report in 1994 suggests that since the end of the cold war, most of the money saved "through cuts in military spending," what it calls "the peace dividend," has gone to balancing the rich countries' budget deficits and to "nondevelopment expenditures."[2] The United Nations Development Program (UNDP) report was quite revealing particularly in reference to the neglect of African nations. Out of the 173 countries it ranked by their levels of success in addressing human needs, 22 of the 25 lowest-ranking countries are in Africa.[3]

Perhaps the most revealing of the poor state of African nations is reflected in the 1996 Human Development Report by the UNDP, which announced the current state of the quality of life in the individual countries of the world. From the report released in July 1996, it became crystal-clear that African nations are also at the bottom of the totem pole of Human Development rating. The annual report, which normally charts a human development index (HDI) in which countries are ranked according to several criteria that are judged to reflect factors that enhance the quality of life in a population, included access to health care, educational standards, and basic purchasing power. The report suggested that sub-Saharan African countries, in general, present the worst situation of many of the developing countries.[4] African countries dominate the list of the eighty-nine countries who report lower per-capita incomes today than they reported ten years ago. In addition, more than two thirds of the nineteen countries listed with less income than they had in 1960 are in Africa.[5] The choice of 1960 as a measure of comparison suggests the importance the documents have for Africa. The 1960s were the period when most African countries obtained independence from colonial rule.

As a response to Africa's endemic crisis, the developed nations claimed that the Structural Adjustment Policy (SAP), spearheaded by the World Bank and the International Monetary Fund (IMF), was the magic wand that would alleviate the social and economic crisis in the post–cold war era. They encouraged the African states to put in place these policies for economic and social recovery. So far, the results have demonstrated that the policies have further demolished Africa's human value and created human suffering unprecedented in the history of the continent. SAP has created social crises such as mass unemployment, poverty, destroyed age-old social institutions that have taken care of human welfare and public services such as the educational institutions.[6] Whereas Ghana has been mentioned by some renowned economists and experts as one of the West-African countries where economic growth is likely to take place and where SAP, often forced down the throat of many African countries, has achieved a high degree of success, the UNDP report list had Ghana as one of the nineteen worst countries whose quality of life was better in its pre-independence period.

The implication for the environment was aptly stated thusly "we have seen that SAP has not only contributed massively to the decimation of the workforce in Africa but now the environment and health and safety of those in employment have come under serious attack from investors who have bought privatized industries such as mines and are out to maximize quick profit."[7] As the standard of living deteriorated rapidly, people resorted to doing anything to survive. In African townships, those who used gas and kerosene stoves to cook have resorted to cutting down trees for firewood and charcoal for cooking. As a teacher in a Nigerian university for ten years, I remember several years ago, my university instructed its faculty to start boiling regular tap water procured from the university dam. Their excuse was lack of money to buy chlorine to purify the dam's water supply. Before the end of the academic session two students died of typhoid fever, obviously caused by impure water.

The African crisis has inevitably led to another serious problem: the migration of unemployed labor from the rural areas to urban cities and the migration of skilled workers (mainly professionals) from African countries to developed countries in Europe and America for economic and political reasons. While the former has created problems associated with unplanned urban migration such as violent crimes, sexual abuse, unemployment, housing congestion, and urban poverty in general, the latter has led to refugee, immigration, and asylum problems in Europe and America.

Part of the legacy of the colonial and postcolonial misrule described above was the numerous ethnic and religious conflicts and civil wars that have plagued the continent since independence. At the present time, wars and civil strifes in Somalia, Sudan, Uganda, Rwanda, Burundi, Liberia, and Zaire have brought untold ecological problems upon these countries' populations. It is estimated that about one third of the United Nations peace-keeping soldiers are stationed in the continent. With hundreds of victims of the wars left unburied on lands and some thrown into rivers and lakes, environmental pollution of great magnitude has been left unaddressed. A case in point was the famous Lake Victoria, which for centuries served as a source of life and nourishment to humans and animals alike. Lake Victoria has been heavily polluted by the dead bodies dumped in River Kagera in Rwanda, when hundreds of Tutsis were massacred by their Hutu neighbors. As if the dumps were not enough, water hyacinths have also been spreading at a fast rate on the lake creating hazards to fishing businesses, water transport, and marine life in general. All of this has led a correspondent to describe Africa's most endowed lake as being "choked by death."[8]

While the above problem of ecological pollution and human migration may rank high in Africa's agenda, overconsumption of her resources by developed countries is equally important and indeed may impinge on the latter. It has been confirmed that the world's largest concentration of oil and gas reserves are in the developing countries. A recent World Bank report indicated that more than 90 percent of the proven oil and gas reserves are located in these countries.[9] As the world faces soaring energy consumption in the developing countries themselves, the exploitation of these resources will increase in years to come. Unfortunately lesser standards of environmental safety are applied to the exploration of oil and gas in African regions. Whereas developed countries have imposed tough environmental regulation such as low or nonpolluting technologies and cleaner fuels, such environmental policies are not mandatory in oil exploration in the developing countries. This has prompted Hussein Razari, the chief of the Oil and Gas Division in the World Bank's Industry and Energy Development, to observe, "In industrial countries, projects are designed and implemented in accordance with clear and transparent standards, but, in most developing countries, there are no standards, for the oil and gas sector."[10] He further observed that oil and gas facilities in many developing countries operate at "suboptimum standards." This causes severe damage to the local and global environment "oil spills and gas leakages which need to be cleaned up as rapidly as possible, are of particular concern."[11]

In 1995 the Nigerian military government sent to the gallows nine prominent indigenes of Ogoniland, the largest oil-producing region of the country, who were protesting the Shell BP poor management of oil exploration in their regions—clearly illustrating the enormous problem that international energy companies and investors create for small defenseless indigenous people and oil-producing African nations. In spite of the world protest against the inhumane killing of Ogoni activists, the British government, whose prime minister had declared the brutal executions "judicial murder," signed a bigger contract for oil exploration in Nigeria barely a month after the execution of Ken Saro-Wiwa and his associates. One commentator remarked after Saro-Wiwa's and others' execution that "killing the land means killing the people . . . the cycle of environmental and human degradation is driven in larger measures by over consumption in the industrialized world."[12] He further remarked that Saro-Wiwa's case in Ogoniland is a "classic illustration of how societies tend to impose the brunt of their ecological damage on the people least able to cope with it—generally, impoverished minorities. . . . Human society's dominant majority; the culture of resources consumption, is gradually driving the minorities, the endangered cultures toward extinction."[13]

NATURE OF AFRICAN RELIGIONS

So far, I have examined the African social and economic impoverishment, the colonial legacy, and postcolonial abysmal mismanagement of its human and natural resources. Next, I shall examine how traditional and modern Africans have faced and will continue to face the realities of their new world situation from the resources of their indigenous religious and thought systems. In other words, how can Africa, through its spiritual resources respond to a crisis that seems to have more telling impact on their continent than on the rest of the world.

Three reasons suggest why this exercise is important. First, it is crystal-clear that as the world community looks for solutions to several global issues (ecological crisis, overpopulation, overconsumption, AIDS epidemic, etc.), Africa is obviously at the lowest end of its scale of preference in terms of finding or gaining access to the solution to the crises. This became quite clear to me at the end to the AIDS International Conference in Canada in 1995, when several of the delegates affirmed that the solution they sought to the crisis was unaffordable to the African people. Yet it has been speculated that 10 million of the 25 million people reported to be infected with the HIV virus are in continental Africa and indeed in some African countries one out of three people are infected with the HIV virus. So, if Africa is to survive at all, it must first look at its own local resources, religious and cultural values, and thought system for solutions. That is, while Africans are encouraged to act globally and be in dialogue with the world community, they must also look inward for local indigenous communal responses to their problems. The second reason this exercise is important is that population and ecological programs and policies cannot be implemented without taking a hard look at these core values and soliciting the support of the guardians of the sacred order in African societies. Seven years ago, Nigeria decided to produce a population blueprint to guide policy on birth control and fertility. To the surprise of all, a week after the government policy was announced in the press, there was a spontaneous country-wide demonstration and protest by religious leaders (indigenous religions, Christians, and Muslims) against what they termed the state's interference in people's private religious duties. Religious leaders, who often do not see eye to eye with one another on other issues, were united to provide a common pressure on the state to drop this plan. The lesson from the incident was clear. The state suddenly discovered that population dynamics, like other social issues, involve deep-seated religious and cultural values and sentiments, which if ignored, lead to their own perils. The third reason Africa needs to look inside for its solutions takes this project beyond a mere academic exercise, to a practical purpose. The reality of the African religious identity must be taken into consideration. Though African religious resources would entail primarily the indigenous religious traditions, we should also bear in mind that the two world traditions—African Islam and African Christianity, which constitute two of Africa's triple heritage—equally shape African spiritual life and behavior today. The roles played by indigenous African Christianity and African Islam, syntheses of African traditions and tenets of the two world religions, are enormous. A sizable number of Africans have converted to these two global religions and in different combinations, the three traditions continue to have strong influence on African society. The dominant influence depends greatly on the pattern of religious demography of a place or region. For example, southern Africa, with predominantly Christian and indigenous African religion populations, would have both traditions influencing life and thoughts, whereas northern African countries, with a predominant Muslim population would have indigenous religious and Islamic traditions shaping cultural patterns and social life.

African religious traditions here will refer in a broad way to traditions, customs, mores that have sacred or transcendent reference. But primarily, they would refer to myths, beliefs, rituals, ceremonies, and symbols that touch upon the ultimate issues of existence and life in African societies. Unlike Western traditions and some Asian religions, African religions are religions of structure,[14] and they emphasize this-worldly salvation, concerned primarily with the here and now. If there is a notion of afterlife, it is one that is seen as a continuation of this world, as is reflected in the core belief of ancestor veneration whose existence and survival depends as much on events of this life as it does on the afterlife. African religions do not have canonical texts or revelations that contain their sacred beliefs. The catechism of African belief systems is their mythical stories and traditions relating to the origin and life of the community and ethnic groups. From the various myths we can discern the entire religious worldview and thought system of a particular people. They spell out how the world was created, the order of the universe, statements about the existence of evil in the world, and they contain stories about the political and economic institutions of the group. Coupled with the sacred myths are rituals and ceremonies that describe the religious practices of the group. Rituals are the most important entry points to the religious life of African communities because they are more visible than mythology. Symbols relate to myths and rituals and are concrete references that convey the deep meanings and values that groups or communities hold sacred. From all these sources, we will now construct an African "theology" of ecology, population, and consumption.

The core of African religious quest as conveyed in the religious traditions of several African peoples, is what among the Yoruba-speaking people of West Africa will be termed the threefold "blessings" or gifts (*ire*) that devotees normally pray for when they propitiate their deities (*orisa*). They are termed *ire owo, ire omo, ire alafia* (the gift of wealth, the gift of children, and the gift of good health, long life, and peace of mind). These highly metaphoric quests correspond roughly to the concerns in the modern time with life in abundance, prosperity, fertility, and growth. We shall now examine how these quests are constructed within the structure of African traditions.

ECOLOGY AND RELIGION

African religious traditions are intricately connected to the environment. In a typical African cosmos, there are three spheres or levels of creation: the sky or heaven, the world, and the earth/land (underworld). There is a link between the cosmos, the spirit world, humans, and nature. This relationship can be described as organic, harmonious, dynamic, and interdependent in character.[15] The relationship between these spheres is not in any way hierarchical, nor does one claim undue privilege or superiority over the other. The link between these spheres is the sacred energy or ritual force, which was produced at the time of creation and becomes an attribute of each sphere. Because the spheres interact very freely, one can take on the attribute of the other; the entire system is a unified whole. The root of traditional African attitude to nature lies in the philosophy of interconnectedness of the spirit world, nature, and humans. Several African cosmogonic myths illustrate this point.

The sky is where the supreme deity and the spirit agencies live, and where the creation of the world was planned before it was carried out in the sphere below. Let us illustrate this with the example of Yoruba cosmogonic myth, the most-cited creation story in Africa.

According to this sacred story, when Olorun (the sky god) the supreme being decided to create the world (*aiye*) he summoned unto his side a senior deity called Obatala (the deity of purity and molder of human body). Olorun gave Obatala the instruments of creation, a rooster, a parcel of earth, a chain, a chameleon, and *ase* (powerful magical object and the most sacred symbol of divine essence). Olodumare sent Obatala out to descend to the lower universe and create the world. On his journey to performing the act, Obatala ran into the assembly of deities who were playing and drinking palm wine. They invited him to join them, he did, and shortly after, he got drunk and fell asleep. Another deity called Oduduwa, who overheard Olorun's message, saw Obatala fast asleep, took all the materials for creation except the *ase* from Obatala. Oduduwa descended into the universe with the aid of the chain, he poured the parcel of earth on the water and placed the rooster on it. As this was done, dry land was created, vegetation was formed, animals appeared, and the world was created. The chameleon was placed on the newly created land to test its solidity. It was after this that other divinities led by Ogun, the fiery god of war, descended into the created world. But because Oduduwa could not remove the *ase* from Obatala, the ritual of creation was incomplete. When Obatala woke up, he rushed to the world to challenge Oduduwa. A great battle ensued, and the struggle almost destroyed the new world; but Olorun summoned both of them to heaven to settle it. He made Oduduwa the ruler over the world, and he became the first sacred king and the only human person who also belongs to the rank of divinities. Obatala was given the new job of fashioning human beings with clay (*amo*). So Obatala molds humans and gives them to God to breathe the breath of life into them before each human soul journeys to earth to be born and live.

This myth of creation touches on several issues that illustrate not only the sacredness of nature but the close relationship between the gods, human universe, and the biosphere. In this ritual of creation, the human world and the world of nature share the same sphere and both were endowed with God's supreme essence and vital power, *ase* or the sacred energy.

The myth illustrates that in the work of creation, both the sky deities and nature, especially animals (a rooster and chameleon), played vital roles in the creative process. The story further illustrates that in the created world, animals, plants, and humans share the same kingdom, and strong kinship relationships exist between the three. The primary element of the African social system, the lineage, clan, village, and town is the kinship system. But the kinship nexus is not limited to relationship between humans alone, it extends to animals and plants. The kinship connection derives its essence and potency from this primordial connection with the natural environment. In several African societies, individuals, lineages, villages, and towns maintain totemic kinship relationship with animals, trees, and plants. For example, as a twin (Ibeji) in Yoruba tradition, I am related to the colobus monkey (it is great taboo for twins to eat or kill this animal). As a result, twins share a common genre of oral poems, called *orin ibeji* (songs of twins) with the colobus monkey. Similar totemic relationship exist between lineage, clans, villages, and towns and other animals, plants, and trees.

The hostile attitude of modern people of the world to the environment stems from humans' appropriation of the environment as mere commodity, not endowed with the same ontological status as humans. This worldview differs significantly from the traditional African worldview. The consequence of the primordial battle between the two gods over the control of the created world was that for a moment everything came to a standstill. The Yoruba explains this potentially destructive state in terms of environmental disaster, famine, infertility, pestilence, and several deaths that were occurring in the newly created world as a result of the standoff between two powerful people: Oduduwa and Obatala. But through the intervention of the supreme being total chaos was averted. The story also indicates the interdependence between the earth and the sky, between the sustaining fertility cult of the land, signified by the people's control of the inhabited space, and the conquering power of modern technology. The Africans do not deny the possibility of potential violence and aggression to the environment; this is accepted as human reality. But there are checks and balances built into their system that ameliorate potential ecological disasters.

SPIRITS, ANIMALS, AND PLANTS

In the African cosmology, animals and plants and humans share a similar spiritual entity. The natural versus supernatural dichotomy characteristic of Western thought is avoided. It behooves humans, therefore, to relate to the other two in a manner that Martin Buber called the "I-Thou" relationship. Unlike the Genesis tradition, where humans are commanded to have dominion over nature, in African religion both humans and nature are imbued with divine essence. For several Africans, it is this spiritual essence and not just the chemical component of leaves that enables humans to use them for medicinal purposes. For example, the Yoruba refer to medicinal leaves as *ewe Osanyin* "the leaves of Osanyin," the god of herbal medicine. These leaves have identifiable names, characteristics, functions, and praise poems (*oriki*).[16] Like humans, their *oriki* are invoked and recited whenever the medicine person utilizes them for healing purposes. Geoffrey Parrinder, a historian of religion, warned scholars unfamiliar with the phenomenology of African medicinal leaves that "these beliefs are scarcely animalistic in the sense of attributing a personal soul to all beings and objects."[17]

Likewise, animals, such as we saw in Yoruba cosmogonic myth, have the divine essence similar to plants. In several West African communities, from western Sudan to the Guinea Coast, the term *Nyame* and its variants is implored to describe the vital force. Nyame may be used as a term for the strength of a god, humans, or animals, and for the mysterious potent force noticeable in medicine. According to Geoffrey Parrinder, Nyame is often conceived as "an impersonal, unconscious energy, found in humans, animals, gods, nature and things." Nyame is not "outward appearance but the inner essence" of any of these.[18] Similar beliefs about vital essence are extended to natural phenomena all over Africa. As John Mbiti remarked, "Nature Spirits are largely personifications of natural objects and forces . . . people give personal characteristics to these objects and forces of the universe, regarding them as if they were living, intelligent beings of the invisible world."[19] Though Mbiti aptly recognized the desire of Africans to regard phenomena that are seen as mere objects, things, and inorganic entities in Western societies, as living spiritual realities in African thought, yet a more proper understanding of the phenomena is to see them as hierophanies through which divine essence or power is manifested. As stated earlier, a typical African cosmos includes three interconnected spheres of creation.

The first of all of these phenomena are spirits connected with the celestial realm (the sky). The sky is the upper layer of the three-tiered universe that constitutes the cosmos in African belief systems. It is the abode of the Supreme Being, variously called names that associate him/her with the sky. The middle layer is the world of humans, animals, and trees. And the third layer, the underworld, is the abode of the ancestors, personified as earth mother goddess. The last realm is important because it harbors the dead and is also where the food that sustains people, animals, and plants that live in the second sphere comes from. In the African worldview, there is a constant interchange or communication between the three spheres. Activities within each sphere relate to the physical and social lives of the human species. From the African point of view, humans see their relationships to the inhabitants of each sphere. This understanding affects their attitude to the biosphere in general.

The sky, the uppermost sphere is the abode of the moon, stars, sun, rain, thunderstorm, wind, lightning—all of which affect the well-being of the world in significant ways. Africans pay both physical and spiritual attention to the behavior and movements of the inhabitants of the sky. Because they believe that the activities of these beings are regulated by the supreme being, they ensure that any disaffection caused to the

Supreme God would bring about problems that will have severe consequences for the biosphere below. Several African communities say that at the beginning of time, the sky was very close to the earth. The separation of the sky from the earth was caused by human errors and polluting habits. As a result of these repeated misdeeds, God withdrew from the easy reach of humans. In another version of this myth of separation, humans, especially women, were blamed for frequently touching the sky with their pestles whenever they ground grains. Out of anger, God removed the sky from the reach of humans. Yet a third version, quite common in Central Africa, says that the first humans to live on the earth set fire to the grassland, and the smoke drove God far away. This has partly given rise to the theory in African religious studies, that the Supreme God is *deus remotus*. But the morality of these stories, symbolized in environmental disasters, caused by humans, gave rise to God's disaffection and withdrawal from direct reach.

The third sphere, the earth/underworld is the habitat of the earth deity and home to the departed ancestors. In the Yoruba imagination, the Earth is referred to as a living person and his head (the ground) is regarded as the most sacred part. A poem says *"Ile afi oko yeri"* (the Earth that combs her head with a hoe), a reference to the African hoe for farm cultivation. The significance of the metaphor should not be missed. Literally it represents the act of cultivating the soil with care and tenderness, just as one shaves the head gingerly without hurting the scalp. In referring to the mysterious ability of the Earth to contain thousands of people that die daily, they say that the Earth consumes or eats people (*Ile nje eniyan*). The Earth's sacred power and moral quality can be invoked as power bond in interpersonal relations both among individuals and at the level of the community. To be trustworthy is to be loyal to the Earth. One who betrays a sacred trust is said to have betrayed the Earth (*o dale*) and the ultimate punishment is mysterious death, which is also described as perishing into the Earth (*o bale lo*). This is not a peaceful death by any means. Someone who dies peacefully may be described as bowing to the call of the Earth (*juba ale lo*). All the above go to prove that the Earth is a sacred entity whose trust is jealously guarded by the African people.

But how does this translate into a more practical attitude toward land cultivation and the modern-day attitude to the use of land? Traditional family and lineage systems were intrinsically tied to an economic production system based on land, observed Emmanuel Obiechina. Land ownership was vested in the lineage by the family, and held in trust by the most senior member. Land tenure was also ideologically based on the ancestral traditions. As he observed "land it was assumed, belonged to the ancestors, especially the founding fathers of the community. The living descendants of the ancestors, are entitled to full use of land while here on earth, but purely as custodians holding it in trust for the ancestors."[20] The African property laws forbid lands to be sold or distributed among members of the family. However, when the colonial government came, the traditional property law was disregarded and replaced by the colonialists' own native laws. It was in British Kenya that the most traumatic foreign land law was imposed with dire consequences for environmental issues and the indigenous people.[21]

This was what is often referred to as the Mau Mau rebellion by the Kikuyu people, a dominant ethnic group in Kenya, who in an armed insurrection challenged the British's unjust appropriation of their land and the abuse of indigenous ecological resources. Against the Kikuyu's notion of communal ownership of land, the British imposed private ownership of land. Considering only the individual interests of the colonial settlers and showing no regard for the Kikuyu's age-old tradition of collective ownership, the British declared a large proportion of the Kikuyu virgin land as "Crown land." The land that the Kikuyus normally cultivated was forcefully acquired by the new settlers for token money, and they were relocated to what was called "native reserves."[22] One statistic claimed that three thousand British settlers forcefully occupied land belonging to four million Africans.[23] The British inevitably introduced a new land-tenure system whereby individuals were allowed to own land permanently quite contrary to the Kikuyu's own notion of communal ownership and belief that land rights ultimately lay with Ngai, the Supreme God.[24]

The British land tenure system had serious adverse consequences for the Kikuyu. As Teresia Hinga rightly observed, the policy ignored traditional land and social values that guide land tenure. This was quite devastating for women, whose needs and rights were completely left out. By introducing individual land ownership as opposed to communal ownership, "land" became a commodity that could be acquired and resold at will. The colonial legacy inevitably led to a permanent artificial "shortage" of land in Kenya as the new land acquired by the British passed on after independence to very rich Kenyans, whose only reason for acquiring the land was for prestige and display of their wealth.[25] Meanwhile, the majority of the indigenes struggled over the limited overgrazed "native reserves." The Mau Mau popular uprising between 1952 and 1954 led to several deaths.[26] The Kenya nationalist Jomo Kenyatta accused of taking part in the revolt, was sentenced to seven years' imprisonment.[27]

If we think that the attitude of foreign settlers to land acquisition ended with the demise of colonial rule, the case of modern Mozambique will demonstrate the contrary. Recently, the World Service[28] reported a new "Boer trek" from South Africa, whereby Afrikaner farmers, losing their privileged position in post-apartheid South Africa are moving in large numbers to the neighboring state of Mozambique. They are taking advantage of the poverty level of the indigenes to buy large areas of land for a new settlement for themselves. The Mozambique government, pressed for hard currency in a postwar period, continues to give its support to the new Afrikaner immigrants to dispossess their own people of their physical, and therefore their spiritual, security. It is predicted that before the end of the twentieth century, more than 20 percent of Mozambique's land will have been taken over by the immigrants, possibly resulting in a new form of apartheid, and inevitably a repeat of the South African experience in the new Republic of Mozambique.

RITUALS OF ECOLOGICAL PRESERVATION

As I argued at the beginning of this chapter, the domain of rituals and ceremonies is the most significant entry point to the transcendent and the sacred in African religions. In like manner, rituals and ceremonies such as festivals address significant ecological matters in African communities. Here, I will focus on two types of ecological rituals found in several African communities in sub-Saharan Africa: first fruit or harvest and rainmaking rituals. My central focus will be to demonstrate the ecological import of these rituals, that is, how the indigenous people use ritual resources to regulate the environment and also how the ritualization of ecology provides a key clue to Africans' attitude to the environment.

Most West African ethnic communities celebrate the new-year festival to mark the beginning of harvest season. In the ritual festival of Iro Mmuo of the Igbo people of Nigeria,[29] performed annually in September–October, the community gathers to offer their appreciation to the gods for the year's bounty harvest. In a rite called "the pleasing of the gods," offerings and sacrifice are made to the ancestral spirits of the village (Ndebunze). After each household has offered its own sacrifices at the shrine of the lineage's ancestral spirit, the entire village assembles at the village square for a joint prayer to the village deities. The focus of this are *Chuku*, the Supreme God; *Ala*, the earth goddess; and *Ndebunze*, the ancestral spirit. In their prayer request, the people will pray for good harvests, increase in children, deliverance from epidemics and from abomination of any kind that could cause the wrath of the gods and ancestral spirits.[30]

A close examination of this ritual would show that in a single festival the Igbo demonstrate their communal, rather than individual, response to environmental and fertility matters. We also notice that the spiritual agencies in the three-tiered universe (sky, earth, and the underworld) are collectively propitiated. Whenever there is a sign of low productivity in farm yields or in periods of epidemics, the Igbo community asks the diviner to detect "what had spoiled the land."[31] If it is due to a communal sin, a ceremony of cleansing is arranged. In this cleansing ritual of a polluted space, the responsibility that individuals and community share in ensuring that the land is sacred and kept "pure" is fully demonstrated. Since individuals' misdeeds are linked to communal sufferings, Africans are able collectively to respond to these problems in very dramatic ways.

Territorial cults play important roles in environmental regulation in Africa.[32] Such a territorial cult in Malawi in Central Africa is the Chisumphi cult of the Chewa people. It is headed by a priestess known as "spirit wife" and guardian of the land. She officiates in the shrines to make regular propitiations to regulate the ecological order. The spirit wife controls the environment in two ways: she presides over the annual "rain-calling" and first-fruit thanking rituals, and she takes charge of the natural resources around the shrine. The annual rain-calling ceremony is particularly revealing in its relationship to environmental control. In this ritual, the priestess wears a dark cloth symbolizing dark clouds. She is accompanied first by young girls who assemble in the priestess's hut where their faces are painted with powdered charcoal and dotted with paste made from maize flour, thus symbolizing rain drops from the dark cloud. One of the girls carries a clean pot containing porridge also made from flour, while a second girl carries a clay pot of water; the former symbolizes food while the latter symbolizes the desired water for sustaining human and agricultural life. Both of course represent the "purity" of land, without which the sky god would keep the rain from falling. The girls at the cult shrine sweep the place clean of impurity, removing vestiges of the old, undesirable order causing drought, and they offer a sacrifice of porridge at the shrine. Once the ritual is complete, they proceed to their houses singing in anticipation of rain. However, whenever the same community witnesses too much rain, the roof of the Chisumphu shrine is opened to let in light. They also remove grass from the thatched roof symbolizing the removal of the dark rain layer, and the chasing away of the deadly rain cloud. By ritualizing the ecology and raising the ontological status of ecological features and natural resources to the supernatural realm, Africans implicitly demonstrate nature's significance to be preserved, maintained, and not desecrated. Whenever desecration of the earth/land occurs, traditional Africans pay very dearly for its refurbishment and rejuvenation as the Igbo's and Chewa's rituals clearly show us.

If the Mau Mau revolt I referred to earlier describes Africa's encounter with and response to ecological crisis caused by foreign colonialists, independence did not assure them of environmental protection. As Africa obtained independence in the 1960s, African fiction writers, in their imaginative and prophetic utterances, employed powerful images of ecological disasters to warn their new nations of inevitable crises ahead, especially disasters of drought, famine, and epidemics. But rather than prescribing quick technological breakthroughs, and rapid industrialization, which they knew were still out of reach for most states, they appealed to the power of tradition to counter disruptive forces on the ecology. Katungulwa Mbitana, a Zambian fiction writer, told a very informative story:

> The earth was hardened and crops began to wither and there was immense famine. Jimo described as a man of "great physical strength" came forward to make rain. He prepared his medicine, in a clay pot filled with water, he then chanted an incantation prayer.
>
> The people who gathered for the rainmaking ritual joined the rainmaker to ask the "Rain Spirit" to descend upon them in torrents.
>
> The rituals involve emploring, commanding, and teasing the cloud. His prayer spell also included casting benevolent curses on those who defy or do not trust in the power of the spirits of the cloud, that is, those who have abandoned believing in the significance of their traditional spirituality because of the enlightenment mentality and modernity acquired through [a] few years of learning in Europe and America. Jimo invoked the spirit to punish these sceptics and prove them wrong by sending down the rain.[33]

The result of the rain ritual, the writer informed us, was that for several nights and days there was torrential rain and the people rejoiced thereafter, though lightning struck dead the rainmaker's wife.

This story captures the reality of African nature spirituality. Not only are the forces personified, they also regulate the rhythm of life. The human-nature relationship is maintained with care and caution. It demonstrates the ambivalent attitude of modern Africans to the spiritual resources within a traditional system to regulate their ecological life. It also shows personal and communal risk involved in environmental protection. Just as Jimo lost his wife in the act of rainmaking rituals, several indigenous peoples have suffered and paid the supreme price for caring for the environment or altering the natural rhythm of nature, even when it is for the benefit of their community.

AFRICAN SPIRITUALITY AND POPULATION DYNAMICS

Two recently explosive problems seem to have complicated Africa's population crisis: old age and migration crises. First, the changing phase of Africa's family structure is the increasing number of problems associated with old age and the care of the elderly. In the traditional setup, getting old was seen as a blessing and a great opportunity to return to the bosom of the family to be cared for and remain till death. As more and more people moved from the villages to the cities in search of employment, and they migrated to places beyond the boundaries of the villages and towns, increasingly the elderly were neglected. Unfortunately, because of this traditional system of caring, no governmental social program is in place to fall back on and remedy the situation. As a Nigerian medical doctor, Yemi Peters, recently noted, "We like to think of people caring for everyone within the family. Although that may have been universally true—and still holds true in most instances—that caring was not always spontaneous. It was a person's duty."[34] He also rightly observed that some of the children were often bullied into caring for their relatives by elderly people in the village. "Nowadays a sense of duty is not one of the social values encouraged by Nigerian Society . . . and our elders are losing out."[35] To back up the current crisis of the neglect of the elderly, it was reported that Lagos city with a population of 6 million people has two old people's homes, providing a mere thirty-two places meant for strictly destitute elderly. There are only thirteen homes serving the entire Nigerian population of over 95 million.[36]

The Nigerian case reflects what is going on across Africa. The depressed state of the economy has meant that only few children will be able to provide for their parents. As able-bodied men and women migrate in large numbers from the village to the townships and cities, and a number of these people face economic and political hardships, emigration to America and the countries of Europe is seen as a viable option and increasingly this is risked. Several of those who emigrate seek asylum in their host countries. So, in an indirect way, population increases have inevitably led to international crises of refugees, asylum seekers, hostile anti-immigration laws, and policies currently in vogue in developed countries. Asylum laws, which in the past have protected African refugees fleeing from political persecutions at home, have been so modified to make it impossible to seek shelter in European countries. A clear case was Britain whose Home Office recently promulgated draconian laws to send refugees back to their native countries. It created a "white list in which a country like Nigeria was described as having a high level of political freedom, a fair judicial system and a general absence of ethnic or other descrimination,"[37] when only a year before, the prime minister of the same Britain had condemned Nigeria's human-rights record and the execution of Ogoni activists, and the pollution of its environment. The lesson from the above examples is that population dynamics inevitably lead to political and racial tensions and are indeed a serious issue in Africa and beyond.

Given the above scenario, how then does Africa respond to the problem of population increase and all the attending issues like women's reproductive health and care of the elderly? How do the African belief system and cultural values take up the above challenge? As I observed in my introduction to this chapter, one of the central concerns of African religious quests is procreation, to have many children, to "protect and strengthen" human life, both for individuals and the community as a whole, and to attain long life and immortality (*ire aiku*), whereby after an elder's physical death, through ancestorhood, he continues to "live" in the spirit world. Death in infancy is viewed as evil because it is an unfulfilled life, and disease and ill heath are viewed as unnatural, to be combatted both physically and spiritually. It is assumed that by keeping to the moral rules of the lineage and ancestors and propitiating the deities regularly, these problems, diseases, and social tensions will be kept at bay and thus guarantee individuals a good life.

Certain diseases and epidemics such as small pox, ebola, and now AIDS are major concerns for Africans because of the ability of these diseases to wipe out a large segment of the community within a short period of time and thus disrupting the flow of life. As a response to the high rate of infant mortality, a number of rituals are directed at every stage of a child's growth to ensure peaceful passage from one stage to the other. These include rituals around birth, menstruation, circumcision, and adulthood, which are performed to accomplish this purpose and prevent sudden death of the individuals during difficult moments.

FERTILITY, MARRIAGE, AND POPULATION CONTROL

African religion is basically pronatal. Marriage in traditional African systems is an important aspect of African social and cultural life. Prolonged bachelorhood is frowned upon and women who do not marry to bear children are accorded less respect than married mothers in the society. Even in the contemporary period, where marriage is fast becoming a personal choice, childlessness is still frowned upon. The reason for this is the African view of humanity. As John Mbiti observed, marriage and the raising of families are viewed as profound religious duties.[38] To be unmarried and childless is regarded "as stopping the flow of life . . . and hence the diminishing of mankind upon earth."[39] A Yoruba song that we learned to sing in my high school confirms the importance of children to the lineage

> If we own twenty slaves,
> sooner or later the slaves will buy their freedom
> If we have several pawns,
> sooner or later the pawns will return to their homes
> But one's children remain with us, they
> are the successors in our homes whenever we die.

This powerful lyric indicates that children are highly prized, valued much more than slaves and pawns because of their significance to the lineage. In traditional African societies, while slaves and pawns may buy their freedom, children remain in the lineage's heritage forever.

Procreation, therefore, is seen as a way of immortalizing the lineage and its values, and hence it is very much linked to the success of marriage. From the time a woman becomes pregnant to delivery, the lineage and community will take every precaution to ensure that the body of mother and child are healthy and their delivery is problem free. Whenever pregnancy occurs, the family, lineage, and village rejoice because it signals the addition of a new member of the community. It is a family affair, not just that of the individual. I was struck when Lady Diana of Britain observed that when she was pregnant with Prince William she felt that all of Britain was carrying the child with her. In African communities this is not just the privilege of the royals, the pregnancy of any village woman has special significance for the community. In addition to keeping special taboos during pregnancy, to ensure the delivery of a healthy baby, a pregnant woman may also be made to wear certain prophylactic charms and armlets of magical substance to ensure that the pregnancy does not abort prematurely. As Mbiti also observed, "great shame falls on anyone who shows no respect to a pregnant woman, who beats her, or does anything harmful to her, whether by word or deed. She carries two lives, and these lives deserve double consideration and care."[40]

The living have an obligation to the departed ancestors, who are regarded as the living dead, to ensure that the tree of life is not broken by individuals through their choice to be childless. "Marriage is regarded as the meeting point for the three layers of human life in African communities, the departed, the living, and those to be born."[41] As a result of this, human procreation is very much a social and religious obligation of individuals, a duty they owe the living and the ancestors.

African marriage systems are complex and very much unlike marriage in Western societies. Polygamy, an important form of marriage, is almost identified with African culture and society. It also remains the most misunderstood aspect of African social institutions. While one does not deny the importance of power relations and its implication to gender relations in this traditional African marriage arrangement, since it generally means that men dominate the social life of the group, from the African perspective, polygamy certainly is closely linked to the emphasis the culture places on procreation. Through polygamy, first of all, an individual or lineage produces lots of children for economic and social purposes. Economically, it provides a large labor force in a farming peasant community that overwhelmingly depends on subsistence agriculture as their main livelihood. Second, polygamy ensures that in spite of the high mortality rate of African children, children are still left to transmit the family and lineage values to the next generation.[42] An Akan proverb says

> Do not let me die in the day (blindness)
> Do not let me die at night (impotency)
> Do not let me die at all (childlessness).

Third, polygamy in traditional Africa symbolizes prestige, affluence, and an indication of wealth. While polygamy is fast disappearing in modern Africa due to Western Christian influences and economic reality, which make it too expensive to maintain, the love for large families is still very common.

The above exposé is an attempt to show why large populations, characterized by high fertility and an uncontrolled birth rate, have characterized African societies. However, in spite of the great demand and love for children in African culture, there is also an equally compelling argument and caution against unplanned families, especially when it becomes evident that they breed poverty and ill health. Most African communities have indigenous family-planning systems, whereby they control childbirth. Because it is assumed that Western contraceptives were the first mode of fertility control introduced into Africa, the indigenous method of birth control has not been examined. In their traditions, the Kikuyu people of Kenya often say many births mean many burials (*maciara mainigi ni mbirira nyingi*)[43] to indicate the sadness that would likely occur in homes where too many children are born since it is almost obvious that there would be infant death. The Yoruba suggest that many births lead to abject poverty of the family (*omo bere, osi bere*). Though the Yoruba regard death at childhood as evil, they also suggest that it is better to die in infancy with honor than to grow old to a life of poverty and neglect (*ki a ku lomode, sanju ka dagba ka tosi*). Though it would appear that preference for more children outweighs the African's concern for controlled population, the reason can be located in their life-affirming worldview.

OVERCONSUMPTION

Consumption and consumerism, the third angle on which we are focus-ing should be seen in the larger context of poverty, wealth, and pros-perity in African culture and society. At face value, the theme of over-consumption may appear irrelevant to the African situation given the fact that several of the issues we raised earlier in this chapter focus on Africa's impoverished and disadvantaged position in juxtaposition to the life of abundance in the developed world. But if Africa portrays sto-ries of impoverishment, it also harbors some of the worst cases of over-consumption, greed, and selfish display of wealth in the world, espe-cially from the angle of the new elite and the postcolonial neocapitalist structure aided and abetted by foreign interests. I shall examine this sit-uation and prescribe Africa's indigenous response to the problem.

Overconsumption should be examined at two levels: internal and external. At the internal level is the African newly rich who have taken advantage of the weak economic system left by the colonial government at the time of independence to enrich themselves. Virtually on a regu-lar basis, there are stories in the media of corruption and the missing millions from the national treasuries of African governments, often ending up in the foreign bank accounts of influential people. The ill-gotten wealth is now openly displayed by these people before the poor to demonstrate the power that their riches have suddenly given them. The creation of an African bourgeoisie in postcolonial Africa was made possible partly by the easy access these African elites have to public assets. This has led to a class war between the "haves" and the "have nots." The results of this is that violent crimes such as armed robbery, and ethnic and religious conflicts, such as the Maitasine riot in north-ern Nigeria, have increased, while money has now become the natural idol of worship and traditional values that cast aspersion at wanton-ness are easily forgotten. Externally, it is important to see how much of the global virus of consumerism has affected African countries and African social institutions. The second angle from which to view this problem is the national expenditure on arms. As a large number of African countries came under military dictatorship after independence, a sizable amount of their natural resources are spent on defense and military hardware even in time of peace. One South African magazine portrays the problem of military expenditure in a cartoon that states one military tank equals equipment for 520 classrooms and one jet fighter will produce forty thousand village pharmacies (dispensaries).[44] While a sizable proportion of the national revenues are spent on defense and national security, a large number of their citizens go with-out adequate food. In the summer of 1996, while in Nigeria, I was informed by a primary school teacher that when a local nurse sent to her school to inoculate the children asked a pupil if he had breakfast that morning, the pupil's response was that it was not his turn to eat breakfast. It was an indication that in this family of six children they take turns eating.

At the basis of this crisis is the change in the fundamental African ethos and value of group and collective solidarity in preference to individual interests. Increasingly with large movements of people to urban centers and cities, there is a weakening of the collective bond of kinship. A Yoruba proverb portrays this new modern outlook thusly: *ko si alajobi mo, alajogbe lo ku* (There is no longer the tie of kinship, what is left is the tie of neighborhood). The latter symbolizes that neighbors who barely know each other in urban cultures have no compulsive reason to be close since they are not kin. In another context, Chinua Achebe, the author of the widely acclaimed novel *Things Fall Apart*, depicted the importance of the bond of kinship in traditional Igbo society and the impact on wealth and poverty in a story plot: At the great feast to celebrate the departure of Okonkwo, the hero of the novel from his maternal village Mbata, his uncle said the following prayer to bid him farewell:

> We do not ask for wealth
> because he that has health
> and children will have wealth
> We do not pray to have
> more money but to have
> more kinsmen.[45]

In traditional African communities, where kinsmen and kinswomen form the core of individual and collective relationship in the community, habits of personal aggrandizement, selfishness, and consumerism tended to be less pronounced. As Emmanuel Obiechina remarked, individual achievements are "related to the well-being of the whole community; there is little room for fame's sake and achievement for achievement's sake; there is little room for purely egotistic calculation as social philosophy."[46] When this is translated into social action or public policy, traditional Africans were able to maintain a collective response to issues and problems that affect the community. Nowadays we see the poverty of many people in the midst of plenty owned by very few. In disparaging societies and communities where the above situation seems to be the norm rather than the exception, the Yoruba of Nigeria would simply say *Igba talaka, olowo kan*, one rich person in the sea of two hundred poor people.

CONCLUSION

I have outlined some aspects of African indigenous thought and ritual activities that can guide humanity and shape public debate on population, ecology, and consumerism. While African religions do have a number of important virtues that will support ecological balance and population control, there are a few unresolved and contested issues that will continue to reappear in the public discourse.

NOTES

1. "Editorial," *South Africa Outlook* [Cape Town Ecological Group] 119.1411 (Jan. 1988): 2.

2. *United Nations Development Program Report*, UN document, 1994, p. 1. The report suggests that even though $935 billion has been saved through cuts in military expenditure, the world still spent $767 billion for weapons alone in that year.

3. Ibid.

4. David Usborne, "358 Billionaires Who Own Half of the World," *The Independent* (London), 16 July 1996, p. 7.

5. Ibid.

6. SAP, *West Africa*, 16–22 January 1995, p. xxx.

7. Ibid.

8. *BBC Focus on Africa* 6.1 (Jan.–March 1995): 14. The article also mentioned that there are speculations as to the origin of the water hyacinths. One suggests that the British brought it from the Amazon region in South America during the colonial period because of the attractions they had for "these beautiful flowers."

9. Hossein Razari, "Financing Oil and Gas Projects in Developing Countries, *Finance and Development* 3.2 (June 1996): 3.

10. Ibid., p. 2

11. Ibid., p. 3

12. Aaron Sachs, "Dying For Oil," *World Watch* 9.3 (1996): 12–13.

13. Ibid.

14. Evan Zuesse, "African Religions, Mythic Themes," *Encyclopedia of Religions*, ed. Mircea Eliade (New York: Macmillan), pp. 70–80.

15. Leonard Barret, "African Religions in the Americas: The Island in Between," in *African Religions: A Symposium*, ed. Nowell S. Booth (New York: NOK Publishers, 1977), p. 185.

16. For a more detailed treatment of the meaning and function of *oriki*, see Karen Barber, *I Could Speak until Tomorrow* (Washington, D.C.: Smithsonian Institution Press, 1990).

17. Geoffrey Parrinder, *African Tradition Religion* (London: Sheldon Press, 1968), p. 72.

18. Ibid., p. 21.

19. John Mbiti, *Introduction to African Religion* (New York: Heinemann, 1991), p. 66.

20. Emmanuel Obiechina, *Culture, Tradition and Society in West African Novels* (Cambridge: Cambridge University Press, 1975).

21. Teresia Hinga, "The Gikuyu Theology of Land and Environmental Justice," in *Women Healing Earth*, ed. Rosemary Ruether (Maryknoll, N.Y.: Orbis Books, 1996), p. 172. See also T. M. Kanogo's excellent book *Squatters and Roots of Mau Mau* (London: James Currey, 1987).

22. Claude Wauthier, *The Literature and Thought of Modern Africa*, trans. Shirley Kay (London: Heinemann Educational, 1978), p. 138.

23. Teresia Hinga, "Gikuyu Theology," p. 172.

24. Ibid.

25. Ibid.

26. More than 12,590 Kikuyus and 58 Europeans died. See Claude Wauthier, p. 139.

27. Elizabeth Isichei, *A History of Christianity in Africa: From Antiquity to the Present* (Grand Rapids, Mich.: W. B. Eerdmans, 1995), p. 259.

28. BBC News Broadcast, London, 20 September 1995.

29. My summary of this festival follows Edmund Ilogu's account of Iro Mmuo, and Ikpu Ala ceremonies in his essay "The Land Is Sacred," in *Traditional Religion in West Africa*, ed. E. A. Adegbola (Ibadan: Daystan Press, 1983), p. 138.

30. Ibid.

31. Ibid.

32. See the works of J. M. Schoffeleers, ed., *Guardian of the Land* (Gwelo: Mambo Press, 1979); Isabel Apawo Phiri, "The Chisumphi Cult: The Role of Women in Preserving the Environment," *Women Healing Earth*, ed. Ruether, pp. 161–71. My description of the Chisumph cult follows Phiri's account.

33. Mufalo Liswanso, ed., *Voices of Zambia* (Lusaka, Zambia: NECZam Press, 1971), p. 5.

34. Elizabeth Obadina, "Ageing," *The New Internationalist* 264 (Feb. 1995): 16–17.

35. Ibid.

36. Ibid., p. 17.

37. *The Economist*, 9 December 1995, p. 16.

38. Mbiti, *Introduction to African Religions*, p. 98.

39. Ibid.

40. Ibid., p. 184.

41. Ibid., p. 98.

42. Kofi Appiah-Kubi, 'The Akan Concept of Human Personality," in Adegbola, *West African Religions*, p. 261.

43. G. Barra, *Kikuyu Proverbs* (Nairobi, Kenya: Kenya Literature Bureau, 1939), p. 44.

44. "Ecology in Crisis," *South African Outlook*, January 1989, pp. 5, 10.

45. Chinua Achebe, *Things Fall Apart* (London, Heinemann, 1958), p. 146.

46. Obiechina, *Culture, Tradition and Society in the West African Novel*.

CHAPTER 13

Conclusion:
An Interreligious Common Front
and Common Hope

Paul F. Knitter

My assignment in this final chapter is to try to knit together common themes and insights from the previous essays and then to suggest what our project might mean for the future. I dare to begin this assignment with what sounds like a gross exaggeration: This book, in the experience and process that it embodies, represents a newly won hope not only for the community of religions but also for the community of nations—I trust that there is more reality than hyperbole in that statement.

The experience and the process that have given birth to this book are as simple as they are profound: a group of extraordinarily diverse people were called together by the pain and problems of our world, and in responding, they discovered that they had formed a new community among each other. The *anguish* of the earth summoned *diversity* and fashioned out of it *community*. More concretely: when two of the most evident and perduring realities of our contemporary global experience—widespread *human and environmental suffering* and *religious diversity*—were mixed in this project, they yielded a new kind of *cooperative community*. If the results of this experiment can be repeated in other contexts and with other diversities, there's hope on the horizon.

In these concluding pages I'd like to explain how all this happened, and why it is a source of hope. The dynamic that took shape, naturally and spontaneously, in the presentations and discussions during our two meetings can be summarized in three movements:

1. We experienced a common *call* that produced in us a shared *response*.

201

2. In so responding, we found ourselves agreeing on a common *analysis* of the problems and suffering that had called us.

3. In our shared response and analyses, we realized that we were a *community* that must stay together and *act together* in the future.

Let me try to describe each of these movements.

A COMMON CALL

A more complexly diversified group would be hard to find. There we were, assembled for the first time in Victoria, British Colombia, in October 1994, eight women and seven men, representing nine different religious traditions, nine ethnic worlds, eight different mother tongues (we conversed, however, in English), and a mild spread of socioeconomic backgrounds from upper middle class to lower middle class. The one common color marking us all was our academic professions or background; but especially in this first meeting in Victoria, our academic training and commitments seemed to sharpen, rather than soften, our religious, ethnic, and gender differences. What drew us together—besides the organizational initiative of the Centre for Studies in Religion and Society, the Religious Consultation on Population, Reproductive Health and Ethics, and the financial support of the Ford Foundation—was our individual concerns about "population, consumption, and ecology," the theme of our project. *This, you might say, was the "central organizing principle" for our coming together:* we were all worried, worried about what was going on in our world and how economic injustice and population growth were threatening not only human life but the life-sustaining capacity of the planet. This project, we were individually assured, was not to be another recondite round of interreligious dialogue; rather, it was to be an interreligious assessment of the mess that humans have created for each other and for the planet. We came together not because we wanted to expand our religious horizons, but because we wanted to feed the hungry, stop violence, save the ozone layer.

Yet these shared concerns did not minimize or sugar-coat our differences. Indeed, during our first sessions there seemed often to be an undertow of resolve, especially on the part of the "minority" religions or ethnicities, to protect their identity and not to be seduced into any grandiose schemes intended for the welfare of all but engineered by the power of the few. Though our shared concerns for the environment gave us a sense of common purpose, we hesitated to step forward shoulder to shoulder. This wariness was nurtured by our shared postmodern awareness of how universal projects tend to shred diverse identities; some of us represented traditions—indigenous religions and Muslims under colonialism, Jews under the Holocaust—that had been so shredded. So while we danced together in this first session, it was usually at arm's length.

But we did dance. We came to know each other, not just as open-minded, sincere (sometimes naive) people, but as persons concerned about the plight of our world. And more importantly, we listened and looked together; we opened our minds and hearts to the reports of experts on the state of the world. We studied, together, more intently the realities of overpopulation, consumption, and environmental devastation. Then we were all sent home to ponder and perhaps pray over these realities, and explore our traditions to see what might be their response, their message of hope or salvation for a so suffering earth.

When we reassembled in Freeport, Maine, in August of 1996 to listen to and evaluate the responses that each of us had prepared in the name of her/his tradition, when we witnessed and felt the depth of concern and the richness of response that each of us was trying to communicate—then, something different started to vibrate between us. *The power of our "central organizing principle"—the earth and its travails—was indeed working.* The undertow of wariness that had kept us at arm's length was giving way to a common tug, a pull, that was nudging us all in the same direction. It was a pull that came from the same source, not from an expressly religious source, but from the heart-wrenching, stomach-turning, shuddering specter of human and ecological suffering that had been presented to us by the experts and our common readings. This pain and suffering had somehow seeped through our religious and ethnic differences and touched a common chord that sounded in all of us.

We found ourselves gasping together, drawing up our resolve together. This was especially the case when those within our group spoke of their own, or their people's, pain, and so concretized and personalized the hard facts of the experts' reports and graphs. When Jacob Olupona spoke calmly but anguishedly of past and present horrors of colonialism for Africans, when Alberto Múnera gave voice to how South Americans feel about being the "backyard" of their powerful northern neighbors, when the women in our group spoke honestly to the men of how patriarchy invades and infects every corner of their lives—we were *all* moved by the same feelings of compassion and responsibility. Compassion connected us to the victims and to each other; responsibility called us to action, to do something.

But something else gradually became evident in these shared feelings. These common reactions of concern and responsibility, triggered by the specter of eco-human suffering, were arising in each of us not just from our common humanity, but also from our individual, very different *religious identities*. We were responding not just because of our human *nature*, but also because of our religious *nurture*! Our hearts were sensitive and responsive to this suffering because they were Hindu, Buddhist, Taoist, Jewish, Christian, Muslim, Native American, and African hearts. Thus, the pain of the world, we were realizing, not only seeped through our religious differences to touch us all in the same way; this pain also stirred our distinct differences and, as it were, put them in a common sympathetic vibration to the world's pain. Despite our religious differences, therefore, there was a diversified, yet common religious reaction to the problems of population, consumption, and ecology.

That all of us were reacting to these problems and pains *as religious persons* and out of (not beyond) our different religious traditions was evident in the way each of us wanted to show the others why and how our tradition *did* have a response to these crises. *Each of us felt, in very different ways, that her/his religious tradition could provide both resources and motivation for dealing with the common specter of eco-human suffering—and that the sharing of these distinct resources and motivations would help us all!* Christians, for example, wanted to show Buddhists why as "good Christians" they must respond, and do have a response, to the pain of poverty. This didn't mean that the Christians, or any of us, had ready answers, simply to be drawn from the database of our historical teachings. As Rita Gross reminded us: "The question is not what *has* Buddhism said about ecology and the environment, but what *could* Buddhism have to say about these subjects." We were realistic, recognizing both that our *individual religious communities* did not have ready-made, follow-the-directions answers for the eco-human problems the world is facing; nor did *all of our communities* have a common program that would empower an interreligious response. Still, what we were feeling together was that *it was possible* to discover or fashion both our individual responses and our common interreligious front.

As I look back on what we were experiencing together, I think the best way to describe it was in terms of a "common call." Yes, I know the language and imagery is Western; still, I think it fits the sense we had of being challenged, beckoned, enabled to do something together as we faced the pain of our species and of the planet. There was no one way of talking about what we felt or where it came from. As Laurie Zoloth put it, we had to fashion, together, "a new language for this discourse."

One of the images that elicited a "yes, that's it" in just about all of us was suggested by Chün-fang Yü when she referred to how Mencius described the spontaneous feeling that most humans sense when, for instance, "they see a child about to fall into a well"; they feel "the mind that cannot bear to see the suffering of others" (Mencius 2A.6). It was this common mind that we were all feeling and responding to. Another image that expresses this same experience was offered centuries later by Wang Yang-ming when he observed that when we feel this "mind" that cannot bear the impending suffering of a child (or, he added, "the suffering of birds and animals about to be slaughtered, plants broken and destroyed, tiles and stones shattered and crushed"), we become aware that we indeed form "one body with the child" and with the animals and elements of the earth. We bear a "humanity that forms one body with all." We were, all of us, commonly sensing this one mind and one body as we looked at the sufferings of the earth.

Another image that for most of us (though not all) harmonized with this sense of a common call was "Jewishly derived" and proposed by Zoloth: We are all on a *Galut* together. Here we have an image that is "metaphorically applicable to all people: the notion of an overreaching, existential Exile, a *Galut*, a journey in the world in which we are all in a difficult diasporic condition that demands terrible obligation from each one of us to the community of sojourners and strangers of which we are a part." All of us, despite our religious differences, felt part of one-community-in-exile, in search of a way to come home to our home.

From my own Christian experience and theological background, I felt that what we were all experiencing as "a call" could also be described, and further understood, by what the Christian theologian Edward Schillebeeckx calls "negative experiences of contrast." By this he points to what he thinks is a universally verifiable phenomenon in all cultures: when faced with the specter of suffering due to human neglect, malice, exploitation—such as is found in the face of a starving child or in a polluted stream—many if not most (which doesn't mean all) human beings react to such experiences of contrast with a resounding sense or cry of "No!" It is an explosive, intruding sense of being called to resist, to assist, to do something. The "no," as Schillebeeckx goes on to describe, leads therefore to some kind of "yes" to the action or effort necessary to relieve such suffering. The no of resistance leads to the yes of action, which is grounded in the gifted sense of hope that indeed it is possible to resist and assist. With Schillebeeckx I would want to ask my religious brothers and sisters from other traditions whether we can call such experiences "religious" or at least "prereligious." In such shared "negative experiences of contrast" we are touching, or being touched by, that which is at the depths or in the heart of each of our very different religious traditions.[1] In the old-fashioned language of my Roman Catholic tradition, we are indirectly but truly sharing in "a communion in the Sacred" (*communicatio in sacris*). The "common call" is the voice of the Sacred appealing to us in the pain resulting from overpopulation, overconsumption, and environmental destruction.

A COMMON ANALYSIS

In sensing what I am terming a "common call," in trying to figure out what it would mean to respond to this call, in seeking to formulate a "yes" of action after we had all felt a shared "no" of resistance, we also realized that we were slipping, not down the slippery slopes of relativism, but toward a *consensus* regarding what are some of the root causes of the earth's eco-human suffering. Again, despite our religious differences, we found ourselves in essential agreement on an *analysis* of what's wrong with and what needs to be done for our ailing planet and species. This was not an analysis that we intended to fashion, but one that, as it were, took shape as we saw in each other's eyes the sparkle of insight or assent. We found ourselves in fundamental agreement on both a "*micro*" and a "*macro*" analysis, that is, on basic malfunctions or mistakes in the way humans understand themselves as *individuals* and as *societies*.

The Micro-Analysis: Problems with the Self

Harold Coward's presentation, both in the simplicity of its case and in the way it touched responsive chords in all of our traditions, served as a lens through which we began to focus our common analysis. In our efforts to tag and then comprehend whatever it is that moves, or allows, some people to cause so much pain for other people and other living beings, Coward helped us formulate what most of us already knew or sensed: it has to do with a notion, we would call it an aberrant notion, of what it means to be a human being. People are simply wrong about who they are and what makes for their real, lasting, well-being. They allow their "individuality" to get in the way of their "commonality." Or, in Coward's terms, they make their "I-self" more important than their "we-self." Because people are, or have been, deceived about who they really are, they act in false and therefore destructive ways. They try to affirm and realize their individual I-self before they realize and live out their communal we-selves. Here's the problem that we all jointly recognized. In Coward's words: we need to recover "our collective sense of self-identity"; this is "essential for an ethical analysis of the population-consumption-ecology problematic."

Agreement that we must recover our "collective sense of self-identity" led us to agreement on further particulars. Especially for cultures and nations of the West (or North), it means that the "human rights" of the individual must be better balanced with the "human obligations" the individual has toward the entire life-community of the earth. Private property and private rights are not sacrosanct; precious as they are, they do not have the last word or veto power over the rights and needs of others; they must be ready to yield to the obligations and bonds we have toward each other. Coward made a statement that we could endorse multireligiously: "Identity is in one's harmonious interrelationships, not in one's choices/rights, powers and privileges." It seemed that all our religious communities, with differing philosophical or theological rationales, could agree that our deeper, or true, or enlightened identity is to be found primarily not in our individual, distinct identities but in our connectedness and participation with others. We are not, as we are often told, innately selfish and therefore in need of a socioeconomic system that will both affirm and control that selfishness. As Rita Gross put it: "to be consumed by *trishna* [greed] is not human nature, not our inevitable lot or inescapable original sin." A popular bumper-sticker is therefore wrong: For humans "to be" is not "to shop." It is "to share."

From this shared micro-analysis of the human being's aberrant and cancerous sense of self, we moved naturally to a shared recognition of what must be one of religion's primary roles in confronting the crises of overpopulation, overconsumption, and abuse of the ecosystem. Religions have it within themselves—that is, within their teachings and sense of purpose—to change, or transform, the way people feel about themselves, which will lead to a transformation in the way they feel about others. One of the urgent and decisive contributions that religions can make to the global crisis is therefore *mystical:* the task of inner, spiritual, personal transformation. In this transformation, in this experience of conversion or enlightenment or new vision, the person realizes to the depths of his/her being and feeling that one's self is an inclusive self, a self that has its being through participation, a self that can and must love others as much as one loves one's self. All religions, in vastly different ways, can provide the challenge and the *motivating power* by which individual self-consciousness is thus transformed. The women in our group reminded us men that such an "inclusive self" will be, and must be, understood and realized differently by inflated male egos than by deflated female egos; for many women, an inclusive self has been an imprisoned self.

Still, there was general agreement among us that without a transformation of how each person feels about him/herself, without some kind of a mystical realization of our profound connectedness, the efforts of politicians, economists, social organizers, environmentalists to remedy our eco-human ills will, probably, be in vain. Thus, as Rita Gross challenged all of us: each of our traditions must seek to bring about such personal, mystical transformation "individual by individual."

This mystical role of the religions would seem to provide a kind of "missing ingredient"—or *missing motivating power*—in humanity's efforts to do something about the social and environmental quagmire we find ourselves in. In a sense, we know what the problem is; we know, too, what must be done. The data, the stultifying statistics and analyses are available: we're draining the lifeblood of the ecosystem and we've got to stop it. That means we have to cut back, reduce, for example, the population of humans and of automobiles. But we don't do what we recognize needs to be done. Why not? The facts have not yet touched our hearts. There's a block between what we see and what we feel. *There has to be some kind of internal transformation before we can really set ourselves to the task of world transformation.* We need what Dan Maguire called a "revolution of affect."

And here is where the religions can make a helpful, if not necessary, contribution. This is what Gross calls "the most important component of a religious response to the environmental crisis." In the personal, mystical, affective "conversion" they are able to bring about in the heart of the individual, religions can equip our hearts with the antennae to "receive" and respond to the messages our world is so persistently and painfully sending us. The ability to receive and feel will come from the transformation of our self-consciousness from monadic, competitive selves to communitarian, cooperative selves. As Gross observed, "the problem for religious environmental ethics is more practical than theoretical." What is needed primarily is not a new multireligious ecological theology but a "profound re-orientation of consciousness" regarding our identity as community beings.

There was general recognition in our discussions that, for the most part, the Asian and primal traditions, at least in the main flow of their histories, seem to offer a clearer vision of, and more practical means to, our identities as "we-selves." In the Hindu image of the Atman as Brahman, the Buddhist message of the "no-self," the Taoist call to abandon ourselves to the flow of the Way, the Confucian recognition of the primacy of the social, and the indigenous spiritualities' placing of humans within the broader earth-family—in such traditions we have the spiritual energy, vision, and practice to animate a "revolution of affect" that will enable us to feel our bondedness with each other. In this regard, evidently, the Abrahamic or Semitic religions will have something to learn from their Asian brothers and sisters.

The Macro-Analysis: Problems with the Market

If we were surprised and heartened by our general agreements on the need for a basic overhaul of people's *self*-understanding, we were even more surprised, and more heartened, by what turned out to be an even firmer consensus about a needed overhaul in our understanding of the market. It was especially the presentations of David Loy and Alberto Múnera that elicited and gave shape to our multireligious agreement that the death-threat that many people and many parts of our planet are today facing is coming not only from the way we understand our individual selves but also, and more threateningly, from the way we understand the global market. While we can never neglect the vital links between the human heart and the social-economic system, neither can we facilely reduce one to the other or think that we can fix both by fixing only one. So, besides calling for a conversion of the heart, we all recognized the need for our religious communities to call for a conversion of the economic system that is presently ruling the seas of international trade.

But addressing the system may be in many ways much more difficult than addressing the individual's heart. Loy helped us understand this. The global market, especially in the self-awareness and consolidation it has taken on after the collapse of the Soviet Union, has not only become what we can call a religion, it has also assumed the characteristics of a *universal* and *absolute* religion. If the so-called new world order has a religion, it is the "free market." The economic system of free markets provides the "plausibility structures," the vision of the way things are, or the way things have to be. Whatever the market requires is understood as the dictates of some kind of a "natural law" or transcendent order that, though it may cause temporary pain, will ultimately make for the salvation of all. To appeal to the dictates of the market nowadays is like appealing to the Bible for a fundamentalist Christian, or to the pope for a conservative Catholic. Here the conversation ends; all complaints are quelled. We bow in pious submission, and in the trust that we will be graced and "saved" by such submission.

Most of us found ourselves whispering both "Amen" and "mea culpa" to Loy's reminder: "the Market is becoming the first truly world religion, binding all corners of the globe into a worldview and set of values whose religious role we overlook only because we insist on seeing them as 'secular'." But this religion of the Market is not only universal; it also understands and proclaims itself as an absolute, an exclusivistic religion. With a conviction and a rigor even greater than that of Christianity at its imperialistic heights, the Market proclaims "outside the church there is no salvation." Only now, the "church" is the marketplace. And therefore, as Loy explained, "aggressive proselytizing" is essential to the life of this market-religion. It must convert the world; it can brook no other religions.

At this point in our conversations in Freeport, we communally bumped into a stark realization. We had embarked on this project in the spirit of "dialogue"—dialogue with each other across our religious boundaries, dialogue with anyone, religious or atheist, who seeks to respond to the pain of the earth. But just as we recognized the impossibility of dialogue with "exclusivistic" religions—communities who consider themselves the only true religion and therefore look on dialogue as either futile or dangerous—so too we had to face the reality that there was little hope for dialogue with the religion of the market. But what did this mean for us, for our project? Should our attitude toward the religion of the market be the same as that toward exclusivistic religions—when we sadly but simply accept the fact that, at least for the moment, a conversation with them is just not possible? Better to occupy ourselves with other, more promising conversations?

While such reasoning might make sense with regard to fundamentalist religions, it cannot apply to our relationship, as religious communities, with the market. The reason why has to do with another shared recognition that resulted from our discussion of Loy's presentation: the religion of the global market, as it is presently functioning, is not only *different* from each of our own religious visions and traditions, it is also in fundamental *contradiction* or opposition to our deepest religious sensitivities. Therefore, if we admitted that interreligious conversation with the market-religion is impossible, we still had to recognize that some kind of interreligious confrontation with it is necessary.

This was a kind of negative consensus. Despite our many doctrinal differences, we were united in a common *religious* resistance to what we all witnessed as the workings and effects of the market-as-religion. Our sense of shared resistance was crystalized by something that, in terms of the Abrahamic religions, has to do with *idolatry:* "All genuine religions are natural allies against what amounts to an idolatry that undermines their most important teachings." In this case idolatry was not just that which usurps the place of God or the Transcendent, but anything that serves to make the well-being of some people superior to, and therefore the "god" of, the well-being of others. That's what was calling us together in a common opposition, or a common effort to identify and then depose the idol.

Contributions from Jewish and Christian members of our project—Zoloth, Múnera, Keller—helped us identify other faces of this idol. From the mouth of idols comes forth *injustice.* If all our religious traditions could not agree on a common definition of God or the Absolute (or even the existence of God!), we found ourselves agreeing on what makes for an "idol": injustice! Yes, each of us would perhaps speak of the causes and effects of social injustice differently; but all of us could smell and react to the monster of injustice, even though we may describe him differently. The odor of this monster was evident to all of us, for example, in the first part of Jacob Olupona's presentation in which he described the effects of the colonial and postcolonial global markets on the peoples of Africa. If all of us could agree with Loy's claim that "all genuine religions are natural allies against . . . idolatry," most, if not all, of us also assented to Zoloth's version of the same claim: "The necessity of justice, for justice to attend to the vulnerable, and to speak to the powerful in an unjust world has long been central to the vision of many religions." Again, although many of us would have different religious perspectives on what makes for justice on earth, we were amazingly unified in responding to what makes for injustice.

As someone in our group observed, a "Mandate from Heaven" was calling us through the specter of injustice and the idols of the marketplace. In an utterly paradoxical way (at least paradoxical for a Christian like me), our common, spontaneous reaction to the idols of injustice was more effective in bringing us together as religious people than any common definition of God or the Ultimate.

Our shared macro-analysis of the religion of the market alerted us to a further contribution that religions must make to humanity's efforts to deal with the crises of overpopulation, consumption, and environmental decay. Using terms familiar to me from my tradition, but acceptable I hope to others, I would say that our group recognized that the religious communities share a *prophetic,* not just a mystical, mission to remedy the pains of our earth. The religious communities must join ranks not just in transforming the consciousness of the individual but also in confronting and transforming the idolatrous, unjust structures of the global political-economic system. Or, formulated more pointedly, we were merging toward a further-shared recognition that "the religious is political." As religious people, we are not only to deepen our awareness and transform our consciousness through meditation and prayer, we are also to get our hands dirty in the grime and ambiguity of politics and social movements.

I use the word "prophetic" to describe this return to the marketplace in order to bring out what we all seemed to be agreeing on: the role of religions is to be *critical* of the way the economic wheels of the global market are turning. Insofar as we agreed on our analysis of the global situation and of the marketplace, we had to agree that *to be religious* in such a world is *to be countercultural.* It is to point out, resist, change the self-seeking, power-oriented, exploitative aspects of so much of the way business is done in our new world order. In Loy's more incisive language, the religious communities of our world must come together to point out and criticize "the religious dimensions of capitalism." "The crucial role that religion can serve [is] to raise fundamental questions about this diminished understanding of what the world is and what our life can be." This means that in order to carry out this "crucial role" of religion, religious people will have to take up the staff and microphone of the prophet. And this can make the role of religion messy, controversial, dangerous. Mystics are stabilizing and pacifying. Prophets are a pain. The high priests of the global market-religion might want to invite mystics for their prayer breakfasts; prophets they will avoid, or remove.

Balancing the Religious and the Political

But in our discussions of what I am calling our "micro and macro" analyses and our religious "mystical and prophetic" responsibilities, there was a definite, if sometimes struggling, effort to keep the two in balance. Some of us (especially those from the Abrahamic and indigenous traditions) stressed that our efforts to transform consciousness "individual by individual" will be faulty or even counterproductive if not complemented by similar efforts to transform social and economic structures; others (especially those from the Asian traditions) readily affirmed this reminder but then added that the critical, activist role of the prophet can be equally ineffective and dangerous if not sensitized and sustained by a personally transformed, mystically nourished center. The vitally urgent contribution that the religious communities can and must make to solving the challenges of population, consumption, and ecological violation must be *both mystical and prophetic*. The religions must help call people to their senses—both their personal-individual senses and their economic-political senses. If religions are particularly well equipped to bring about the "altered state of consciousness" that is so necessary for people to be liberated from the prison of a narrow, selfish self, religions are also equipped to bring about an "altered state of society" in which neither humans nor any sentient beings will ever be treated as mere instruments or objects of profit. In our ailing, endangered world, religious communities, we realized, are being called to be agents of spiritual and social transformation—mystics and prophets.

The kind of dialogue we were experiencing in our interreligious discussions of population, consumption, and ecology was embodying for all of us, it became clear to me, what David Tracy of the University of Chicago has recently been saying: one of the most pressing and promising requirements for the understanding and practice of religion in our contemporary world is to explore how prophetic and mystical forces animate all religions and how these forces can be related between the religions.[2] From his own study, Tracy believes that "in all religions . . . [there is] a search for new ways to unite these mystical and prophetic trajectories."[3] This is what was happening in our project: in coming together as committed members of different religious communities in order to turn our common gaze and concern toward the human-environmental crises facing humanity, we were helping each other search for new ways to unite the mystical and prophetic energies *within* and *between* our communities. As we delved into what I have called our micro- and macro-analyses of human hearts and human societies, we kept reminding ourselves that, like the up and down of a teeter-totter, both a mystical and prophetic, both a personal and political, response was needed from our religious traditions. And it seemed that we could better realize this balance between the mystical and prophetic *together* as an interreligious community than we could isolated in our own religious backyards.

The balance I am trying to describe was felt with special richness in our conversations about how we should respond to the market-as-religion. While the "prophets" among us were describing the inequities and injustices and ecological devastation that our market-economies were producing, while they were urging all of us, as religious people, to confront and resist such human and environmental exploitation, the "mystics" in our group would gently but firmly remind us that in taking such necessary action, we must never look on those whom we are confronting as "the enemy" or as "evil." If our prophetic, political action was coming from not just our social analysis but also from our mystical, selfless centers, then such action will never be violent and hateful; it will never be the efforts of "the good guys" versus the "bad guys." Political action balanced with mystical personal transformation will always be *relational;* in confrontation and denunciation, mystical prophets will seek to maintain connection with their opponents, a connection rooted in compassion, respect, and love.

We were realizing that religious contributions to the global concerns of population, consumption, and the environment were both richer and better balanced when they were *interreligious* contributions.

A COMMON FRONT

Our project, and this book, which tries to give it voice, represents an experiment and an experience that can, we feel, be repeated in interreligious and intercultural contexts throughout the world. And so it embodies a hope that—we hope!—will become contagious. From our experience of a "common call" that spoke to us out of the pain of the planet, from the "common analyses" that we found ourselves agreeing on as we tried, together, to answer this call (not that other such interreligious experiments will have to come up with the same analyses), we realized at the conclusion of this stage of our project that we had attained what many of our colleagues in the postmodernist academy would say is impossible: we had formed a *common interreligious front*!

By a "common front," please understand, I am not saying that we were marching lockstep to the very same drumbeat, or that we were ready to sign a common, interreligious "mission statement" (or even, at this stage, Hans Küng's "Global Ethic").[4] Rather, we found ourselves, as people with extremely different religious experience and history, *desiring, hoping, trying* to address common concerns *together*. We wanted to work together on a common agenda, even though we don't know, yet, just how the work will proceed, or what the details of the agenda are. We knew where the suffering and dangers exist, we had a general common take on what some of the primary causes of this suffering are, we had a sense of direction for where we must search to find solutions—and we felt impelled to step forward together. That is our common front.

And this is the message we want to "announce from the rooftops" to our religious brothers and sisters in our different communities—and to the world: In a kind of good-news/bad-news paradox, the specter of human-environmental suffering and dangers (that's the bad news) can become the arena for a new kind of dialogue among the religions of the world (the good news). This paradoxical message contains three interlocking realizations that became clear to us over the course of our discussions:

1. The crises that our species and planet face, and that we have tried to decipher under the threefold rubric of overpopulation, overconsumption, and overuse of the environment, will be understood and remedied only with the *contribution of the religious communities* of the world. That doesn't mean that religion is the panacea, the deus ex machina, that will save us when everything else fails. It means simply yet decisively that if religious vision and energy are not added to all the other contributions—scientific, economic, political, cultural—that must interconnect to save our people and planet from growing destruction and violence, then such efforts will certainly lag and probably fail. This, I think, is the sense and the power of Hans Küng's kerygma: "No world peace without peace between the religions."[5]

2. When individuals in the different religious communities look at and examine the human and the ecological pain that is searing and frightening so many of us, especially when they carry out this examination in the presence of persons of other religious traditions, they realize that they all are being *affected and connected in similar*

ways. This is what I tried to describe as our experience of a *common call* and a *common reaction*. The images and the voices of suffering beings somehow were able to plunge into and go below the waters of our different religious streams to an undercurrent that passed through all of them. Our differences weren't removed. But when these differences were focused on the pain and the crises of our threatened global village, they somehow reacted with similar concerns and similar resolves. Different though we were, we wanted to stay together in order to work together.

3. The third aspect of our discovery and our message for others was only a dawning realization, or an exciting hope. We were experiencing *a new kind of dialogue* that was leading us to new ways of hearing each other, new ways of learning from each other, new ways of working and carrying on together. All the members of our project had been participants in various forms of dialogue; most of these encounters with others were either academic, based on scholarly study and exchange, or spiritual, grounded in shared prayer or religious practices. What we experienced in this project was something different. It was a different way of dialoguing. By beginning with the global issues that *surround* all of us, instead of first trying to communicate the wisdom and experience *within* each of our traditions, we found ourselves energized and sensitized to communicate with greater care and intensity. After having felt the call of the suffering earth together, after having attempted, together, to understand and respond to this suffering, we discovered that we were linked in new ways, that we were brothers and sisters despite our different religious neighborhoods. And this linking or bonding enabled us, when it came to talking about our religious beliefs and differences, to "hear" each other more effectively, to appreciate the depth of what at first seemed so strange, and to learn from each other. In more academic terms, our shared actions led to deeper understanding; praxis facilitated and gave life to theory.

This, then, is the message that we hope we can communicate to the religious communities of the world. It is a message that must be delivered and lived not only "from the top down" (by professors or religious leaders in books like this) but also, and especially, "from the bottom up"—on the so much more fertile soil of grassroots religious communities: By accepting the *obligation* of responding together to the crises and challenges of global issues such as population, consumption, environmental degradation, the religions of the world can not only make a genuine contribution to the resolution of these crises, but they will discover a new *opportunity* to work with, talk with, and thus learn from each other. And in the process of such "globally responsible dialogue" each of the traditions will be enriched, possibly transformed. And most importantly, the religious communities will be promoting the "salvation" of our beautiful but endangered world.

NOTES

1. Edward Schillebeeckx, *The Church: The Human Story of God* (New York: Crossroads, 1990), pp. 5–7.

2. See *Dialogue with the Other: The Inter-Religious Dialogue* (Grand Rapids, Mich.: Eerdmans, 1990).

3. "God, Dialogue, and Solidarity: A Theologian's Refrain," *The Christian Century*, 10 October 1990, p. 100.

4. Hans Küng and Karl-Josef Kuschel, eds., *A Global Ethic: The Declaration of the Parliament of the World's Religions* (New York: Continuum, 1993).

5. Hans Küng, *Global Responsibility: In Search of a New World Ethic* (New York: Crossroads, 1991), p. xv.

ABOUT THE AUTHORS

Nawal H. Ammar is Associate Professor of (Criminal) Justice Studies at Kent State University. She received her Ph.D. in cultural anthropology from the University of Florida, Gainesville in 1988. Nawal works in issues of justice and public policy. Some of Nawal's publications include: "Discrimination against Women under the Nationality Laws: Case Studies from Egypt and Lebanon" in Muraskin's *Women and Justice: Policy Implications—Domestic and International* (Harwood Press, 1999); "Domestic Violence in Egypt: A Move away from Silence towards Systematic Studies" in *Women and Criminal Justice* (March 1997); "The Status of Childless Women in Islam: Issues of Social and Legal Construction" in *Humanity and Society* (November 1996); "On Being a Muslim Woman: Laws and Practices" http/www.consultation.org./consultation/ammar.htm (October 1996); "Islam and the Environment: A Legalistic and Textual View" in Coward's *Population, Consumption, and the Environment: Religious and Secular Responses* (1995); "Women in Islam," *The Reader's Companion to U.S. Women's History* (1995); "Islam and Fertility: A Legalistic and Textual View," in Brauen and Zweifel's *Bread for All* (1994).

Harold Coward is a Professor of History and is the Director of the Centre for Studies in Religion and Society at the University of Victoria. He received his Ph.D. from McMaster University. With a teaching focus on India, comparative religion, and ecology, he has supervised numerous students for their M.A. and Ph.D. degrees both at the University of Victoria and at the University of Calgary. He is a Fellow of the Royal Society of Canada. He has been the recipient of numerous research grants from SSHRC and the Ford Foundation. He has been a Visiting Fellow at Banaras Hindu University and the Institute for Advanced Studies in the Humanities, Edinburgh University. He has written sixty-two articles and is author/editor of thirty-two books, including: *Hindu Ethics* (1988); *The Philosophy of the Grammarians* (1990); *Derrida and Indian Philosophy* (1990); *Mantra: Hearing the Divine in India* (1991); *Population, Consumption, and the Environment* (1995). His current research is focused on medical and environmental ethics.

217

Rita M. Gross is the author of *Buddhism after Patriarchy: A Feminist History, Analysis, and Reconstruction of Buddhism* (1993) and *Feminism and Religion—An Introduction* (1996). A Professor of Comparative Studies in Religion at the University of Wisconsin—Eau Claire, she is also a senior teacher for Shambhbala, an international network of Buddhist meditation centers founded by Chogyam Trungpa.

Catherine Keller teaches constructive theology at Drew University, focusing on the feminist, ecological, and pluralist potential of progressive Christian theology. She is the author of *From a Broken Web: Separation, Sexism and Self* (1986), and *Apocalypse Now and Then: A Feminist Guide to the End of the World* (1996).

Professor of Theology at Xavier University, Cincinnati, *Paul F. Knitter* received a Licentiate in theology from the Pontifical Gregorian University in Rome (1966) and a doctorate from the University of Marburg, Germany (1972). Most of his research and publications have dealt with religious pluralism and interreligious dialogue. He is the author of *No Other Name? A Critical Survey of Christian Attitudes toward World Religions* (1985), *One Earth Many Religions: Multifaith Dialogue and Global Responsibility* (1995) and *Jesus and the Other Names: Christian Mission and Global Responsibility* (1996). He is also General Editor of the Orbis Books series "Faith Meets Faith." Over the past decade, he has also been active in various peace groups working with the churches of El Salvador.

David C. Korten, President of the People-Centered Development Forum, can be found on the website at http://iisd1.iisd.ca/pcdf.

David R. Loy is Professor in the Faculty of International Studies at Bunkyo University, Chigasaki, Japan. His work is primarily in comparative philosophy, particularly comparing Buddhist philosophy with modern Western thought. In addition to papers in various journals, he is the author of *Nonduality: A Study in Comparative Philosophy* (1988) and *Lack and Transcendence: The Problem of Death and Life in Psychotherapy, Existentialism and Buddhism* (1996), and the editor of *Healing Deconstruction: Postmodern Thought in Buddhism and Christianity* (1996).

Daniel C. Maguire is a Professor of Ethics at Marquette University. He is President of the Religious Consultation on Population, Reproductive Health and Ethics, and the past President of the Society of Christian Ethics. He is the author of *The Moral Core of Judaism and Christianity* (1993) and of *Ethics For a Small Planet*, coauthored with Larry L. Rasmussen, with an introduction by Rosemary Radford Ruether (1998).

Alberto Múnera, S.J., is Consultant for the Social Foundation in Colombia. The last twenty-five years he has been Professor of Moral Theology in the Jesuit Javeriana University of Bogota. He was Dean of the Faculty of Theology, of the Faculty of Education, and of the Faculty for Interdisciplinary Studies in the same university. He was elected three times Vice-President and twice President of the World Conference of Catholic Theological Institutions. He is author of *Teologia Moral* (1975), *El Misterio de Dios* (1978), *Pecado Personal desde el Pecado Original* (1985), *De una Moral de los Manuales a una Moral Liberadora* (1990), and many articles on moral theology. As member of the Colombian Association of Theologians, *Koinonia*, he has participated in the very difficult process of liberation theology in his country.

Vasudha Narayanan is Professor of Religion and the Gibson Term Professor in the College of Liberal Arts and Sciences at the University of Florida. She has written and edited five books and nearly fifty articles and encyclopedia entries. Her books include *The Way and the Goal* (1987), *The Vernacular Veda: Revelation, Recitation, and Ritual* (1994), and (with John Carman) *The Tamil Veda: Pillan's Interpretation of the Tiruvaymoli* (1989). Her research support has included grants and fellowships from the National Endowment for the Humanities and the John Simon Guggenheim foundations.

Jacob K. Olupona, a historian of religion, is John Simon Guggenheim Fellow and Professor in the African American and African Studies Program at the University of California, Davis. He is the author of *Kingship, Religion and Rituals in a Nigerian Community: A Phenomenological Study of the Ondo Yoruba Festivals* (1991), the editor of *Religion and Peace in Multifaith Nigeria* (1993) and the coeditor of *Religious Plurality in Africa: Essays in Honor of John S. Mbiti* (1993) and *Religion and Society in Nigeria: Historical and Sociological Perspectives* (1993). He is currently the Chair of the African Association for the Study of Religion.

Chün-fang Yü is Professor in the Department of Religion at Rutgers, the State University of New Jersey. She received her Ph.D. from Columbia University. She works primarily in Chinese religious traditions, with particular emphasis on Chinese Buddhism. She is the author of *The Renewal of Buddhism in China: Chu-hung and Late Ming Synthesis* (1981), editor of *In Search of Dharma: Memoirs of a Modern Buddhist Pilgrim* (1992), coeditor of *Pilgrims and Sacred Sites in China* (1992), many articles on various aspects of Ch'an and Pure Land Buddhism, and is finishing a study on the cult of Kuan-yin in China.

Laurie Zoloth is Associate Professor and Chair of the Jewish Studies Program at San Francisco State University. She received her Ph.D. from the Graduate Theological Union at Berkeley, in 1993. Her research is primarily in ethics and social justice, with an emphasis on bioethics from the perspective of the Jewish tradition. She is the author of *The Ethics of Encounter: Community and Conscience in Health Care Reform* (1997), and a number of articles about feminist theory, clinical ethics, and postmodern Jewish philosophy.

INDEX